THE FATHER OF AMERICAN CONSERVATION

THE FATHER OF AMERICAN CONSERVATION

GEORGE BIRD GRINNELL
ADVENTURER,
ACTIVIST, AND AUTHOR

THOM HATCH

TURNER PUBLISHING COMPANY

Turner Publishing Company
Nashville, Tennessee
www.turnerpublishing.com

The Father of American Conservation
Copyright © 2019 Thom Hatch

Cover Design: Lauren Peters-Collaer
Book design: Meg Reid

Library of Congress Cataloging-in-Publication Data

Names: Hatch, Thom, 1946- author.
Title: The father of American conservation : George Bird Grinnell,
    adventurer, activist, author / by Thom Hatch.
Description: Nashville, Tennessee : Turner Publishing Company, [2020] |
    Includes bibliographical references and index. | Summary: "Award-winning
    author, Thom Hatch presents the definitive biography of George Bird
    Grinnell (1849-1938), who was recognized in his time as "The Father of
    American Conservation." This book chronicles not only Grinnell's life,
    but also offers a history of his accomplishments in saving the wildlife
    and natural resources of this country"— Provided by publisher.
Identifiers: LCCN 2019025022 (print) | LCCN 2019025023 (ebook)
ISBN 9781684423330 (paperback) | ISBN 9781684423347 (hardcover)
ISBN 9781684423354 (ebook)
Subjects: LCSH: Grinnell, George Bird, 1849-1938.
Conservationists—United States—Biography.
Naturalists—United States—Biography.
Classification: LCC QH31.G74 H38 2020 (print) | LCC QH31.G74 (ebook)
    DDC 333.72092 [B]—dc23

LC record available at https://lccn.loc.gov/2019025022
LC ebook record available at https://lccn.loc.gov/2019025023

Printed in the United States of America
19 20 10 9 8 7 6 5 4 3 2 1

For my lovely and talented wife, Lyndy,
my beautiful and brilliant daughter, Cimarron,
and our faithful border collie, Emily,
who are my daily inspiration.

CONTENTS

The pleasures, the values of contact with the natural world, are not reserved for scientists. They are available to anyone who will place himself under the influence of a lonely mountaintop—or the sea—or the stillness of the forest, or who will stop to think about so small a thing as the mystery of a growing seed. I believe natural beauty has a necessary place in the spiritual development of any individual of any society. I believe that whenever we destroy beauty, or whenever we substitute something man-made and artificial for a natural feature of the earth, we have retarded some part of man's spiritual growth.

—*RACHEL CARSON*

INTRODUCTION

EVERY NOW AND THEN A BOOK COMES ALONG THAT IS NOT only timely but has a chance to make a substantial difference. The book you are holding in your hands is that sort of book.

One dedicated visionary, George Bird Grinnell, led successful public crusades to gain justice in myriad aspects of conservation in the days when animals and birds were being slaughtered at will; unique natural land formations were being destroyed and looted; our public lands were being ravaged by commercialization; and lobbyists for powerful business interests owned Congress.

And today, we are in danger of history repeating itself. Rollbacks of government regulations have weakened protections and threatened the future of our country's abundant wildlife and fragile environment. Our natural resources are under siege, and many of the changes are being carried out surreptitiously and without debate.

In order to better understand this alarming direction, we must be aware of the historical aspects of the battle between corporate and government interests against the natural balance of our planet. There are methods to be learned from those who have already committed their lives to fighting for justice in the natural world.

Otherwise, history could repeat itself and it may be too late to reverse the damaging trend.

This book takes you back to the days and times of George Bird Grinnell (1849–1938), who was recognized in his era as "The Father of American Conservation." A remarkable man, Grinnell was known as a model of intellectual diversity, integrity, and professional dedication. He was a daring adventurer and explorer; crusading magazine publisher and editor; prolific author; accomplished outdoorsman; notable paleontologist, ethnologist, ornithologist, and anthropologist; presidential advisor; advocate for Native American rights; and this country's first environmental activist, whose contributions in that arena are unparalleled in American history.

Although small in stature, George Grinnell had an air of dignity about him, with his immaculate dress and neatly trimmed mustache, and he stood tall when it came to causes in which he believed were righteous and worthy. He did not merely speak out or write about the need to preserve this country's wildlife and natural resources or suggest fair treatment of Native Americans. He was the catalyst for change, a tireless crusader who rallied the support of common people as well as presidents and Congress to take action in a wide range of conservation issues to protect the land and the wild animals that he loved and to defend Native Americans, who at the time were in serious danger of extermination.

Grinnell created the Audubon Society; co-founded the Boone and Crockett Club; worked to save the last wild herd of buffalo in the country; successfully lobbied Congress to pass the protection of wildlife and natural resources in our National Parks; pushed for setting aside national forest and wilderness land; negotiated fair treaties for Native American tribes; as well as being a vigorous advocate for rules and regulations to establish sensible hunting laws that exist to this day.

But this book is more than merely a biography of an extraordinary man whose accomplishments in the area of environmental protection have affected our modern society. We travel back to an era when the country was rapidly growing—and for the first time concerned conservationists came forward to struggle with those growing pains that were affecting nature. It was a time of unchecked abuse for commercial purposes of our natural resources and a near extermination of animal and bird species for profit, not to mention the systematic ostracism if not annihilation of Native American culture.

We begin our journey in Brooklyn at the rural estate of the late John James Audubon, where Lucy Audubon, the widow of that famous painter, home-schooled young George Bird Grinnell and gave him his first lessons about the natural world around him.

And then, after college at Yale, we are off on daring adventures, heart-stopping escapes, and momentous discoveries throughout the wilderness American West that shaped Grinnell's perspective of the challenges facing the land and animals—a groundbreaking paleontology expedition; the last buffalo hunt of the Pawnee tribe; the search for gold and unknown natural resources with Custer and the Seventh Cavalry in the Black Hills; the first documentation of the birds and mammals in the wilderness of Yellowstone National Park—and the first official condemnation of their treatment; an unprecedented exploration of Alaska in a floating scientific university; negotiating fair treaties and rights for Native Americans; fighting for migratory bird laws that presently exist; the creation of Montana's Glacier National Park, with Grinnell's Glacier as its centerpiece; and, as the pitchman once said, much, much more.

And through it all we follow the tireless activism of George Grinnell as editor of *Forest and Stream*, the leading sportsman's magazine of the day, and a prolific editorial writer working to inform and inflame the public about any threat to the natural world while offering concrete ideas about how to fight it.

Along the way, we are introduced to such luminaries as his close friend President Theodore Roosevelt, scout and entertainer Buffalo Bill Cody, Lieutenant Colonel George Armstrong Custer, naturalists John Muir and John Burroughs, famed photographer Edward Curtis, painter Albert Bierstadt, Lakota Sioux Chief Red Cloud, Yale paleontology professor O. C. Marsh, Army scouts Frank and Luther North and Charley Reynolds, General Phil Sheridan, railroad moguls Edward Harriman and Jay Cooke, trapper Liver-Eating Johnson, and many other contemporaries of George Grinnell, both famous and lesser known but each playing a relevant role in this country's legends and history as heroes or villains.

Although this book is intended to be enjoyable entertainment and not homework, it is my wish that it will serve to inspire and motivate people to become passionate about environmental issues in their own communities as well as nationally and involve themselves in protecting those precious resources that are being threatened.

With that in mind, it is my belief that anyone who reads this book will recognize the urgent need to revisit the battles that the visionary George Grinnell waged and not allow his work to be in vain. Hopefully, readers of this book will forever after choose *sensible* preservation and protection over *unrestrained* corporate greed when evaluating environmental issues, and the public will respond the way it did when George Grinnell called upon responsible people to stand up and defend our precious natural resources.

Perhaps due to his unassuming personality and lack of self-promotion while alive, Grinnell has not enjoyed the acclaim of other early conservationists. His life story, one of great adventure and remarkable accomplishment, however, virtually cries out for attention and recognition. And now, as his story unfolds on the following pages, George Bird Grinnell should finally receive the credit he deserves and assume his place in history with the title that was bestowed upon him in his day: "The Father of American Conservation."

Thom Hatch
Ellicott, Colorado
April 1, 2019

CHAPTER ONE:
THE BUDDING NATURALIST

Come forth into the light of things, let nature be your teacher.
—WILLIAM WORDSWORTH

IN *1849*, *GENERAL ZACHARY TAYLOR*, *THE CONQUEROR OF* Buena Vista in the Mexican War, was inaugurated as president of the United States. He stated in his inaugural address: "We are at peace with all the world and the rest of mankind." That statement was true for the victors of that recent bloody conflict, but not so for the losers.

In the West, the old Spanish missions in the territory conquered by the United States were deprived of their wealth and influence. That expansive new territory would eventually encompass most of the western states from Kansas to California. The Apache, Navajo, Cheyenne, Sioux, and other tribes in those regions posed immediate trouble for white men who sought to build homesteads, or communities, or travel to the gold fields.

Those gold seekers from all over the world, called "49ers," tracked across the plains and poured into California by the thousands in search of riches dug out of the earth. The once-quiet port at San Francisco Bay was soon surrounded by a huge, raucous settlement of tents and sheds.

Back on the East Coast, thousands of recent inventions had utterly transformed methods that had been employed almost unchanged for hundred of years in manufacturing, transportation, mining, communications, and agriculture. Machinery, first driven by water-power and subsequently steam engines, produced commodities in great factories on a large scale. The leading commodities used for food, clothing, and shelter had been caught up in this industrial revolution with astounding results in output. For the fiscal year, the total value of machine and hand manufactures, including fishing and mining, was placed at almost two billion dollars—more than four times the total national wealth in 1787.

This revolution spanned a rapid growth of population in old cities and the appearance of new cities as well. In 1790 only five towns—Boston, New York, Philadelphia, Baltimore, and Charleston—had more than eight thousand inhabitants. By 1849, the population of New York City, including surrounding districts later drawn under its jurisdiction, was approaching the one million mark.

One of these districts surrounding New York City—located directly across the East River from Manhattan—was an area first settled by Dutch farmers in 1636 called Brooklyn. Home to the Brooklyn Naval Yard, where missions to suppress the slave trade off the coast of west Africa were launched, Brooklyn was populated by a diverse mixture of working men, professionals, college professors, shopkeepers, artists, and master craftsmen.

Immigrants dominated the workforce, with those of German, British, and Irish descent the most prominent. About forty percent of Brooklyn's wage earners worked in New York City, which put a strain on the ferries carrying passengers to and from work. Among the eighty thousand denizens were those middle-class mothers and daughters who did not work outside the home, rather, if anything, performed such tasks as seamstresses and laundresses. These ladies were perceived by their peers as the moral guardians of civilized society.

It was into this growing and changing society on September 20, 1849, that *Mayflower* descendant George Bird Grinnell was born in Brooklyn. He was the eldest of five children born to textile manufacturer George Blake Grinnell and the former Helen Alvord

Lansing. The family had been well represented in the history of the fledgling country. Ancestors included a congressman—George Grinnell, who served ten terms—and five colonial governors, as well as Betty Alden, who had been the subject of Jane G. Austin's book, *Betty Alden: The First-Born Daughter of the Pilgrims*.

George's family moved to Manhattan when he was four years old. He remembered sleigh rides through Central Park, which at the time was a wilderness of rocks and pastureland. But his most memorable times back then were at his grandfather's home in Greenfield, Massachusetts. His uncle, twenty-year-old Thomas P. Grinnell, owned a huge collection of birds and mammals that he had preserved, and enjoyed telling young George exciting stories about hunting and fishing. In this manner, George was introduced to the great outdoors in his earliest years by his Uncle Tom, who also loved to draw pictures of birds. George was enchanted by his uncle and recalled that he "had no pleasanter hours than those spent among Uncle Tom's birds" in what was called the "bird room."

The construction and extension of railroad lines at that time, however, enabled people to depart congested areas and build houses farther out in the country. In the year George Grinnell was born, the Hudson River Railroad completed its line between New York's 30th Street and the village of Peekskill, about forty miles. This form of transportation opened attractive places along the eastern shore of the Hudson River. People immediately began to settle northward along the river—and George Grinnell's parents enthusiastically joined in the migration.

When George was age seven, the Grinnell family relocated to Audubon Park, an area that was never officially a "park," located along the Hudson River between what would become upper Manhattan's 155th and 158th streets. This estate had been built by painter and naturalist John James Audubon, who had died six years earlier. The book *Birds of America* had made Audubon famous on both sides of the Atlantic. It also made him wealthy enough to afford that twenty-acre parcel of land and to build a family home.

This estate was located within a virtual wilderness. New York City—with its Tammany Hall politics, high finance, and busy harbor—was about an hour and a half away over a hilly wagon road. The

Audubons, however, were never rich. After John's death, his widow, Lucy Bakewell Audubon, made money by renting out portions of the property, as well as marketing her husband's original watercolors.

The Grinnell family rented one of the houses on the grounds, and later built a home of their own there when Lucy began selling parcels of her land. Their house stood at present-day 157th Street and Riverside Drive, with their garden plot located at what is now the subway entrance on Broadway.

George thrived in this rural setting—swimming, crabbing, fishing, hunting, ice skating, and roaming the countryside in search of natural wonders. "The fields and the woods were left in a state of nature," Grinnell would fondly remember. Stands of hemlocks, oaks, and ancient chestnuts, amid dense foliage, were interspersed by a few country roads. Wildlife was everywhere, as were domesticated horses, and cows, and pigs, and other farm animals and smaller game like rabbits, foxes, and hawks. Brazen eagles would make kills right there on the manicured front lawns.

The area was home to a horde of youngsters who took full advantage of all the activities that the outdoors afforded them. George, his brothers, and the neighborhood boys would tramp through the woods with bow and arrow in hand and shoot small game. George's uncle, George Bird, had bought him a hickory bow and arrows from the nearby Saratoga Indians, and the boy would use plumes from a feather duster as a pretend headdress. Some days they would cast with a rod and line for game fish or scour the tide pools in the river for clams and other interesting species, or frolic in the various swimming holes and beaches of that river. In the winter, there was ice skating, sledding, and spirited snowball fights.

One of the favorite playgrounds for the boys of Audubon Park was the loft of John Woodhouse Audubon's barn. John, who had continued his father's work, used the barn as a storehouse and art studio. Piled up against the walls were rows of wooden boxes full of bird skins collected by the famous naturalist and his son. The boys were careful not to disturb anything in this fascinating barn for fear of losing the privilege of being allowed in there, and spent much time studying and discussing the odd species found inside those walls.

John, who was a close friend of George's father, would often set

THE FATHER OF AMERICAN CONSERVATION

up his easel and paint inside that barn. The boys would stand at a respectful distance watching as his subject grew under his skillful brush. But for George there were occasions more special than that at the barn. John would receive natural history specimens, and the boys would "gather about him with breathless interest waiting to see what wonderful things he would draw forth from those boxes. I recall especially a great white Arctic hare that he held up for us to see. With the hare were some dark colored birds—Spruce Grouse and some white ptarmigan—strange creatures from the north."

Like many boys with freedom to wander, George and his companions were occasionally prone to mischief. One time, the boys ignored an ordinance calling for swimmers to wear "tights," and were arrested and taken off to jail for skinny-dipping within sight of passing uptown trains. "An hour or two of this confinement," Grinnell recalled, "gave us plenty of time to ponder on the sorrows of life." A judge soon released them with a stern warning. Other mischief included stealing chickens and roasting them over a fire deep in the woods. Grinnell later wrote that "the little boys of Audubon Park—all of them—ought to have been sent to some reform school."

One of George's closest friends was Jack Audubon, grandson of the painter. The two boys were enchanted by stories they had read about the outdoors. The primary influence on them were tales of adventure written by Captain Thomas Mayne Reid (commonly known as Mayne Reid), an Irishman who had arrived in America in the 1840s. Reid had begun writing novels after being seriously wounded during the Battle of Chapultepec while serving in the US Army. He wrote about Native Americans and the horrors of slavery, but the volumes that captivated George the most were those about boys out hunting. Reid's books were quite popular in his day, although they have not stood the test of time.

"I had been brought up, so to speak, on the writings of Captain Mayne Reid. His stories had appealed to my imagination," Grinnell recalled. "It must have been 1860, or possibly 1861, when I was eleven or twelve years old, that I first began to go shooting." George, within his impressionable romantic heart and mind, believed in Reid's philosophy that responsible hunters were a type of biologist as well, and should learn all they could about animals and their habitat. Captain Reid always emphasized that the boys in his stories were "hunter-naturalists," who respected nature and all the wildlife living within it.

The adventurous boys would roam the woods and act out the stories they had read, at first using a borrowed musket so heavy that they could barely handle it. "Small birds were the chief game pursued...meadowlarks, robins, golden winged woodpeckers and occasionally a wild pigeon." The songbirds were brought down not just as easy targets, but with intentions of studying them, just as John James Audubon had done. George would later receive a shotgun from one of his uncles, but the weapon he coveted most was owned by Jack Audubon. His friend carried the same rifle that his famous grandfather had trusted when he went into the wilderness to the West across the Mississippi River to seek out and sketch bird species.

However, it was not all fun and games for the children of Audubon Park. They received an element of structure in their lives by attending an informal home school on the estate grounds. The schoolmistress was none other than Mrs. Lucy Bakewell Audubon, the widow of the naturalist. This school that Lucy conducted for her grandchildren in her second-floor bedroom welcomed neighborhood children as well. This was the first "formal" schooling attended by George Grinnell. Lucy Audubon, known as "Grandma" to the children, would become a dominant force in young George's formative years.

Grinnell had great respect and affection for Grandma Audubon, who acted not only as his teacher but as a surrogate mother figure. He fondly remembered her as the most "kindly, gentle, benignant woman...loved and admired by everyone. [She] was a fit mate for her great husband, for her steadfastness and determination supplied qualities which in some ways he lacked. I believe that of the two she was the stronger—as she was the better balanced—character. If she did not have her husband's vivacity, charm, versatility, and artistic talent, she possessed characteristics more important: the force to keep him up to his work, the faith to cheer his heart when discouraged, the industry and patience to earn money that he might continue his struggle, and the unyielding will to hold the family together. It was largely through her assistance and support that he at last won success."

Lucy had been born on January 18, 1787, in England to William Bakewell and Lucy Green. She was well-educated, first by tutors and then by attending boarding school. She was a voracious reader and loved to spend time in the outdoors, riding horses and exploring her natural surroundings. In 1801, the Bakewell family immigrated to the United States and settled on an estate outside of Philadelphia, Pennsylvania. John James Audubon had spent his childhood roaming the French countryside. He trained briefly as an artist in Paris, where he started observing and painting birds. In 1803, Audubon's father sent him to America to oversee the family plantation, which adjoined the Bakewell estate.

Lucy Bakewell and the young Frenchman eventually met, fell in love, and were married in 1808. She taught him how to speak English; he taught her how to paint; and together they enjoyed long walks in the nearby forest to observe and discuss nature and the wild creatures they encountered. The couple would spend their early years of marriage on the Kentucky frontier where Lucy gave birth to two sons—Victor Gifford in 1809 and John Woodhouse three years later.

After suffering a failed business and being briefly jailed for debts, Audubon decided to turn to his artistic talents to support his family. He announced his intention to paint every bird in North America for eventual publication. As a self-taught ornithologist and talented artist, he had researched birds in their natural habitats since childhood. Over the years, he had gained an intimate knowledge of these birds and their surroundings in the field. But his real genius was in his ability to translate his vision into breathtaking paintings. Audubon hungered to observe those birds that lived in distant places. He left his family in Kentucky and embarked on an expedition down the Ohio and Mississippi Rivers in 1819.

During this time, Lucy, who had been raised by a wealthy and privileged family, became the family provider, which freed her husband to do his work. In 1821, she moved to Louisiana with her sons and began teaching in a local school, which was one of the proper and acceptable professions for a woman in those days. Later, she conducted classes for young ladies, instructing many of the daughters of prestigious plantation families.

In 1823, it was Lucy who traveled to New York City looking for financial support to publish her husband's artwork, but her effort was in vain. She then encouraged Audubon to visit the United Kingdom, where his work might be more appreciated. In 1826, he carried with him three hundred of his original illustrations and embarked on a tour of Europe. Audubon's bird watercolors and his lectures became a sensation overseas, and finally produced a book.

The *Birds of America*, a volume with 435 images, portrayed every bird then known in the United States—each one painted in life size. John James Audubon began touring both America and Europe to lecture and display his work, which caused problems at home.

Lucy did not resent the growing fame of John whatsoever. They had worked hard for years to achieve this result. She simply wanted him back in her arms. She had sacrificed for years, working to support her absentee husband while raising their children. Lucy wrote letters to him expressing her bitterness about art taking priority over family.

Audubon finally came to his senses and reconciled with Lucy. He promised her that she would share fully in every future project and they would work and live together from then on. The publication of *Birds of America* had secured Audubon's reputation as America's leading ornithologist and artist, and he and Lucy went on to become popular figures on both sides of the Atlantic.

John James Audubon died on January 27, 1851, after suffering a stroke. Lucy lived on, preserving her husband's legacy, having supported him both monetarily and emotionally throughout his career.

Lucy, by intimately assisting her husband with his work, had become proficient in the natural sciences. Along with basic school subjects, she was able to relate her knowledge of nature to her Audubon Park pupils, which fit well with the surroundings. Natural history was cutting-edge science in those days, fueled by Charles Darwin's recent study, *On the Origins of Species by Means of Natural Selection.*

The Audubon estate was a virtual natural history museum, and the curriculum included the study of existing specimens and those that frequently arrived for John Woodhouse Audubon. Grinnell would write: "The interior of the Audubon House was attractive— an old-fashioned country house, worn and shabby from the tramping and play of a multitude of children. In the hall were antlers of elk and deer, which supported guns, shot pouches, powder flasks, and belts. Pictures that are now famous hung on the wall. In the dining room facing the entrance from the hall, was the portrait of the naturalist and his dog, painted by John Woodhouse Audubon. The painting of pheasants startled by a dog—now in the American museum—was in the parlor south of the hall, and the picture of the eagle and the lamb upstairs in Madame Audubon's bedroom. Everywhere were vivid memories of the former owner of the land."

That painting of the eagle and the lamb was the favorite of young George. He discussed the work at length with Lucy Audubon. At one point, she told him that after she passed away the painting would be his to own. Grinnell treasured that memory for many years. And, in fact, she kept her promise. Grinnell received a note from Mrs. Audubon just before she died, reminding him that the picture would be given to him in her will. He took possession of the painting after her death, and proudly displayed it in his home.

The influence of Lucy "Grandma" Audubon laid the foundation for Grinnell's lifelong focus on conservation. She once said, "If I can hold the mind of a child to a subject for five minutes, he will never forget what I teach him." She found that open mind in George Bird Grinnell. Her impact on Grinnell's direction in life and future career as an active conservationist cannot be understated. She recognized that the boy had a great interest in the natural way of things, especially those creatures with feathers and wings, and nurtured the budding naturalist inside of him. It was Grandma Audubon who gave young George his first lessons about birds and their habitat and habits. She would privately school him on every species found in that area to the point that he could not remember a time when their common names were not known to him.

One of his earliest memories was being called from the breakfast table one morning to witness a huge flock of now extinct passenger pigeons feeding in a dogwood tree near the house. Young George watched with amazement as the birds tried to land on the branches, but the tree could not hold them all. Many were fluttering about in the air while others were eating berries that had been knocked to the ground. It was one of those magical spectacles of bird behavior that he would never forget.

One winter's day George was on his way to school when he came upon a flock of birds that he could not identify. He caught one of them in a crab net and rushed up to Grandma's room to show her his catch. She told him that he had caught a young Red Crossbill and went on to explain the peculiarities of the bird and even showed him a picture of it. "Then after a little talk, she and I went downstairs and out of doors, and set the captive free."

This episode was typical of Lucy's patience and willingness to share her knowledge with George Grinnell. Perhaps he made her think of her late husband's inquisitive nature about the ways of natural things. Regardless, Grandma Audubon, who died in 1873 before Grinnell had achieved his greatest accomplishments, would have been exceedingly proud of the man he had become and his dedication to preserve and protect nature.

One of George's prized possessions as a youth was a pony that his father had bought for him. His initial ride, however, was anything but pleasant. "The little animal was brought up one summer afternoon and having been saddled and bridled, I was put on it, feeling considerable trepidation. When the person holding it let go the bridle, for some reason the beast bolted and running under the low branches of a hemlock tree close to the saddle, I was swept off, the saddle turning at the same time." The pony was caught, the saddle tightened, and George was soon riding again. "The pony had a trick of galloping along at a good rate, and stopping suddenly, and I invariably turned a summersault over his head and alighted on my back in the road. Sometimes the wind was knocked out of me for a little while, but nothing serious ever occurred."

Whether it was out of necessity or just plain stubbornness, George stayed with that pony and later rode full grown horses and became an excellent horseman. His early training would serve him well when he grew older and his adventures would lead him to places on horseback that he could only dream about as a child.

At age twelve, George began attending Manhattan's French Institute, and two years later was enrolled in Churchill Military

School, a prestigious facility located at Sing Sing. His grades there over three years were never honor roll material, but he did manage to be promoted to the position of commanding a company of students. "I started in as a small boy as a private in the rear rank, and finally got to be an officer in command of the company." Grinnell likely took his studies and behavior most seriously due to national events that affected every American—the Civil War.

At that time back home in Brooklyn, the city was playing a major role in supplying troops and matériel for the War. The Brooklyn seaport and manufacturing center was contributing greatly to the Union cause—the ironclad *Monitor* had been built in Brooklyn. The *Monitor* engaged in history's first duel of ironclads when it encountered the Confederate-manned *Merrimack* at Hampton Roads, a harbor at the mouth of the James River, on March 9, 1862. The *Monitor* would prevail in that brief battle but was later lost— along with sixteen crewmen—in a gale off Cape Hatteras, North Carolina, on New Year's Eve 1862.

Closer to home, George's father was the head of a textile firm that partnered with Southern planters. At the outbreak of the War, the firm's customers were unable to pay their bills, and the textile company went broke. The elder Grinnell settled with most creditors and promised the others that he would pay the remainder that he owed. He then applied his expertise at business on Wall Street and opened what would become a highly profitable investment company.

No doubt George Grinnell and those adventurous teenage boys who had grown up at Audubon Park who were too young to join up closely followed the actions of their hometown regiment. The famous "14th Brooklyn Red-Legged Devils" regiment, named for their red attire and the only regiment in the army named after a city, fought for the duration of the War. It distinguished itself in engagements at the First and Second Battles of Bull Run, Antietam, Fredericksburg, Chancellorsville, Gettysburg, The Wilderness, and Spotsylvania Court House. It was acclaimed for never having withdrawn from a battle in any manner but an orderly fashion.

The unit provided relevant lessons for Grinnell and his contemporaries who were learning about the ways of military life along with regular studies. The boys would excitedly joke about the panicked

cries of Confederate general Thomas "Stonewall" Jackson at the
First Battle of Bull Run when the regiment repeatedly charged up
Henry House Hill to engage the Rebel soldiers: "Hold on boys!
Here come those red-legged devils again!"

In 1865, during George's spring vacation from Churchill, the
news that President Abraham Lincoln had been assassinated
shocked the nation.

*The same morning, I went down to New York City with my mother
and still remember the air of gloom that pervaded the whole city, the
eagerness with which people purchased fresh editions of the newspapers, and the tears which rolled down the faces of the women, and even
some of the men, as they walked along the streets. No one old enough
to observe can ever forget that day. My father took me to the City Hall
where Mr. Lincoln lay in state, and on that occasion I had pointed out
to me a number of well-known men of the day, especially soldiers who
had been in command of large bodies of troops during the war.*

After the war, George was not interested in college, but his
wealthy parents insisted that he attend Yale, the alma mater of several ancestors. "I did not in the least wish to go, and tried to escape
it, but I was not in the habit of questioning my father's decisions."
In preparation, George was enrolled in a boarding school, but faired
poorly. Eventually, through the efforts of several private tutors, he
managed to fulfill the entrance requirements.

George entered Yale in 1866, but due to his spirited nature his
scholastic career became a running flirtation with disaster. He paid
little attention to studies, instead engaging in hazing, hat-stealing,
and clowning around—and once, in an act of bravado, he climbed
the lightning rod on the tower of the Lyceum and painted the numbers of his class year on the face of the clock. George, now nicknamed "Birdie," was suspended from Yale for one year after his
sophomore year for hazing a freshman. "Barely seventeen years old,
and quite without any sense of responsibility, I was perpetually in
trouble."

Young Grinnell and several of his accomplices in crime were sent
to Farmington, Connecticut, for tutoring, but wiled away the year

hiking, boating, and enjoying nature. "At Farmington, we had a very good time, doing very little studying, and spending most of our time out of doors. We took long walks, paddled on the Farmington River, and on moonlight nights in winter used to spend pretty much all night tramping over the fields." Despite the valiant efforts of the supervisor, Reverend L. R. Payne, himself an 1859 graduate of Yale, George lacked the discipline and maturity to take his studies seriously.

Predictably, George failed the tests for readmission the following spring. He may have been happy not attending college, but his parents remained steadfast in their desire for him to graduate from Yale. George was then subjected to intense tutoring by one Dr. Hurlburt, a physician friend of the family. Hurlburt made Grinnell accompany him on his early-morning rounds, and while riding in that buggy had the boy learn lessons and study on his own when the doctor was inside a home visiting a patient. This intense effort by a man whom Grinnell called "not only a good tutor but a good handler of boys" paid off. George easily passed his exams and was readmitted to Yale. "That I did so was not at all to my credit, but was wholly due to Dr. Hurlburt."

George's junior year was unremarkable but at least he stayed out of trouble and maintained acceptable grades. The summer before his senior year, he toured England, France, Scotland, and Switzerland with his parents. Apparently, this tour of the Continent had little appeal or affect on him. The family must have visited all the cities, monuments, and landmarks cherished by foreign sightseers, but George failed to write about any fond memories regarding his adventures or those places that he had toured.

During his senior year, he was elected to Scroll and Key, a secret society at Yale. Otherwise, he maintained his discipline and stayed out of trouble. His studies, however, were another matter. But in 1870, despite the fear that his degree might be "withheld on account of my poor scholarship," Grinnell graduated with an AB degree and no solid plans regarding a future career, although he had nurtured the idea of becoming some sort of naturalist—but there was one major obstacle that dampened his dreams.

Now that the school year was winding down and George Grinnell was assured of receiving his degree, he was faced with a dilemma.

He understood that he was expected to abandon any thought of becoming a naturalist and accept a position as an unpaid clerk in his father's Wall Street office. The elder Grinnell was presently the principal broker for Commodore Cornelius Vanderbilt and intended to groom his son to one day assume control of the profitable investment firm. It was common practice for the sons of fathers who had attained high standing in business to carry on with the family tradition.

For a young man with an adventurous spirit, being chained to a desk inside a drab building when he yearned to be exploring the wonders of nature was a most disagreeable prospect. No doubt George had investigated his options before resigning himself to such a fate, but he was a dutiful son and, in the end, knew that he would obey his father's wishes. A possible temporary reprieve, however, was about to present itself, and, to George Grinnell, it would be the opportunity of a lifetime.

Short and stocky, with a receding hairline, thirty-nine-year-old Othniel Charles Marsh (who preferred to be called "O. C.") was a product of the Yale Scientific School, and then had spent a year studying at Heidelberg and Berlin. He had returned to Yale as a professor of the new science of paleontology and director of a scientific museum his uncle George Peabody was in the process of building for Yale. At that time, the collections at the Smithsonian and Harvard were the leading natural history museums. The year that George Bird Grinnell had entered the school, Marsh had been awarded the first chair of paleontology in the United States.

The particulars of paleontology were relatively unknown at the time. This science had welcomed in a new era of discovery. It was no longer good enough to just locate and map a mountain or a river. Now, it was necessary to closely examine those mountains and waterways to determine what sort of life had existed there before recorded history. That meant digging into the earth's crust to extract the remains of early life. Marsh would form expeditions out West to gather and then study the fossilized bones of extinct creatures to try and understand the origin and development of the planet.

In the summer of 1868 Marsh had discovered fossil fragments of an extinct horse near Antelope Station, Nebraska, which had convinced him that the West was a great untapped reservoir of fossil remains. He had planned to mount an expedition to explore that area in 1869, but widespread Native American uprisings made it impractical.

In this summer of 1870, however, with support from Generals Philip H. Sheridan and William T. Sherman, who promised a military escort, Marsh would lead an entourage of Yale graduate students on the first of a series of western expeditions. His party of volunteers would travel to a part of the country that was relatively unexplored, and then commence the backbreaking work of digging into stubborn rock or soil to extract those precious fossils. There would be danger in the form of hostile Indians, wild animals, unpredictable weather, and, of course, the prospect of arduous travel through the unknown wilderness. It was hoped, however, that this new sophisticated approach to exploration would be as beneficial to the scientific community as traditional reconnaissance had been to the military and commerce.

Word of the expedition made its way around the Yale campus and to the ears of George Bird Grinnell. "When I heard of this proposed expedition," he wrote, "and learned too that the party would be made up from recent graduates of the college, I determined that I must try to be one of these. After several days' consideration, I at last summoned up the courage to call on Professor Marsh, and tell him what I desired. He discouraged me at our first interview, but said that he would inquire about me."

Marsh's statement should have struck fear into the heart of George Grinnell. His academic performance at Yale had been lackluster at best, and any serious inquiry would likely result in disappointment. George, however, met with Marsh on several occasions, and perhaps because of his unbounded enthusiasm or assistance from an unknown benefactor, he was selected with eleven other recent graduates to accompany Marsh to the West. George, just two months short of his twenty-first birthday, had been spared, for the summer at least, the mundane existence of a brokerage clerk.

Professor Marsh intended for his expedition to follow the recently completed transcontinental railroad. From various staging points, they would embark on extended side trips north and south of the line into the rugged badlands of Nebraska, Kansas, Colorado, Wyoming, and Dakota Territory. Railroad officials went out of their way to aid the party, even to the point of lowering or eliminating fares.

On the last day of June 1870, armed with pistols, rifles, Bowie knives, and great quantities of camping paraphernalia, the Yale contingent departed New Haven "bound for a West that was then really wild and woolly." Marsh carried a letter of introduction written by General William Tecumseh Sherman that would gain him assistance and support at every military post on the frontier.

The train ride through the settled portions of the country was uneventful, but as the party neared Omaha, it was apparent that they had reached the edge of known civilization. The group boarded a stern-wheel steamer to cross the Missouri River from Council Bluffs, and George was intrigued by a fellow passenger "who carried a long rifle and wore moccasins. I believed that now I was on the frontier, and I was not far wrong."

Marsh and his young fossil hunters spent a few days getting outfitted in Omaha and familiarizing themselves with their brand-new Henry rifles. Targets were set up on the prairie in what is now downtown Omaha and the young men practiced their marksmanship. The results were initially disappointing, but after some time firing the group decided that they had at least a chance of survival if attacked by hostile Native Americans.

They proceeded by train across eastern Nebraska, where they were halted twice by herds of buffalo that blocked the tracks, which was a common occurrence. On the second occasion, the train would set idly for three full hours before the last buffalo had passed. "We supposed they would pass by," Grinnell recalled, "but they kept coming in numbers so great that they could not be computed."

This sight of thousands of buffalo parading before his eyes must have reminded him of the passage he had read in John James Audubon's journal about the shaggy beast being slaughtered on the plains: "What a terrible destruction of life, as if it were for nothing...as the tongues only were brought in, and the flesh of these fine animals was left to beasts and birds of prey, or to rot on the spots where they fell. The prairies are literally *covered* with the skulls of the victims." The sight of this endless stream of buffalo and

Audubon's prophecy were perhaps a contradiction to George at the time. Little did he know then, but the struggle to save the buffalo from extinction would become an important part of his later life.

Finally, the Marsh party reached Fort McPherson, Nebraska, located on the Oregon Trail near the confluence of the North and South Platte rivers. This frontier fort would be their first staging point. To the north were the rippling sand hills of Nebraska, and then prairie that stretched to Dakota Territory. To the south was the endless rolling prairie of Kansas, and to the west, the barren plains of Colorado Territory.

No sooner had the Yale men climbed down from the rail coaches, when three antelope hunters thundered into the fort, one of them with an arrow stuck in the arm of his blood-soaked buckskin shirt. This hunting party was led by William F. Cody, who was known by the nickname "Buffalo Bill." The hunters had been attacked by a party of a dozen Sioux warriors and engaged in a fight in which one Native American was killed.

This episode of death-defying danger and escape may have been commonplace to those hardy, veteran frontiersmen who frequented those remote forts. But the battered and bloody welcoming committee must have been quite an eye-opening and disquieting shock for a group of freshly graduated, clean-cut young men from the East, only a week removed from the comforts of home. This expedition was merely a summer's interlude before beginning normal lives as lawyers or businessmen, and none of them at that time believed that they would ever participate in such an experience again in their lifetime.

It would be reasonable to assume that at least a few, if not all, of the young men had second thoughts about this excursion far away from the comforts and security of New Haven and wondered what dangers the West might have in store for them. What they did know, however, was that Marsh's expedition would be the adventure of a lifetime—if only they survived it.

CHAPTER TWO

A TENDERFOOT IN THE WEST

*Do not go where the path may lead, go instead where there is no path
and leave a trail.*
—RALPH WALDO EMERSON

IT WOULD BE PROBABLE THAT ALL THESE NEWCOMERS HAD
heard of William F. Cody. At the tender age of twenty-four, Buffalo
Bill was fast becoming a living legend, courtesy of a series of popular dime novels written about him by Ned Buntline. Although his
adventures were usually fictionalized and greatly exaggerated in
print, Cody had plenty of real-life credentials to brag about, especially to an eastern tenderfoot.

At fourteen, Cody had ridden for the Pony Express, and during
the Civil War had served with a "jayhawker" militia company in
Kansas, participating in numerous skirmishes against the Rebels
and the Confederate-allied Kiowa and Comanche tribes. In 1867,
he had contracted to supply buffalo meat for workers on the Kansas
Pacific Railroad, and his proficiency had earned the nickname
"Buffalo Bill." The following year, Cody had served as chief of
scouts for the Fifth Cavalry during General Sheridan's winter campaign against the Cheyenne tribe, and it was said that he had taken
part in at least sixteen fights with Native Americans.

George Grinnell was impressed by the appearance of this young
but seasoned frontiersman. "He was a tall, well-built, handsome

man who wore his blonde hair long and was a striking figure; above all on horseback. Like many outdoor men on the plains and in the mountains in those early days, he wore buckskin clothing, and in such dress Cody's splendid physique made him very noticeable."

General Sherman had written to Cody asking him to serve as the guide for the Marsh expedition. Now, however, the post commander wanted Buffalo Bill to hunt down the Sioux that had attacked the hunting party. Thirty-year-old Major Frank North, another experienced scout and plainsman, was chosen to guide the Marsh party.

North, a native New Yorker, had immigrated at a young age to Nebraska, where he became acquainted with the local Pawnee tribe and learned their language. After a brief stint hauling freight to the Colorado goldfields, North returned home to work as interpreter for the Indian agent at the Pawnee reservation.

Frank North gained fame throughout the West as the commander of a battalion of Pawnee Indians during the Civil War, which saw action and gained recognition against their natural enemy, the Sioux, in Dakota Territory. In the fall of 1865, North and his company returned to the Pawnee reservation, and on Christmas Day, he married twenty-year-old Mary Louise Smith, with whom he had one daughter. He reorganized the battalion several years later for the purpose of protecting crews building the Union Pacific Railroad and was presently scouting for the army. The effort of assembling the Pawnee Battalion into a credible fighting force was notable because the prevailing thought had been that Native Americans could not be taught to fight together as a unit. They were accustomed to fighting "every man for himself" during battles. Frank North proved them wrong.

Cody and North had spent part of the previous summer serving as guides for the Fifth Cavalry at Fort McPherson, which had pursued a fierce and resourceful band of Cheyenne Dog Soldiers, led by Chief Tall Bull. In July 1869, after a five-hundred-mile chase, the army had engaged in a battle and defeated their enemy at Summit Springs. When the fight ended, fifty-two Cheyenne had been killed, among them Tall Bull, who had died at the hands of either North or Cody. A pony herd of over four-hundred animals had been confiscated, and the entire village was destroyed. This major victory had effectively crushed Cheyenne resistance on the plains and forced the tribe onto reservations.

Two days after their arrival at the fort, George Grinnell and his companions were escorted by Cody and North out to the corral to select the horses that they would ride on the expedition. By that time, the young men had heard countless firsthand accounts about the Summit Springs battle from the Fifth Cavalry officers and men, and likely were in wide-eyed awe of the two army guides. Their excitement heightened when they were told that the mounts from which they would choose were Cheyenne ponies that had been captured from Tall Bull's village during that famous fight.

On July 10—with the rattle of arms, creak of wagon wheels, and clink of spurs—the Marsh expedition rode out of the fort on their Indian ponies. Every volunteer sported a rifle, a Bowie knife, a revolver or two, and a geological hammer and shovel. Major North and two Pawnee scouts led the way, and then came the Yale party, followed by a company of the Fifth Cavalry commanded by Lieutenant Bernard Reilly Jr. There were six army wagons loaded with provisions, feed for the horses, tents, and extra ammunition. Buffalo Bill Cody, who was curious to see how the tenderfeet would handle themselves, rode along with the fossil hunters for the first day. In all, there were seventy men in this historic fossil-hunting expedition.

Grinnell recalled: "Except through what they had read, Professor Marsh and his party knew nothing about the West. It was an entirely innocent body of 'pilgrims' starting out to face dangers of which they were wholly ignorant. The Sioux and Cheyenne occupied the country of western Nebraska and that to the north and northwest, and they objected strongly to the passage of people through their territory, and when they believed they had the advantage—they attacked."

The procession moved slowly and with difficulty across the Platte River, northward through the sand-dappled hills. The Pawnee led the way, creeping up over mounds and peering out from behind bunches of grass for sign of the Sioux. Major Frank North had the responsibility of guiding them along the smoothest and safest path, yet the going was precarious. The wheels of the heavy wagons could easily crack through the thin cover of green and rust-colored grass and stall in the sand beneath.

Professor Marsh was enthralled by this rugged country and lectured to his students from the saddle about the origins of that vast wilderness. He told them how at one time all the hills within sight had been at the bottom of a great freshwater lake, and how even before that an inland sea had covered most of the West and lapped at the foot of the young Rocky Mountains.

The route followed by the party of paleontologists and soldiers led them over treeless sand hills, where the temperature shot up to as high as 110 degrees. "We were 14 hours in the saddle without a drop of water except what we carried in our canteens," Grinnell wrote to his parents. "I never realized what thirst was before. Your mouth becomes perfectly dry and your lips split."

For five days, they would endure the intense heat, broken only by an isolated thunderstorm, from which the party filled their hats and drank. Then the expedition turned west along the Platte to its headwaters, at which point they again headed south and struck the North Platte River near the mouth of Bird Wood Creek and continued to the Loup Fork River. At that point, the rippling sand hills ended abruptly and gave way to a series of white cliffs. Also, winding away from the river were numerous small canyons with walls of bare rock. It was here that Professor Marsh decided that their geological investigation would commence.

Fossils were found in rocks such as sandstone, mudstone, and limestone that have hardened over long periods of time. Since most fossils were created when the layers of sediment from a river or lake covered a dinosaur's body, the trained paleontologist would search for places where the sedimentary rock appeared to be as old as a dinosaur. Usually the sides of river canyons were the best place to start because the layers of rock were well exposed—as it was here on the Loup Fork.

Each day, the soldiers stood guard, and the wagons and the rest of the column would move slowly up the river to keep pace with the efforts of the fossil hunters as they dug into the earth and rock in search of bones.

Marsh's volunteers chipped away at the layers of loose rock with their hammers and dug into the subsoil with a shovel or trowel or by hand, brushing away the dirt with delicate strokes to expose the fossils, some of which were quite fragile. The exact location of each find was registered as precisely as possible, then the objects were meticulously removed, cleaned, analyzed, and stored for safekeeping. The work was hard, the heat relentless, and the volunteers were aware that danger lurked just beyond the horizon.

The column had been shadowed day and night by Sioux war parties. The Native Americans regarded the presence of these whites as an intrusion into their territory. Sign that the Sioux were nearby could be found everywhere. Grinnell and his companions thought they could hear the thundering hoof beats of Indian ponies in the night. Smoke signals were commonplace during daylight hours.

There had been no direct contact or actual sightings of Native Americans that would indicate an immediate threat, however. The Sioux might attack a few antelope hunters—such as Buffalo Bill's party—but would generally avoid confrontations with a group of seventy armed men, even if some of them were tenderfoot Yale men. Everyone, however, was warned not to wander away from camp, even in small groups.

There on the Loup Fork, where the river had eroded away the strata, Grinnell and his fellow volunteers, often on hands and knees, dug into the rock and clay surfaces along the stream beds seeking specimens of ancient fauna. Their efforts were soon met with extraordinary success.

Along that stretch of the river, the party collected an array of Pliocene mammals—primitive horses, miniature camels, rhinos, birds, and a mastodon. Marsh was particularly interested in fossils of horses and had told his workers to concentrate on finding as many of those as possible. They responded by unearthing six different horse species.

The enthusiasm of the volunteers for their work was contagious. Eager, off-duty soldiers were caught up in the fossil frenzy and frequently volunteered to join in the digging. The Pawnee, who believed that the bones belonged to an ancient race of giants, at first refused to take part. Marsh, however, set them at ease when he held up the jawbone of a fossil horse close to the jaw of one of their ponies, showing how the two were similar. From that time forward, the Pawnee scouts brought in many fossils to Marsh, whom they called the "Bone Medicine Man."

Grinnell was fascinated by the two Pawnee scouts, and studied them with the eye of a future ethnologist. "Both of them were celebrated, the oldest as a warrior and the youngest as a hunter. They wore their hair long and had their scalp locks neatly braided, and sometimes they would decorate them with a piece of bright colored cloth or a feather. They were jolly fellows, both of them, and they would sing and dance for us frequently."

The party also came across several Sioux funeral platforms. One of them contained the crusty remains of a women lying beside a scalpless man, whose face was streaked with war paint and a rusty shotgun had been placed in his hands. The young men somberly observed this morbid scene with reverence—ancient fossil bones were one thing, but relatively fresh human remains were another matter. Perhaps they were more than a little shocked when Professor Marsh said, "Well, boys, perhaps they died of smallpox; but we can't study the origin of the Indian race unless we have those skulls." The skulls were removed and added to the Yale collection.

The nights in camp, with fires burning, meals cooking, and guards posted, were quite pleasant. The young men relaxed, wrote letters home, smoked their pipes, discussed the day's dig, listened to western stories told by the soldiers, and often engaged in frivolous activities similar to an overnight camping trip back home.

Grinnell wrote about one such night: "We all put on our blankets and marched in single file to the Indian tent, where we sat in a circle and smoked the pipe of peace. Then the major made a speech in Pawnee, [the younger Pawnee] answered him, and then one of our fellows made a stump speech to the Indians, which, as they did not understand English, delighted them. They sang the buffalo song…we sang some college songs, and then the council broke up."

Huge herds of game were everywhere, the most abundant animal being the pronghorn antelope. Every day Major North would take along one of the Yale boys when he went out to hunt. "No member of the party killed anything," Grinnell admitted, "which is not surprising in view of the fact that none of us knew anything of hunting or rifle shooting. Major North and the Indians kept us supplied with fresh meat."

Also found in great numbers was the majestic animal that the easterners regarded as the grandest of western trophies—the elk. One herd of elk was spotted on the north bank of the Loup Fork, and Grinnell, in the company of two soldiers, set off to hunt. By the time they had crossed the river, however, the elk had disappeared over a bluff and the hunters dared not follow due to the possible presence of the Sioux.

The Indians had thus far remained out of sight and had not bothered the party in any manner. One night, however, as the sun set amid black thunderclouds, they observed a line of orange light that danced across the darkening plain. The Sioux had decided to test the meddle of the white men and had ignited a prairie fire on both sides of the Loup Fork that quickly advanced toward the fossil hunters' camp.

Each gust of wind from the rising storm would sweep whole hill-sides into a sheet of flames, as stands of cottonwood and pine trees flared up, and eventually created a rain of cinders and debris that fell upon the camp. The men anxiously watched the spectacle of the fire moving toward them as they beat out the cinders with blankets.

The fire approached more rapidly on the south bank of the Loup, directly across the river from the camp. "At last, when the fire got just opposite us, it rushed down the bank into a clump of cedars and burnt furiously," Grinnell wrote. "We were afraid that it would cross and destroy everything."

Lieutenant Reilly, aware that the Sioux could attack behind the wall of flames, was hesitant to deploy his troops to fight the fire. He finally ordered that a backfire be set to burn the prairie between the camp and the main fire, and a detail of troops were dispatched to battle the onrushing flames. The situation remained dangerous until the wind shifted, and the thunderstorm moved in to drench the camp and extinguish the fire. The Sioux had remained distant, perhaps believing that their mischief would serve as a warning and encourage the column to turn back.

The subject of returning to relative civilization was discussed that night, but not due to the Sioux harassment. As the expedition had moved along, the Loup Fork had turned into a trickle and water was becoming scarce. The morning after the fire, the column assembled and passed over the smoldering, charred prairie, with its roasted plant life and toasted grasshoppers, heading south toward the Platte River.

The party emerged near North Platte, Nebraska, and, in an act of tomfoolery, the Pawnee scouts led the Yale boys on a mock raid of the town. When this strange cavalcade of Indians and the by-now-shaggy paleontologists approached the town at the gallop, hooting and hollering, the entire population turned out with rifles in hand, fearing that Indians were swooping down on them. Grinnell and his companions were greatly amused—not so the good citizens of North Platte. All was soon forgiven, however, and the party sat down to dinner with china plates for the first time in more than two weeks and bought items at the general store.

Back at nearby Fort McPherson, the Yale men dined with the army officers, and listened once again to the thrilling, and unquestionably embellished, tales of frontier exploits, while preparing their fossils for shipment to New Haven.

Marsh and his volunteers then shifted their base of operations farther west, taking the train to Cheyenne, Wyoming, and then making their way to Fort D. A. Russell. "Here I had my first experience with a bucking horse," Grinnell mentioned, "and was twice ingloriously thrown."

The party, accompanied by a thirty-man detachment of soldiers from Company I of the Fifth Cavalry under the command of Lieutenant James McB. Stembel, set off from the fort into a region of northeastern Colorado lying between the north and south forks of the Platte River. This was a previously unknown, unexplored badlands, composed of hard, white-rock washboard cliffs that appeared to be of the same age and character as the Dakota badlands, some two-hundred miles to the northeast.

Here again Marsh and his fossil hunters had extraordinary success. South of the White River of South Dakota, they located a Miocene formation which had never been seen before. This site yielded great quantities of bones—prehistoric turtles, rhinoceri, birds, rodents, and the curious remains of oreodons, which Grinnell described as "a remarkable animal combining characteristics of the modern sheep, pig, and deer." They also found a specimen of a gigantic horned Titanothere (*Titanotherium proutii*), a grazing beast that looked like a rhino and stood as tall as an elephant, whose jaw alone measured four feet in length.

Professor Marsh was so excited that he immediately sent a letter describing these discoveries back to Yale for publication in the next edition of the *American Journal of Science and Arts*.

The party moved into western Nebraska and stopped at Antelope Station, where they scoured the nearby cliffs and found three more species of fossil horses. In this area, the main threat to their well-being was not the Sioux but rattlesnakes. Three draft animals were killed by snake bites, and the young men endured a constant rattling serenade as they worked.

Marsh then headed south toward Scotts Bluff on the banks of the Platte River. They traveled across a bizarre prairie of volcanic ash, with bluffs and cones rising from the floor, that had been created as ancient silt and gravel had washed down from the uplands. These bluffs looming on the western horizon, which towered five-hundred feet over the mesa, were a welcome sign to wagon train pioneers on the Oregon Trail. It indicated that they had covered six-hundred miles of their 2,000-mile journey, a distance that would usually take about two months from their starting point of Independence, Missouri.

The professor located another patch of badlands—deep ravines choked with sagebrush—and, with the soldiers standing guard, George and the other volunteers searched for fossils as they made their way in the direction of Fort D. A. Russell down Horse Creek, a small stream that flowed into the North Platte.

On the early morning of August 20, Professor Marsh asked Grinnell and John Nicholson to ride off by themselves down the creek and bag enough ducks for the evening meal. They were assured by an army officer that the creek ran parallel to the direction of the moving wagon train, which would cover perhaps twenty miles that day. "We were told," Grinnell wrote home, "not to pay any attention to the movements of column but to follow the creek until we came to the night's camp."

By noon, Grinnell and Nicholson had followed the creek for about fifteen miles and had taken enough ducks for the evening meal. The two young men, as they moved down the creek, had not observed the wagon train since they had departed and were now quite anxious to discover its whereabouts. They were keenly aware that they were roaming through country inhabited by hostile Sioux and Cheyenne, and cautiously left the creek to try and find the trail of the wagons. The two Yale men rode up onto a ridge to look for any signs of movement or a camp, but saw nothing but endless, barren prairie.

Unknown to that army officer, who was supposed to know such things, Horse Creek made a great bend that would lead the duck hunters away from the destination of the column.

To add to the anxiety, Grinnell and Nicholson happened upon another Sioux burial platform, on which a man rested who had only recently died. "His knife, which was by him, was not rusted, and his long black hair looked fresh," George wrote. Always the naturalist, however, he also observed that "a pair of barn swallows had commenced a nest on the underpart of the litter he was laid on."

After examining the Sioux corpse, Grinnell and Nicholson traveled southwest for seven or eight miles and were astonished when they struck Horse Creek again. They calculated that the creek had bent around almost at right angles with its former course and decided instead of venturing off onto the prairie once more that they would follow the waterway.

"About this time, 2 or 3 p.m.," Grinnell wrote, "we saw smoke in the east. At first we were afraid it was an Indian signal fire, but after watching it awhile we saw that it was the prairie burning."

The two young men hurried along the creek, but when the flames were within a half mile of them, Grinnell dismounted and set a backfire in the creek bottom, which appeared to slow the raging fire. They rode several hundred yards down the creek, when Grinnell decided to set another backfire.

"I dismounted and gave my horse to Jack to hold, and also my gun," Grinnell stated. "I had set the fire in two places and was lighting a match for the third, when suddenly I heard Jack scream to me 'mount Birdie mount.' I knew by his tone that there was danger, so without looking round I jumped on my horse and then turned to take my gun from him. At that moment the fire was not twenty feet from us, the flames were 5 or 6 feet high, and the air was so hot and filled with smoke that we could not breathe."

Grinnell and Nicholson raced away and finally outran the wall of fire, which Grinnell said came "near enough to singe the hair on our faces and on the horses."

They had escaped the prairie fire but were no closer to locating the camp. By sunset, they had given up all hope of finding their companions in the near future and rode down into a small gulch to stop and assess the situation.

"We watered our horses and picketed them where they could get the best food," Grinnell explained, "and then Jack and I cleaned and ate a saw duck. We had no wood, and if we had, we would not have dared to build a fire for fear of Indians. After our duck Jack and I had a talk over our chances, and we decided that they were very small. We thought that in all probability, the Indians had been watching us all day from the bluffs, and that at night they would come down and lift our hair."

By now, it was pitch dark, and Grinnell and Nicholson decided to move, with intentions of following their own back trail to the route of the wagons. They stealthily rode down the stream bed for several hundred yards, and then cut across the prairie for about a mile and a half, where they decided to stop and make camp for the night. The ground was quite soft, so they could not adequately picket the horses. Instead, they tied the lead ropes around their legs, and attempted to sleep. Every time a bird or animal rustled in the bushes, however, they would sit up and listen.

The horses were as restless as the young men, and at one point during the night, according to Grinnell, Jack was "dragged twelve or fifteen feet out into the prairie, while I, under the impression that this was the beginning of an Indian attack, sat up with my shotgun across my knees, determined to sell my life as dearly as possible."

At dawn, Grinnell and Nicholson headed down the creek, halting at the Sioux burial platform, where they built a small fire and cooked another duck for breakfast. "It is true that the entrails had turned green," Grinnell remembered, "but nevertheless, I think that I never ate anything that tasted so good."

The food, however, had failed to raise their spirits. Grinnell wrote that "we were now getting rather tired, and the constant anxiety was so great that Jack was almost done up, and I myself was feeling pretty badly discouraged. I wanted to hurry right on, while Jack had given up in despair. He wanted to stay where he was and wouldn't come on."

But George Bird Grinnell was not about to concede defeat and simply wait to be discovered by the Sioux. After considerable coaxing, he managed to get Nicholson into the saddle. Grinnell led the way, searching for the trail, while Jack was "doubled up on the saddle, paying no attention to anything."

Finally, perhaps miraculously for this resolute but inexperienced easterner, he struck the trail of the wagons. By late afternoon, the two men straggled into the camp of the main party.

Grinnell told about the reaction of their companions: "Of course we were received with congratulations, for no one in camp ever expected to see us again. Early the day we got in, some of the soldiers picked up an Indian pony, and it was supposed by everyone in the outfit that we were killed, and that the Indians after taking our horses and traps, had turned this pony loose because he was lame."

Although no doubt shaken by his experience and overwhelmed with relief, Grinnell displayed youthful exuberance when he wrote:

I am happy to say that though there were scouting parties out after us all day, we made our way into camp without any assistance from anyone.

Even Buffalo Bill would have approved. Grinnell had faced a variety of perils in this bleak wilderness, and had survived, perhaps earning him the right to shed his status as a "tenderfoot."

The fossil hunters reached Fort D. A. Russell on August 23 and boarded a Union Pacific train headed west. The next phase of the expedition would operate out of Fort Bridger, which was in southwestern Wyoming on the edge of the Uinta Mountains.

"Fort Bridger was not an active place," Grinnell wrote, "but its situation was delightful. A few soldiers were stationed there, and it was still a military post. From time to time, groups of Indians from south or north camped near it, stayed for a little while, sold their furs or purchased goods at the trader's store, then went on. To people who had just come in from two or three months spent on the hot dry plains to the eastward, the post with its timber, its green grass, and its trout streams, seemed very attractive."

At the end of August, Marsh's party, escorted by a detachment from the thirteenth Infantry under the command of Lieutenant W. N. Winn, headed south through the sand and clay soil of Bridger Basin. The going was once again difficult, as the wheels of the heavy wagons sank into the soft earth. At one point, they tried to lighten the wagons by caching a load of grain. That, however, was not enough to alleviate the problem. Finally, O. C. Marsh sent back to Fort Bridger for packsaddles. The provisions and equipment were then distributed on the backs of sure-footed mules, which was an improvement over the cumbersome wagons.

The expedition traveled down the Green River, with its emerald waters bound by flaming red cliffs, the same region that explorer John Wesley Powell had navigated the previous year. They would travel a circuitous route—down the Green to the junction of the White River, up that waterway for an undetermined distance, then head north for the return trip over the mountains back to the fort.

Grinnell was greatly impressed by the Green River country, and eloquently wrote:

From where it rises—a little brook in Fremont's Peak—the Green River rolls southward an impetuous torrent, its volume constantly increasing as it receives the tribute brought by a thousand channels from the lofty mountains through which it flows. Its waters are dark and black as it sweeps through some narrow passage where the sun's rays never penetrate, but assumes when spread out in the clear light of day the pale green color from which it takes its name. It is a glorious river. The territory through which it passes presents some of the most majestic scenery that our country can afford. For miles it rushes through deep and gloomy canyons, whose precipitous sides offer no inequality that might serve as the resting place for a bird; or through stony valleys, where the water leaps and dashes against the rocks as though they were enemies. It roars between high mountains, rock-ribbed and dark with their evergreen foliage, or sublime with their mantles of everlasting snows, and glides pleasantly through fertile valleys, where nature is the only husbandman.

The horse that George Grinnell had been given to ride on this leg of the journey was a green colt that was only partly broken, and it became quite a handful for him to manage at times. It was suggested that he could possibly purchase a more reliable mount from some trappers who were camped over on Henry's Fork.

One morning, he set off to locate this trappers' camp. "I recall pleasantly," he wrote, "the ride through the cool fresh day to Henry's Fork. The mountains and their animals were new to me. I was young and enthusiastic and enjoyed all that I saw."

Grinnell paused on his ride to observe the antics of a beaver, the first he had ever seen, and reached Henry's Fork at sundown, where he located three buffalo-skin lodges standing near the water's edge. He was warmly greeted by the resident trappers and was introduced to their Shoshonie wives and "a large flock of children of various sizes." One of the trappers "gave me robes and blankets for my bed; then by the small lodge fire, which was needed for light only and not for warmth, we talked far into the night."

These mountain men were the rugged western individualists that George Grinnell had hoped to encounter on this trip, the type of men that he had read and fantasized about as a boy, and he made the most of his time with them.

In the morning, the young easterner accompanied one trapper as he checked his traps, and then watched with interest as the man skinned the two beavers that he had caught. He tagged along as the trappers hunted deer; one of them pointing out to him a wildcat perched on the branch of a tree. Many hours were also wiled away in camp, with Grinnell asking endless questions and listening intently as his hosts related stories about the lore of the wilderness West that stirred his romantic blood.

This new experience with the trappers—of all the events on the expedition—made the greatest impression on the young man. He wrote:

These men lived in just the fashion of the old-time trappers of early western days. They possessed that independence which all men seek. Theirs was everything a man needs—food, clothing, shelter, and family. They were masters of their own lives. Their mode of life appealed strongly to a young man fond of the open, and while I was with them I could not imagine a more attractive—a happier—life than theirs. I desired enormously to spend the rest of my life with these people, but, of course, the knowledge of the grief this would give my parents pulled me back again.

The next day, riding a newly purchased horse, Grinnell regretfully left the trappers' camp and returned to the main party.

The Marsh expedition meandered south through mountain passes that were already covered with snow—one pass rose to an elevation of eleven-thousand feet—and headed in the direction of Fort Uinta, in southern Utah, over a crude route recently opened by the army to supply the Uinta Indian Agency. They would stop here and there to dig at Marsh's direction, excavating the earth in several areas to reveal its fossil treasures. Each specimen was diligently cataloged and stored in the saddlebags of the mules.

In traveling through this primitive mountain region, the party experienced a firsthand view of various aspects of western life. George Grinnell and his companions hunted elk, duck, grouse, and other wild game to supplement the menu. John Nicholson, out duck hunting again, was chased by a grizzly bear. They passed a hunting party of Ute Indians, with horses pulling their lodge poles and children strapped to cradleboards that were slung over saddle pommels. When rations ran low, the group feasted on a mule that had the misfortune of breaking its neck when it stepped in a badger hole.

At one point, they spoke briefly with a posse that was tracking some horse thieves who were known as the Brown's Hole gang. A short time later, the thieves themselves were encountered, and Marsh noticed that these outlaws had located and stolen the Yale grain cache. Marsh approached the men with intentions of getting his grain back. When face to face with these desperadoes, who were "armed to the teeth," however, Marsh apparently thought better of demanding that his property be returned and resorted to small talk before the expedition moved on. The fact that these men were not confronted by the soldiers perhaps attests to the extent of their notoriety.

As they exited the mountains, the expedition came upon a fantastic scene—an expanse of stark Eocene rock, signifying the Uinta badlands. In this desolate, wild, and broken place, so lifeless and silent that it seemed the ruins of the world, they dug for fossils along the edges of ragged ridges and bluffs of every conceivable form, and drank from cool, pure streams that flowed from dark canyons carved into mountainsides. Here, Marsh and his volunteers opened Tertiary lake-bed formations that for years to come would yield endless specimens of dinosaurs and other ancient reptiles.

George Grinnell, perhaps yearning to emulate the mountain men with whom he had bonded, described a typical evening in their camp:

> *Around the glowing fire a dozen men are stretched upon the ground. Bearded, bronzed by exposure to all weathers, and clothed in buckskin, you might take them all at first glance for a party of trappers; but their speech betrays their occupation, and shows you that they are members of some scientific expedition. The evening meal over, they have lighted their pipes, and are discussing with animated voice and gesture the various prizes obtained during the day. Some exult in a new fossil; others examine some rare bird; others still are looking over their tools. Soon after the sun goes down we wrap our buffalo robes around us and ere long are soundly asleep.*

The party finished its work in the Uinta badlands and retraced their route through the mountains, arriving back at Fort Bridger around the middle of September. Once again, the volunteers carefully packed the precious fossils, which were then shipped east to the Peabody Museum.

Shortly after returning to the post, Grinnell had:

> *…the interesting experience of driving stage for the distance of eleven miles, from the Fort to Bridger Station on the Union Pacific Railroad, and back. The driver, whom I remember as Charley, and whom I had accompanied on one or two trips, got hurt and I took his place for a few days. The mules we drove were pack animals, unbroken to harness. They had to be roped, tied up, harnessed, and by force hitched to the*

stage. For the first six or seven miles of the road, the frightened animals ran as hard as they could, and the drive was exciting, but coming back from the railroad station they went quietly enough.

After such an arduous trek through the Uinta Mountains, Marsh and his volunteers turned to more civilized endeavors. They traveled to Salt Lake City, where Grinnell and the other young men "flirted with twenty-two daughters of Brigham Young in a box at the theater."

Professor O. C. Marsh engaged in conversations with Young regarding the fossil horses that had been unearthed. It was clear to Brigham Young that Marsh had found the ancient horses described in the Book of Mormon, which had previously been somewhat of an embarrassment to nineteenth-century Mormon prophets. Marsh's discovery soon became celebrated throughout the desert as one more demonstration that the lost tribe of Mormon had indeed existed in North America.

The next stop was California, where they visited San Francisco and took a side trip to Yosemite and the Mariposa Grove of sequoia trees. After five months exploring the West, George Grinnell and most of volunteers returned to New York City in time for Thanksgiving. Marsh and a few of his assistants returned to the plains of Kansas for one more fossil search and would return home in December.

Professor Marsh and his volunteers had amassed a fossil collection that filled thirty-five boxes. It consisted of over one hundred species of extinct vertebrates new to paleontologists, which created quite a sensation in the scientific world and with the public. This collection would be the nucleus of exotic creatures around which the Peabody, one of the world's great natural history museums, would be constructed, and became the foundation of Marsh's later writings. This group of bones alone would sustain Marsh's studies for many years.

The Marsh Expedition of 1870 marked the beginning of a cycle of rediscovery by a generation concerned with a more sophisticated exploration than their predecessors. The bones were not merely specimens to be hidden away in museum drawers, rather were treated as pieces used to try and complete a puzzle of learning about the dramatic changes that had occurred over the ages. The trip had not only introduced a new form of science to America but had changed forever the life of one of its members.

For George Bird Grinnell, being part of such a groundbreaking expedition was certainly a source of pride. But, more importantly, he had undergone an awakening in those five months. His love of nature had merged with an admiration for the West and its colorful history.

This mysterious land that he had read about had more than lived up to every expectation. He had embraced life on those dusty plains and grassy prairies, and high atop jagged mountain peaks as if he had been born to it. The diverse characters that he had encountered— plainsmen, soldiers, mountain men, and Native Americans—had appealed to his romantic vision of this vast wilderness. And the dangers that he had faced served as fuel to stoke the fire of his adventurous spirit. No longer would he consider himself merely an easterner but, in his heart and soul, he was now a westerner as well.

On the train ride home, George Grinnell likely brooded about his impending entrance into the business world. When an impressionable young man who already appreciated nature had witnessed those moon-blanched silver mountain peaks against a deep blue sky; heard the mournful murmuring of the night wind through a pine tree forest; and experienced the dance of wild expectation in the earth's quivering pulse, not to mention the thrill and the joy of heart-stopping action in dangerous moments, there was always a yearning for more of the same. The skyscrapers of New York and the bustle on the sidewalks could not compare with the romance of the untamed wilderness. Grinnell vowed that he would find a way to get back to the West again very soon.

CHAPTER THREE:
BUFFALO HUNTING WITH THE PAWNEE

*Pursue some path, however narrow and crooked, in which you can
walk with love and reverence.*
—HENRY DAVID THOREAU

GEORGE BIRD GRINNELL DUTIFULLY—AND PERHAPS GRUDGINGLY
—accepted a position as a clerk in his father's Wall Street office. The
elder Grinnell was the principal broker for Commodore Cornelius
Vanderbilt, who controlled the New York Central system of railroads. He expected his son to one day assume control of the profitable firm, Geo. Grinnell and Company. It was without question
an excruciating experience for Grinnell to spend his days indoors
being schooled about the intricacies of buying and selling stocks.

His father was a patient tutor, however, and soon young Grinnell
was involved in high-stakes transactions, such as buying stocks "on
margin." The brokerage would borrow money at rock bottom rates
and lend it to the investor to buy stocks at a slightly higher rate. As
long as the stocks rose in price there was no danger. If stock prices
dropped and customers could not repay when the brokerage had a
"margin call," entire fortunes could be wiped out in an instant—and
brokerages could go bankrupt. At the time, George Grinnell had no
qualms about this risky practice, believing that prices always "would
go much higher."

Like most brokers, Grinnell and Company invested heavily in railroads, which was regarded as the growth industry in those days. Railroads were expanding across the country, and no one believed that their stocks would not continue to gain in worth. But the firm had a security blanket just in case. When the elder Grinnell or his son extended credit to a client, it was with the knowledge that should trouble occur it would be tempered by the deep pockets of partner Horace F. Clark, who was the son-in-law of the company's biggest client, Cornelius Vanderbilt. "So long as Mr. Clark was living," Grinnell wrote, "any additional margin required was always forthcoming."

Grinnell put in long hours and learned the business inside and out. However, he yearned to be involved in scientific investigation. In his spare time, he scoured New York and Connecticut for fossils and unusual birds, and often spent his free time practicing taxidermy. He confessed that he would "spend two or three hours of the evening down in the cellar, where I had an excellent outfit for mounting birds."

He also maintained his relationship with Professor O. C. Marsh, and occasionally performed small tasks for him at the Peabody Museum. He would seek out unusual fossils and osteological material—bones and skeletons—that would somehow end up for sale in various shops around the region. He would barter on a price and then provide the item for Marsh to study at the museum.

In time, however, Grinnell needed a break from the world of business and high finance. "In the summer of 1872," he wrote, "I was anxious again to go out West." To that end, he wrote to Major Frank North, the guide for the Marsh expedition, and asked if a buffalo hunt might be arranged. "These hunts of the Indians had been described to me with the graphic eloquence that filled me with enthusiasm as I listened to the recital, and I had determined that if ever the opportunity offered I would take part in one."

Major North replied that he was not available, but his younger brother Luther, nicknamed "Lute," would serve as guide. Accompanied by Jim Russell, a friend from the 1870 expedition, Grinnell traveled to Nebraska and was met by Lute North with horses, provisions, a cook, and a supply wagon. The party then set off to rendezvous with the Pawnee tribe—four-thousand strong—which was preparing to engage in their annual summer buffalo hunt.

Twenty-six-year-old Luther North had been born in Richmond County, Ohio, and moved to Omaha at age ten. Lute had tagged along with his older brother, Frank, as the elder North worked at clearing land for new settlers and hauling freight, which by 1861 brought them to the Pawnee reservation near Columbus, Nebraska. Lute became proficient in the Pawnee language and was accepted and respected by that tribe.

In 1863, during the Civil War, Lute enlisted in the Second Nebraska Cavalry and accompanied General Alfred Sully's Sioux Expedition in Minnesota. The following year he hauled freight between Columbus and Fort Kearny, and then signed on to scout for the army—nearly losing his life in a skirmish with the Sioux. In 1866, Luther joined his brother on a scout with the Pawnee battalion, and the following year became captain of one of their companies. The Pawnee scouts were involved in numerous battles and skirmishes over the ensuing years, including that monumental July 1869 Battle of Summit Springs. After the war, Luther established a successful business guiding easterners on hunts throughout the West. George Grinnell was in capable hands with Lute North as his personal guide.

The Pawnee reservation where they were headed was located along the Loup River in Nebraska. This tribe, formidable both as fighters and hunters, was one of the tribes that dominated the heart of the grasslands during the early and middle decades of the nineteenth century. The world in which they lived, however, was one of swift and violent transition. They fought hard to maintain territory rights, often raiding other tribes for horses—and for captives.

There was one ritual that had set the Pawnee apart from other Plains tribes—human sacrifice. Only the ancient peoples, such as the Aztec and Maya, had practiced the ritual killing of another human being. Other Plains tribes would enslave enemies or use them for trading purposes but did not kill them in a ceremony. Not so the Pawnee.

On their raids of other tribes, the Pawnee would take captives.

All the captives except one would be adopted into their tribe. One unlucky captive would be sacrificed to their creator god Ti-ra' wa and to the Morning Star, which was actually the planet Venus, to ensure, among other things, a plentiful harvest.

The captive who was chosen to be sacrificed would usually be a woman selected for her physical appeal, and she was treated like an honored guest before the ceremony. She was served the best food and looked upon respectfully but was kept isolated. The keeper of the sacred Morning Star bundle would sing songs meant to symbolically transform this captive into an earthly embodiment of the Morning Star. The meaning of this Morning Star related to past spirits and ancestors who were represented as stars.

The Pawnee would dance and feast for four days during the Morning Star ceremony. On the fifth day, the captive would be secured spread-eagled and naked on a wooden frame scaffold outside of the village and a fire would be built below. The ceremony commenced when the warrior who had captured the woman would shoot an arrow into her heart. Her body was then struck with arrows fired by every man and boy in the camp while they circled the scaffold four times. The arrows would then be removed. The dead woman's breast would be cut open and the elder who had supervised the ceremony would smear her blood on his face. She would be touched by everyone before her body was burned. During this time of incineration, they would all place their hands in the smoke and pray to Ti-ra' wa for good crops, victory in battle, and good health. But the Morning Star ceremony also could be regarded as much a fertility rite as anything, and from the Pawnee perspective, the young woman was not a victim, but a messenger.

As word of this repulsive ritual spread, the Morning Star ceremony was opposed by the US government, and eventually a number of Pawnee leaders saw the shame in human sacrifice. The practice was finally abolished in 1838—after one last ritual sacrifice of a young Oglala Sioux maiden.

The Pawnee were also unlike many Plains tribes because they were not nomadic. Instead, they preferred to reside and farm in permanent villages and then hunt buffalo during the summer. They lived in large, dome-shaped lodges which they constructed from four solid posts—each representing the four directions of the compass—covered with willow branches, grass, and packed earth. As many as fifty people would live in one lodge.

The Pawnee were a matriarchal people with descent recognized through the mother, and women were permitted to speak their minds in the political arena, although men would always make the final decisions. These people were deeply spiritual and maintained their balance with nature by placing much significance in their Sacred Bundles. They also practiced astrology and planted their crops according to the position of the stars. They harvested corn, beans, squash, and pumpkins, which they not only ate but traded to other tribes. But the staff of life for the Pawnee had always been the buffalo, or bison. Every lodge displayed an altar of buffalo skulls, and their religious ceremonies required offerings of buffalo meat.

The Pawnee and the other Plains Indian tribes not only regarded the buffalo as sacred—a gift from the creator—but these subsistence hunters viewed a herd of these shaggy animals with the same prospects that modern consumers might contemplate a spacious shopping mall or superstore. There within one centralized location was nearly every item required not solely for basic survival but as a dependable source for those luxuries that provided a comfortable standard of living.

Best of all, this shaggy beast covered the plains in abundance, reportedly after wandering across the Bering Land Bridge half a million years earlier. During the early nineteenth century, buffalo herds were estimated to total upwards of seventy-five to one hundred million, an impressive figure considering that each animal weighed around a ton, with most bulls tipping the scale at a ton and a half. Nowhere else in the annals of food resources can such an infinite provider of sustenance be documented.

There has been a continuing debate about whether the by-products derived from the buffalo were indeed vital to the health and welfare of the average Plains tribes. Granted, there was an abundance of other wild game, and those animals were assuredly a part of the menu and wardrobe. But these people sustained a thriving self-sufficiency by ingeniously utilizing every part of the buffalo but the bellow.

The most obvious, and important, benefit was food. The buffalo was truly a four-legged commissary. Parts of the animal were eaten raw as soon as it was killed. The liver and kidneys, along with the heart, tongue, and nose were considered delicacies. The muscle was high in protein, and other parts supplied more than the daily requirements of vitamins and minerals. After a hunt, the aroma of fresh chunks of meat hung on skewers from tripods over the fire permeated the village. What was not readily consumed could be preserved for the long winter months. One manner was by drying the meat under the sun; another by pounding berries and fruit into that dried meat to create pemmican—a treat that provided every element necessary for a balanced diet.

In addition, the women would clean and shape the entrails into sausage cases, stuffing them with marrow fat and strips of meat that had been seasoned with wild onions and other herbs, such as sage. They would also make stew by tying the ends of a buffalo's stomach lining to four poles to form a kettle and then fill it with the meat and various vegetables and boil the water by dropping hot stones into the pouch. Other favorites were blood soup, calf brains, and marrow dug out of bones.

But there were many more uses for this animal than simply food. Within the village proper, the first thing to catch the eye would be the structures, the lodges or teepees, which were constructed mainly from cured buffalo hides. Inside those lodges were warm coats and sleeping robes also fashioned from those same hairy hides, and summer blankets made soft by scraping off the hair and tanning both sides. These dressed hides were also sewn into shirts, leggings, moccasins, and women's dresses.

Green skins made serviceable kettles for drinking and cooking. Buffalo hair was braided into ropes, lariats, and reins for ponies. Horns were used for ladles, cups, and other containers. Bull boats to traverse the rivers were made water-tight with stretched hides. Hooves were boiled down to make glue for many applications. Bones could be carved into arrowheads, spear tips, awls, or needles. Sinew made strong bowstrings. Skins protected battle shields. Axes and hoes were designed from shoulder blades. Sledge runners were made from ribs. Paint from blood. Hair to stuff pillows. Fly swatters and whisk brooms from the tail. The black beard was an ornament to adorn clothing. Fuel for campfires came from buffalo chips, the dried droppings. Primitive toys, including baby rattles, were constructed from various parts. And the list goes on and on.

Another advantage was that the buffalo was relatively easy to kill in whatever numbers desired. As white hunters quickly discovered, when one fell the others simply continued grazing. If the herd should happen to stampede, it could be directed toward a cliff and chased over to die at the bottom.

Other game together may have collectively provided the bulk of the above-mentioned products, but the buffalo offered everything in one specially packaged container. It was the difference between shopping at a mall versus the corner convenience store.

The buffalo was a hardy animal with a thick coat and could survive even when the thermometer dropped to fifty below. These animals, however, had little defense against progress, and were rapidly falling to the guns of white hunters. Had the Plains Indian tribes known that cheap transportation provided by new railroads would eventually deprive them of their shaggy commissary, they might have offered more resistance. By the time George Grinnell arrived in the West, the southern herds were being steadily decimated, and the northern herds were soon to follow.

In fact, the Kansas Pacific Railroad had begun advertising that passengers could actually shoot buffalo while the train moved along the tracks. The thousands of carcasses that littered the nearby landscape attested to the truth of that claim. The train brought many dignitaries, such as congressmen, wealthy businessmen, and even P. T. Barnum to depots along the line, each of them desiring to hunt buffalo. In January 1872, while heading east toward Saint Louis aboard the Kansas Pacific, Russian Grand Duke Alexis on his historic visit to America climbed atop the baggage car and counted six buffalo kills from the train, which was moving at about twenty miles per hour.

There has been an enduring theory that the white man had formed a conspiracy to secretly exterminate the buffalo, which would in turn exterminate the Plains tribes. This theory may have been discussed by some people, but it would be highly unlikely that any concerted effort was made to kill off all the buffalo. For one thing, the white hunters hoped that they had a resource that would keep them in hides and tongues forever. No one wanted their profession to disappear.

On the other hand, there were those whites who wanted the buffalo exterminated for selfish reasons. With millions of buffalo roaming the prairies, there could be no farms, no crops planted, because fences could not hold back these huge animals. They went wherever they pleased and would destroy anything that was planted. Consequently, no town could be safe if the buffalo was free to wander.

In addition to having their own lifestyle that included being excellent buffalo hunters, the Pawnee warriors displayed courage and diligence in defending Nebraska Territory—saving the lives of hundreds of white settlers—by campaigning as a military unit. In 1864, the Sioux and Cheyenne began raiding white immigrants— ranches and wagon trains were burned, stock run off and butchered, and brutal murders shocked the settlements. Frank North, only twenty-four years old at the time, was called upon to form a company of Pawnee scouts to try and combat this onslaught of violence.

The Pawnee had been run off their traditional land over the years by the more aggressive Sioux and Cheyenne, and now was their chance for revenge. The Pawnee scouts knew the location of the enemy camps and would stampede Sioux and Cheyenne ponies and attack their enemy from ambush. Eventually North established four companies of Pawnee, with fifty warriors in each company. They were armed with new Spencer seven-shot repeating rifles and received the assignment to guard workers on the Union Pacific Railroad, which was under siege by the Sioux. The Pawnee, mounted on sturdy government horses, took their assignment seriously. The Sioux were so surprised to find themselves fighting the Pawnee that their raids on the railroad became rare.

The battle that established their reputation, however, came in July 1869. Sioux Chief Tall Bull and his warriors had roamed Kansas and Nebraska Territories for a long time, murdering, robbing, burning, and eluding the soldiers that had been sent after them. Major Frank North and his Pawnee scouts, with brother

Lute leading a company, guided General Eugene Carr and the Fifth Cavalry to Tall Bull's camp hidden in the sand hills just west of the Nebraska line. The subsequent Battle of Summit Springs completely wiped out Tall Bull and his band. That defeat of Tall Bull's band of raiders earned the Pawnee scouts the gratitude of the pioneers of Nebraska. The legislature passed a formal vote of thanks to Major North and his brave warriors. In 1871, the scouts were mustered out of the service. Frank North remained in the army as a scout and guide.

Despite the Pawnee's ingenious traditional adaptation to their environment and their service in the army, their lives were ones of uncertainty now that they were no longer the masters of their land. Death, in the form of hunger, pestilence, or marauding enemies, was a growing possibility—mainly due to the intrusion and meddling of the white man. But nothing was going to stop them from their summer buffalo hunt.

North, Grinnell, Russell, and a companion raced across the plains of northern Kansas hurrying to catch up with the Pawnee tribe, which was already on the move. Although the tribe was normally confined to a reservation, the army allowed them to visit their traditional hunting grounds twice a year. "For a little while," Grinnell wrote, "they returned to the old free life of earlier years, when the land had been all their own, and they had wandered at will over the broad expanse of the rolling prairie."

The territory through which the hunters passed, with its clear flowing streams and abundant wildlife, created a great impression on Grinnell. They traversed hundreds of square miles of uncultivated prairie interrupted now and then by hills, buttes, valleys, streams, ravines, canyons, or the occasional small settlement. Rolling mounds of grass stretched as far as the eye could see beneath dramatic skies. Sunrises and sunsets were always spectacular. When storm clouds rolled in, the sky became quite sensational, providing breathtaking horizon-to-horizon rainbows. The air was always fresh with pleasing natural scents. Out there, the rhythm of the earth's breathing could be sensed.

Of course, there were those natural obstacles that could cause discomfort or even death. It was a place where clouds could suddenly pile up and burst into violent storms. Black skies would flare with lightning that sizzled to the ground, and rolling thunder would shake the prairie and everything in it. Sudden blizzards could cover the earth in no time at all, burying any sign of life beneath. Conversely, the terrain could become parched and sandy in summer months. The sun could be blistering and the nights frosty. The wind would often whip up the soil into clouds of stinging dust that battered the faces of travelers, making their eyes sting and their lips puff and split.

Grinnell had experienced this land before, and, to him, the dangers and hardships were worth the privilege of riding through some of the most majestic country known to mankind. In addition, he trusted Lute North to choose the safest route and to guide them to their destination.

He was so thrilled to be back, however, that he wrote at length with the heart of a romantic poet about the natural beauties around him upon awaking at dawn on his third day out.

The sun pushing aside the rosy curtains of the east commences to renew his daily course, bringing again light and life to all animated nature. He touches the more elevated bluffs with flaming light and suffuses the whole heavens with a ruddy glow. The leaves of the low willows, frosted with a coating of tiny dew-drops, glisten in the light, and each silvery globule that hangs from the high grass reflected his image like a polished mirror. The waters of the Republican, dark and turbid seem to become purer as they are touched by his beams, and flash and gleam as they whirl along toward the Missouri. The mellow whistle of the meadow lark is heard from the prairie, the short cry of the migrating blackbird falls from on high, a flock of ducks on whistling wings pass over us on their way to those genial climes where frost and snow do not penetrate, and where the rigors of winter are not felt.

Lute North led his party to the temporary Pawnee camp—some two-hundred buffalo-hide teepees and over four thousand people— set up on Beaver Creek. Although they normally lived in permanent structures, the Pawnee would use portable buffalo-hide teepees

47

when they were on the move to and from their buffalo hunts. Grinnell, the aristocratic easterner, was immediately enchanted by the ancient rituals of the hunt, the bustle and warmth of the camp atmosphere, and the splendor of the Pawnee people. "The women and girls were busily at work bringing water, chopping wood and cooking, while the men strolled about the camp smoking and talking, or clustered together on the bluffs and gazed at us as we approached." He learned that on that afternoon the Pawnee had encountered their enemy, the Sioux, and had captured four horses. The men were carefully guarding their herd for fear that the Sioux might reciprocate.

At dawn, the day after Grinnell arrived, Chief Peta-la-shar broke camp and started a procession consisting of the entire Pawnee tribe led by "eight men, each carrying a long pole wrapped round with red and blue cloth and fantastically ornamented with feathers, which fluttered in the breeze as they borne along." The long poles to which Grinnell referred were known as "buffalo sticks," and were a reverent part of the ritual. "The success of the hunt was supposed to depend largely upon the respect shown to them."

Behind the buffalo stick handlers rode several dozen tribal dignitaries, and then came the lead group, which included George Grinnell and Lute North riding in an honored position beside the chief. At the end of this long line of people were the women, children, and older men, most of whom were walking. Many of the warriors were on foot as well. North explained to Grinnell that the hunters were keeping their horses fresh by saving them for the chase when they sighted buffalo. Warriors chose and maintained their mounts with more care than they gave to their wives. Their pony was a source of pride and the essential instrument for buffalo hunting.

The procession halted and set up a temporary campsite. It was not long before the object of their hunt was located some ten miles away by scouts. Great excitement ran throughout the camp—the women struck the teepees and gathered up family belongings to move closer to the hunting ground; the men stripped down and readied their horses and weapons; and George Bird Grinnell watched the wonder of it all as he, too, prepared for the hunt while keeping a studious eye on his Native companions.

He explained the joyous commotion of the camp this way:

The scene that we now beheld was such as might have been witnessed here a hundred years ago. It is one that can never be seen again. Here were eight hundred warriors, stark naked, and mounted on naked animals. A strip of rawhide, or a lariat, knotted about the lower jaw, was all their horses' furniture. Among all those men there was not a gun or a pistol, nor any indication that they had ever met with the white men. Their bows and arrows they held in their hands. Armed with these ancestral weapons, they had become once more the simple children of the plains, about to slay the wild cattle that Ti-ra' wa had given them for food. Here was barbarism pure and simple. Here was nature.

Grinnell rode with the lead Pawnees, ahead of eight hundred determined horsemen, and quickly deduced that it was not an every-man-for-himself hunt, but there existed a traditional protocol. Some warriors rode one horse and led another, while others rode double. And there was a method to the hunt that had been dictated for centuries. Certain men had been designated as "Pawnee Police," and they were the ones who set the pace, making certain that an anxious warrior would not dash ahead and frighten the herd. These official guardians were not about to allow one warrior to spoil their chances at six month's worth of food from the hunt and were capable of using violence if necessary to keep everyone in line.

After riding ten miles, they topped a rugged ridge. Grinnell wrote: "I see on the prairie four or five miles away clusters of dark spots that I know must be buffalo."

The Pawnee did not ride directly toward the herd but concealed themselves along a line of bluffs and stealthily approached. In time, they arrived at a point that led them onto a two-mile-wide open plain bordered by high bluffs. "The place could not have been more favorable for a surround had it been chosen for the purpose," Grinnell marveled. "At least a thousand buffalo were lying down in the midst of this amphitheater."

The Pawnee had long ago devised a strategy that afforded them the best opportunity at killing as many buffalo as they needed to make the hunt successful. It was a lethal battle tactic called a "surround." Warriors on the fastest horses would ride through the herd, and then turn about to face the shaggy beasts. The buffalo would instinctively turn away from these lead warriors. Meanwhile, the main party of hunters waited for the animals to turn straight toward them. Within the moments, the frightened buffalo were on their feet and, with a thunder of hooves against ground, were rushing toward the distant bluffs. It was time to hunt.

When the word was given, Grinnell watched as "like an arrow from a bow each horse darted forward. Now all restraint was removed, and each man might do his best." Grinnell would have been thrilled to watch the horsemanship of these young warriors who raced recklessly across the plains on their ponies much like today's teenagers would drive hot sports cars.

"The better mounted riders spur out from the line, this time myself among the number. The buffalo see us, stop, and then separate and flee in wild confusion. Half a dozen Indians and myself start after part of them and follow at a full run as they dash madly down a steep ravine, throwing up dense clouds of dust in their furious career."

The two columns of hunters converged at the gallop, shrieking and waving their arms, which caused the confused and terrified lead buffalo to turn back into the herd. With the buffalo swirling in circles, the hunters rode around the perimeter of them, firing arrows at will. The trapped buffalo fought back, and lashed out with their horns, occasionally goring a horse or throwing a rider, who was then in danger of being trampled under the pounding hooves.

Grinnell rode onward, losing ground to the fast Pawnee ponies. He strived to navigate this field of swirling, blinding dust, and held on for dear life as his horse surged forward. "I soon found myself in the mist of a throng of buffalo, horses and Indians."

He watched with admiration as the warriors expertly used their bows and arrows to kill the animals. They would come upon the buffalo and aim their arrow just behind the shoulder, trying to puncture its diaphragm and collapse its lungs by hitting a spot behind the last rib. Now and then the force of their arrow would cause it to pass almost all the way through the sturdy animal. The Pawnee ponies had been trained to ride alongside the dangerous beasts and would instinctively veer away if threatened.

Grinnell began chasing and shooting. "I put spurs to my horse, and as soon as I get within easy distance, fire, and the ball entering near the root of the tail ranges diagonally forward and come out at the shoulder. The huge beast drops to the shot, and I pull up to examine my first buffalo." He downed at least two buffalo while galloping alongside.

Later, the procession had moved about ten miles away when another herd was sighted. Grinnell rode with his Pawnee companions and killed several more buffalo while galloping within the panicked herd. He did have one close call when a buffalo cow charged him and only a violent yank on the reins saved his horse from being gored by the enraged beast.

After his brush with sure death, Grinnell decided that he had experienced enough action for one day. He rode up a slope and watched as the final stages of the hunt unfolded around him. The prairie was littered with hundreds of downed buffalo, each of which was soon being field dressed by several hunters. Before long, the women arrived at the hunting grounds and commenced processing the meat and hides. The hide was stripped from the carcass, the meat separated from the bones, and everything loaded on pack animals and carried back to camp.

By participating in the Pawnee buffalo hunt, George Bird Grinnell had enjoyed an experience few white men had ever witnessed. He was doubly proud of himself—he had also achieved success in killing several buffalo on his own that he donated to the tribe for food. He joined his Pawnee friends that night for a celebration of feasting and dancing. All the while, his exhilaration at being in his present surroundings with his fascinating companions was tempered. "And so the evening wears away," he wrote, "passed by our little party in the curious contemplation of a phase of life that is becoming more and more rare as the years roll by."

Lute North made the event more memorable by relating Pawnee traditions and customs, a subject that enthralled Grinnell and initiated a lifelong study of various Native American tribes. One can only wonder what Grinnell might have thought about the Morning Star ceremony that had been abolished only one generation before his visit. It would stand to reason that some of the older warriors sharing his campfire had participated in that final Morning Star ceremony and likely additional human sacrifices for years before that one.

North introduced Grinnell to influential Pawnee leaders, which established relationships for future visits with that tribe. But there was one relationship that flourished more than any other. Grinnell and North had found kindred spirits in each other. By the time the trip was over, the two young men had established a close friendship that would last a lifetime. Grinnell called North his "guide, philosopher, and friend," and looked forward to future hunts with him.

This time spent with the Pawnee had a profound effect on Grinnell. Here was a man of great intellect, who had attended the finest schools, and lived an aristocratic life. Around him in that camp was a race of mankind who were, in civilized terms, crude, uncouth, savage, even barbaric. Yet, George Bird Grinnell viewed these people as his equal. He did not look down his nose at their primitive ways. Their knowledge and talents were unique to him, and, just as he dreamed of doing with those trappers on his first excursion West, he could envision himself living this wild and free life.

To Grinnell, the lure of the west had been strengthened by these new, exhilarating experiences, and when he returned to New York his interest in business—for which he "had always had a settled dislike"—had declined still further. His heart remained on those spectacular Great Plains, with the buffalo, and the Indians, and the rugged individuals, and the primitive lifestyle that so appealed to him. No doubt he began immediately to plan his next trip to explore the West.

In early August 1873, devastating news from the western plains made its way to the New York offices of Geo. Grinnell and Company. The Pawnee had gathered for their annual summer buffalo hunt—350 men and 250 women and children. Their hunt had been successful, and eight hundred ponies were laden with freshly butchered meat and hides. The tribe had just broken camp on the morning of August 4 and were headed north up the divide between the Republican and Frenchman Rivers. The procession had proceeded about a mile up the canyon when the lead riders spotted a band of Sioux warriors.

These Sioux—some 1,500 strong—attacked the outnumbered Pawnee before they had a chance to react, either to make a stand or to retreat to a defensible location. In a matter of minutes, the Pawnee were overrun. The Pawnee warriors put up a brave fight, but the odds were heavily against them. The Sioux eventually surrounded them and commenced killing them one by one. The Pawnee fought to break free and escape down the canyon, leaving behind their dead and their precious buffalo meat and hides in their haste. The Sioux fired at the panicked Pawnee from both banks of the canyon, inflicting serious casualties.

In time, a few of the fleeing Pawnee happened upon a camp of soldiers from Camp McPherson under the command of Captain Charles Meinhold. The soldiers immediately rode off in search of this massacre site. The horsemen passed stragglers from the fight as they rode, and upon finding the canyon quickly discerned what had happened. From all indications, it was evident that many of the Pawnee warriors had made a stand and fought throughout the day. But by the time Meinhold and his troopers had arrived the field was strewn with dead bodies and they could hear the moans of the wounded. They counted over one hundred Pawnee killed, raped, scalped, and mutilated—and the precious buffalo meat and hides that would feed them throughout the winter was gone.

A few weeks later, a detail returned to what was now being called Massacre Canyon and buried the remains of an estimated 156 Pawnee victims of the Sioux attack, many of them women and children.

Massacre Canyon would be the last great engagement between Plains tribes in Nebraska. As a result of the fight, the Pawnee would be forced to relocate from what they regarded as their rightful home in Nebraska to a reservation in Oklahoma. These Native people who had welcomed George Bird Grinnell into their midst and entertained him on a grand scale would never again hunt buffalo. Grinnell could only shudder to think about how he could have been a victim of this vicious Sioux attack had it occurred this year instead of last year—and he would mourn for those treasured companions from the Pawnee tribe who had lost their lives to their traditional enemy.

Perhaps this tragedy compelled Grinnell to seek the comfort of Lute North to hear firsthand what exactly had happened at Massacre Canyon. Several weeks after the massacre, Grinnell traveled to a place about one hundred and fifty miles west of Omaha and rendezvoused with North for an elk hunt. Both men were quite apprehensive given the earlier events, but nonetheless they traversed a trail on their hunt that was occasionally used by the Sioux on their raids. The hunt had been successful—and uneventful with respect to the hostiles—and soon Grinnell was back on the Union Pacific line headed to New York.

In September 1873, George's father was preparing to retire and turn the business over to his son. The longtime cashier, Joseph C. Williams, would run the company, to be named "George Bird Grinnell & Co." But these plans ran into a major obstacle—the Panic of 1873.

In that month of September, the respected brokerage firm of Jay Cooke and Company failed and precipitated the country into a depression. Thirty-seven banks and brokerage houses closed the same day as Cooke. Two days later the stock market shut down for an unprecedented ten days. Railroads and other banks were soon forced to close, affecting the fortunes of thousands of merchants and farmers.

This Panic of 1873 caused five-hundred businesses to fail in the first year and over ten thousand more would soon be forced to close. The economic fall was essentially caused by years of over-trading, over-production, over-speculation, over-issues of paper money, and inflated prices. The economy had been running at fever heat for over a decade and a letdown was inevitable. The failure of Cooke was merely the snowball that started the avalanche; it was not in itself responsible for the conditions that led to the disaster. Unforeseen problems in financing the Northern Pacific Railroad, a projected second transcontinental line, wrecked this otherwise honorable company.

This Panic was a psychological watershed in the fortunes of the country. A portion of the continent's unbridled optimism had leaked away forever. In its place the need for cooperation emerged as a necessary factor in the affairs of both labor and management, which would be called upon to work together to rebuild the economy.

Those were desperate times for Geo. B. Grinnell and Company. Their benefactor, partner Horace Clark, had died in the spring, and Cornelius Vanderbilt, who could have bailed out Grinnell, bore a grudge against another partner and refused to help. Predictably, Grinnell and Company failed, and became mired in bankruptcy proceedings. Grinnell wrote that the "winter was one of great suffering for the family."

During this time, perhaps as a pleasant distraction, George began writing stories for a year-old weekly newspaper called *Forest and Stream*. Grinnell's experiences that summer with the Pawnee had a unique quality to them that he knew would fascinate eastern readers. He related the highlights of his exciting visit with the tribe and the particulars of their traditional hunt. He did, however, offer an opinion that was both prophetic and dire.

Grinnell was troubled by the fact that buffalo had disappeared from some traditional ranges. The hunt in which he had participated would feed the Pawnee through the winter, but white hunters had been slaughtering the animal solely for tongues and hides and leaving the meat to rot. "How different would have been the course of a party of white hunters had the same opportunity," he wrote. "They would have killed as many animals but would have left all but enough for one day's use to be devoured by the wolves or to rot upon the prairie." Now that he had witnessed firsthand this slaughter and the empty prairies where buffalo had always lived, he had not doubt about the future of this endangered animal.

Although countless numbers still roamed the Plains, he wrote:

Their days are numbered unless some action is speedily taken not only by the States and Territories, but by the National Government, these shaggy brown beasts will ere long be among the things of the past.

This was one of the first serious public protests about the senseless killing that was taking place. And he would not have experienced any guilt in his own killing of two buffalo because those animals had remained as part of the Pawnee's winter stores.

Apparently, Grinnell had the uncanny prophetic ability to place events he had witnessed into historic perspective as they happened. He had been melancholy while witnessing the festive nature of the Pawnee on the night of the hunt and now he was already writing off the buffalo from the Plains while millions of them remained. This thought pattern could be regarded as the initial elements of developing into full-blown activism, a hunter-naturalist seeking to sustain the wild things he loved.

The first step was to recognize the problem, and Grinnell—at a young age—had a unique perception of discerning what may lie ahead. Perhaps he had gained this pattern of thinking from his mentor, Lucy Audubon, who had brought him closer in touch with nature and fostered an appreciation for all things wild and free more so than the average boy. And he had also read her husband's dire journal warnings. Everything of note that he experienced was assuredly contemplated and analyzed, and then placed in a readily retrievable compartment in his mind for future reference.

Meanwhile, the elder Grinnell worked hard to try and save the company and pay off the debts from this financial disaster. Fortunately, he eventually managed to collect enough money to satisfy creditors. His efforts even gave the firm a little operating capital left over to remain relevant. Young Grinnell wrote that "this was the first known occasion when a man who had creditors had later paid these forgiven and often forgotten debts. I remember hearing at the time that my father's action was commonly spoken of as something previously unheard of." When the crisis had passed, at age fifty, the elder Grinnell retired to the comfort and refuge of his home at Audubon Park, and young George took charge of operations.

Grinnell and Company had managed to squeak through the economic panic of that year, but this financial disaster evidently served as a stern warning for George Grinnell—as well as an opportunity.

Grinnell, not wanting to be part of this risky game of high finance any longer, believed that after his father retired, "there was nothing to hold me to Wall Street." Much to his father's disappointment, George dissolved the firm in 1874. He had never wanted to be a Wall Street businessman in the first place. His heart had always been afield, with a burning desire to learn about bones, birds, and mammals. Now, he had the freedom and the means to devote himself to scientific pursuits, and he decided to pursue graduate studies at Yale while working as an assistant to Professor Marsh at the Peabody Museum. He would now follow a path that led away from the bustle and stark realities of Wall Street business and into the fascinating natural world to explore, discover, analyze, and feed his curiosity about all things that lived or had ever lived.

Shortly after his departure from business, rumors swept across the country about an expedition into the Black Hills of Dakota Territory, "then an unknown and mysterious region," that would be conducted by Lieutenant Colonel George Armstrong Custer and the Seventh Cavalry. Those rumors also included the word *gold*, which excited a nation mired in the depths of a recession.

General Philip Sheridan wanted this expedition to be a rapid reconnaissance and had not planned to include a scientific corps in its ranks. Sheridan understood that scientists would be disappointed at the pace because a fast-moving column would not allow them ample time to investigate the terrain through which they traveled. The general, however, was personal friends with Professor O. C. Marsh and extended an invitation to Yale's paleontologist to accompany the expedition. Marsh politely declined the invitation but suggested that his young assistant take his place.

George Bird Grinnell jumped at the chance to return to the West. He arranged for his friend, scout Lute North, to serve as his assistant on the expedition. The two men would go along with the understanding that they were to create no expense to the government. Their expenses would be covered by Marsh at Yale. The fact that Marsh would pay the way for his young assistant said a lot about his belief that Grinnell had great potential as a future naturalist.

The next stop for twenty-six-year-old George Bird Grinnell would be Fort Abraham Lincoln in the wild and untamed Dakota Territory where the elite Seventh US Cavalry was garrisoned along with their commander, the popular and enigmatic national celebrity, George Armstrong Custer.

CHAPTER FOUR:
CUSTER AND BLACK HILLS GOLD

The nature lover is not looking for mere facts but for meanings, for something he can translate into terms of his own life.
—JOHN BURROUGHS

THE HISTORIC IMAGE AND REPUTATION OF GEORGE ARMSTRONG Custer has been established from the tragic events of one day in his life—the day he died. Every other aspect of his career has been overshadowed by that lone fight on the frontier. In his time, however, Custer was not a symbol of defeat but a national hero on a grand scale due to his achievements in both the Civil War and his standing as the country's premier cavalry officer on the Plains.

In the Civil War, he captured one of the first enemy battle flags taken by the Union army and accepted the Confederate white flag of surrender at Appomattox four years later. In between those notable events there existed a series of intrepid acts of almost unbelievable proportion as he personally led electrifying charges that resulted in victories for the Union and earned the twenty-three-year-old swashbuckling general the admiration of his men and captured the fancy of newspaper reporters and the public. He became known as a brilliant battlefield strategist, and his ambition, energy, and flair for being in the thick of the most important battles became his trademark.

On the Plains, Custer had a shaky start chasing marauding Sioux around the Kansas plains during the ill-fated Hancock Expedition of 1867, where he was under the command of over-matched General Winfield Scott Hancock. However, Custer as the field commander went on to score a smashing, if not controversial, victory over Black Kettle's Cheyenne at Washita two years later, and bested Crazy Horse, among other Sioux warriors, during skirmishes on the Yellowstone Expedition of 1873.

Now, Custer was being called upon once again to make national headlines as he would travel deep into country controlled by the fierce Lakota Sioux tribe. The Panic of 1873 had compelled the US government to view the Black Hills of Dakota, which was part of the Great Sioux Reservation, in terms of its valuable resources. The nation had been plunged into a deep economic recession, and rumors of gold in those hills had caused an overwhelming public outcry for admittance into this forbidden territory.

Those rumors had begun as early as 1833 when a prospector named Ezra Kind led a party into the area and allegedly found gold, but apparently, he and his partners never made it out with their fortune. It was said that the men had run into a band of hostile Sioux and were murdered, or they may have succumbed to the natural elements while eluding the hostiles. All that remained was an inscription carved by Kind on a stone that read: "Got all the gold we could carry our ponys all got by the Indians I have lost my gun and nothing to eat and Indians hunting me."

With national interest riding on the outcome, George Armstrong Custer and his Seventh Cavalry had been ordered to lead an exploratory expedition into the mysterious Black Hills. The published purpose of Custer's controversial scheduled two-month reconnaissance was to identify likely locations for a military post. It was a poorly kept secret, however, that Custer was also interested in verifying claims of valuable mineral deposits—gold in particular—within the Black Hills.

Consequently, the expedition would not be without danger. They would be riding through an area called sacred by the Lakota Sioux—land that had been granted that tribe as part of their reservation in the Fort Laramie Treaty of 1868. Custer wrote: "The expedition is entirely peaceful in its object, [but] the Indians have long opposed all effort of white men to enter the Black Hills and I feel confident that the Sioux will combine their entire strength and endeavor to oppose us."

The white man had been engaged in fighting the war to gain independence from England when a small band of Sioux led by warrior Standing Bear—prompted by their nomadic instinct— had walked from their homeland in Minnesota to visit for the first time the Black Hills, a wilderness region along the South Dakota-Wyoming border that runs roughly one hundred miles north to south and sixty miles east to west.

This group of adventurers were members of the Teton or Lakota Nation of Sioux who, along with their brethren the Dakota and Nakota Sioux, had migrated from the South in the sixteenth century to settle the headwaters of the Mississippi in northern Minnesota.

Standing Bear's Lakota Sioux hunting party was not by any means the first American Indians to view the Black Hills, for its dominion had been the matter of contention between local tribes for centuries. These explorers, however, regarded the discovery as if it had been preordained by their Creator. There was apparently an awakening within their souls that spoke to tell them that the innate spirits that dwelled within the Black Hills had reserved that place for them—as if some mystical magnet was calling home those who had wandered for so long. Although other tribes may have discovered this place before them, the Lakota were the first to recognize that it was sacred land.

Standing Bear returned home from his trek and spoke in glowing terms about his wondrous discovery. His assessment of the Black Hills affected his people with such a seductive force that they abandoned the north and journeyed en masse to that unknown territory to establish a homeland for the Lakota Sioux Nation. The Dakota and Nakota remained in Minnesota.

The emigrating Lakota Sioux declined to settle permanently inside the boundaries of the Black Hills, for it was considered sacred land. For three-quarters of a century they would rarely make camp out of sight of this place they now called *Paha Sapa*, "Hills That Are Black," and would enter only to hunt, cut lodge poles, hide out after raiding parties, or to perform ceremonies.

The seven principal Lakota Sioux bands—the Blackfeet, Brulé, Hunkpapa, Minniconjou, Oglála , Sans Arc, and Two Kettles—thus became the final group of Indians to arrive in that part of the country. It established its own territory throughout Montana, Wyoming, Kansas, Nebraska, and the Dakota Territory, but enjoyed greater numbers than their rivals due to their supportive alliance between bands and became the strongest tribe on the Great Plains. They acquired proprietorship of the area by force from the Cheyenne who years earlier had pushed aside the Comanche who years earlier had pushed aside the Crow and other weaker tribes.

This treaty that gave ownership of the Black Hills to the Lakota Sioux had come about due to one of the most shocking events between Native tribes and the United States government—a total surrender on the battlefield by the United States Army.

While George Armstrong Custer had been chasing tribes around the Kansas plains, another conflict was being waged to the north. In 1862–63, explorer John Bozeman had pioneered a route to the Montana goldfields that passed directly through prime Sioux buffalo hunting grounds. In 1865, the government built a road from Fort Laramie, Wyoming, to Montana along this Bozeman Trail. Oglala Chief Red Cloud and other Sioux bands retaliated by attacking miners, army patrols, and wagon trains that trespassed onto this land that had been promised them under terms of the Fort Laramie Treaty of 1851.

In 1866, the army attempted to negotiate a nonaggression treaty but balked at Red Cloud's demand that no forts be built along the Bozeman Trail. In fact, the army commenced construction on two new forts—Phil Kearny in Wyoming and C. F. Smith in Montana—and reinforced Fort Reno in Wyoming. Red Cloud responded by intensifying hostilities. He masterminded hit-and-run tactics to harass the soldiers with his two thousand warriors, which included ambitious young braves Crazy Horse, Gall, and Rain-in-the-Face, and kept Fort Phil Kearny under constant siege.

On December 21, 1866, Captain William J. Fetterman, who had once boasted that he "could ride through the entire hostile nation with eighty good men," commanded a detachment of eighty men from Fort Kearny as escort for a woodcutting wagon train. Crazy Horse and a band of Sioux appeared and pretended to flee from the soldiers. When Fetterman took the bait and chased after this decoy, he and his men were ambushed by another force of Sioux and annihilated.

On August 1, 1867, Crazy Horse and a group of warriors estimated at five-hundred to 800 strong attacked a detachment of nineteen soldiers and six civilians that were guarding a hay-cutting detail near Fort C. F. Smith. In the ensuing three-to four-hour battle—known as the Hayfield Fight—two soldiers and one civilian were killed, and two soldiers wounded before troops from the fort arrived and the Indians broke contact.

The following day, Company C of the twenty-seventh Infantry was guarding a woodcutting detail about six miles from Fort Kearny when they were attacked by warriors under Crazy Horse. In what became known as the Wagon Box Fight, the soldiers took refuge in a corral crudely constructed from wagon beds. The Indians alternated sniping and charging for a period of about four hours before reinforcements arrived from the fort to drive them away. The soldiers lost six killed and two wounded.

Red Cloud's constant harassment made the soldiers virtual prisoners in their forts, and safe travel along the Bozeman Trail was impossible. The US government finally yielded to Red Cloud's demands and the Fort Laramie Treaty of 1868 was drawn up to end hostilities. The army agreed to abandon the three forts and to provide the Sioux a reservation that encompassed nearly all present-day South Dakota west of the Missouri River, which included the Black Hills, as well as other concessions. Whites were expressly forbidden to trespass on Native American land.

More than two-hundred chiefs and sub-chiefs signed the treaty at Fort Rice on July 2, 1868. Chief Red Cloud, however, waited until November 6 to sign—after the three forts had been abandoned by the army and burned to the ground by Sioux warriors.

There was a technicality to the Fort Laramie Treaty, however, that permitted the army to explore the reservation for roads or for any other national purpose, like a necessary fort to distribute annuity rations or to protect travelers. It could be loosely interpreted that a military expedition onto this reservation was within the rights of the US government. The Sioux, however, thought otherwise and dubbed Custer's route through the Black Hills the "Thieves' Road."

George Bird Grinnell would have certainly been warned of the dangers that faced him on this expedition. After all, the Sioux had recently slaughtered his Pawnee friends on their buffalo hunt—and he was heading into Sioux territory once again. His primary focus, however, was that he had another wonderful opportunity to explore the western wilderness to seek bones, birds, and animals—this time in an official capacity. He craved adventure and, like John James Audubon before him, he had that burning desire to see what kind of wildlife existed over the next hill. His ambition as a naturalist far outweighed his fears of torture or death at the hands of hostile Sioux. He traveled by rail to Fort Abraham Lincoln in Dakota Territory by way of Chicago to rendezvous with George Armstrong Custer and the Seventh Cavalry, mentally prepared for whatever hardships or dangers he would face.

During the three weeks before the expedition departed Fort Lincoln, Grinnell socialized with the officers of the Seventh Cavalry—as well as Lieutenant Colonel Fred Grant, the president's son who would serve as Custer's special aide. Grinnell took his meals at "Autie" Custer's table, and found Mrs. Libbie Custer to be "extremely kind and hospitable." He listened for hours to his host's hunting tales and shared his own intimate knowledge of the flora and fauna that he had studied.

Custer and Grinnell would have found a common thread from their college days—both had been class pranksters, Custer at West Point and Grinnell at Yale. Custer had maintained that mischievousness, as evidenced by his love of practical jokes, and Grinnell may have recognized a bit of himself in this enigmatic military man. The two men shared many interests and would have enjoyed a familiarity right from the beginning of their relationship, although Custer was almost ten years older.

During this time, George Grinnell became fast friends with the celebrated scout "Lonesome" Charley Reynolds. This thirty-two-year-old adventurer from Kentucky had been a trapper, soldier, trader, prospector, and buffalo hunter before becoming an army scout, and was proficient in the Sioux language. He was a modest, unassuming man who did not smoke or drink, and was highly respected by both whites and Indians for his frontier skills, endurance, and resourcefulness. The Sioux called him the "White Hunter Who Never Goes out for Nothing." Grinnell was drawn to Reynolds for the same reasons that Custer had been—in addition to his outdoor talents, Charley was interested and well-versed in geology, zoology, and was a voracious reader. He had attended college in Illinois before being lured to the Colorado goldfields by the call of "Pikes Peak or Bust." He knew the territory as well as any man from his extensive travels to trap or hunt, as well as having been on Custer's Yellowstone Campaign the previous year.

George Grinnell also became acquainted with the colorful officers that made the Seventh Cavalry the finest unit on the frontier. Introductions included those members of the "Custer royal family." In addition to Custer's brother Captain Tom Custer, who had been the first double Medal of Honor recipient in the Civil War, there was First Lieutenant Jimmy Calhoun, who had married Custer's sister, Maggie. Captain George Yates, a close friend of Custer from Michigan, was a heavy drinker and gambler. Company commander Captain Myles Moylan was a Custer favorite, but shunned by some officers because he had once been an enlisted man. First Lieutenant Algernon "Fresh" Smith's wife was close friends with Libbie Custer. Younger brother Boston Custer had been hired as a civilian guide, but, in truth, he could barely find his way to the latrine.

Captain Thomas McDougall was the son of a brevet Brigadier General and physician. First Lieutenant Edward S. Godfrey would go on to become an army general before retiring. Second Lieutenant Charles Varnum, Second Lieutenant Henry Harrington, and Second Lieutenant George Wallace all graduated from West Point in the same class. First Lieutenant Owen Hale was a descendant of American patriot Nathan Hale. Captains Thomas French and Verlan Hart, First Lieutenant Edward Mathey, Canadian native First Lieutenant Donald "Tosh" McIntosh, West Pointer Benjamin Hodgson, and First Lieutenant Marion Gibson rounded out the junior officer ranks.

Every outfit needed a villain, and the out-spoken Custer critic Captain Frederick Benteen fit that role for the Seventh Cavalry, although he was known as an excellent soldier. Conspicuous missing on the expedition was Major Marcus Reno and Irish soldier-of-fortune Captain Myles Keogh, both of whom were on detached duty on Northern Boundary Survey. Custer's second in command would be West Pointer Major Joseph G. Tilford and commanding a battalion would be Major George "Sandy" Forsyth, who had been wounded three times in the 1868 Battle of Beecher Island.

In addition to his social life at Fort Lincoln, George Grinnell spent much of his free time collecting birds along the bottoms of the nearby Heart and Missouri rivers and the adjacent high, dry prairie. He was always accompanied by Luther North, who was listed as an assistant zoologist but whose real task was to serve as the personal guide for Grinnell. North was not completely inexperienced—he had led a fossil-collecting expedition into Colorado the previous year. No doubt Grinnell was pleased to renew his friendship with Lute North. The two men had formed a strong bond during the Pawnee buffalo hunt two years earlier.

On July 2, 1874, with the regimental band playing "Garry Owen" and "The Girl I Left Behind," George Armstrong Custer, wearing a buckskin shirt, gray campaign hat, and his trademark red scarf, rode out of Fort Abraham Lincoln at the head of a column composed of ten companies of the Seventh Cavalry, two infantry companies, a train of over one hundred wagons, a beef herd, three Gatling guns, scouts, interpreters, two professional miners, numerous journalists, and four members of the scientific corps.

In addition to Grinnell and Lute North, the two other members of the "Bug Corps" were botanist A. B. Donaldson and geologist Horace Winchell. Donaldson, a forty-three-year-old Ohioan, was described as a "big bodied, big-hearted old fellow, a professor in a western college. His character is noble, yet funny, for in it are mixed the most generous, manly emotions, and a simple childishness it does one good to see." Winchell was raised in Dutchess County, New York, and educated in Salisbury, Connecticut. He had graduated from the University of Michigan and moved on to Minnesota, where he became the state geologist and a professor at the University of Minnesota.

George Grinnell's observations during this historic trek would become part of the *Annual Report of the Chief of Engineers for 1875,* published by the Government Printing Office. The man responsible for this report would be Lieutenant Colonel William Ludlow, chief engineer of the department.

Ludlow had a rather unusual connection with George Armstrong Custer. Both men had been cadets at West Point when Ludlow and another cadet had engaged in a fight. Fighting was strictly prohibited, and it was the responsibility of the officer of the guard to break it up. That officer of the guard—Cadet Custer—instead of stopping the fisticuffs, called out, "Stand back, boys, let's have a fair fight!" Two officers appeared, and Custer was arrested, stood a court martial, found guilty, but was only reprimanded. There were no hard feelings, however, between Custer and Ludlow. In a letter to his wife on July 15, Custer mentioned that "Col. Ludlow is a great favorite." The two men socialized together, and Ludlow, along with Grinnell, North, Grant, Reynolds, and Custer's two brothers, Tom and Boston, would dine as Custer's guests at the headquarters tent during the expedition with the regimental band supplying musical entertainment during the meal.

Another notable member of the entourage was Englishman William H. Illingworth, who was living and working in Saint Paul, Minnesota, when he had been hired by William Ludlow to serve as the expedition photographer. Ludlow provided the camera and necessary chemicals and equipment, rations, a wagon and horse, and paid all expenses. In return, Illingworth promised to deliver six sets of prints to Ludlow but could retain the negatives for his own purposes.

The two miners, Horatio Nelson Ross and William McKay, were not officially attached to the command. Their names were purposely deleted from any muster roll for the expedition, but they were not inconspicuous by any means. All eyes would be watching them as they scoured the Hills for gold. Both were experienced miners and knew their way around wilderness country. Ross had overseen a high-producing gold mine in Colorado, and McKay, who had been an early settler on the frontier, was a member of the Dakota territorial legislature. The two men furnished their own team, wagon, and equipment, and Custer personally saw to their rations. Everyone knew that the reason these men had come along was to locate gold deposits.

Grinnell was afforded the privilege of riding at the front of the column with Custer and his headquarters staff. "General Custer," Grinnell wrote, "was friendly, sociable, and agreeable." They would march for the better part of every day, and "camp was not reached until 8 o'clock at night, sometimes not til midnight, and sometimes not at all." He also noted that "Gen. Custer was a man of great energy. Reveille was usually sounded at 4 o'clock; breakfast was ready at 4:30; and by five tents were down and wagons packed, and the command was on the march."

Grinnell and Winchell were disappointed to locate only a few freshwater shells and no fossils within a week of leaving the fort. One of the correspondents, William Elroy Curtis of the Chicago *Inter-Ocean*, wrote that "Four scientific gentlemen have been wandering about with bags and hammers for nearly a week, and not yet have they found one [fossil] of importance. It seems that nothing ever died in this region, and one is inclined to the opinion that nothing ever existed here until foolish, restless man penetrated these barren plains."

After a march of about three hundred miles, Custer and his column entered the north-western edge of the Black Hills on July 20 by traveling along a well-worn Indian trail. Two days later at Inyan Kara, an extinct volcano, some of his Arikara and Santee scouts warned him that if he did not turn back there would be severe retaliation from the Sioux. Custer ignored their protests and, perhaps because these scouts had never been to the region before and would have little to offer with respect to information, he released them. Those Indians who did remain with the column included the Sioux-Arikara named Bloody Knife, Custer's favorite scout.

Before leaving Inyan Kara, Custer, accompanied by chief engineer William Ludlow, botanist A. B. Donaldson, and several others, climbed to the 6,500 foot summit of this mountain. Ludlow, with hammer and chisel, created a monument of sorts when he chipped an inscription into a rock that read: '74 *CUSTER*.

Without capable scouts to guide them, Custer personally rode ahead of his column and blazed the trail, which eventually gained him the reputation of always being able to locate a passage through even the most difficult terrain. He would assume this responsibility throughout the entire the expedition.

Grinnell found plenty of time to go out hunting with Charley Reynolds and Lute North. "The company never suffered for lack of fresh meat," Grinnell reported, noting that as the terrain changed from prairie and badlands to pine-covered mountains, the fauna was transformed. Deer replaced antelope as the most numerous animal.

Due to Custer's fast pace, the column would get strung out, and occasionally take a couple of days to entirely close up. Grinnell, North, and scout Charley Reynolds took advantage of this time by going out hunting together with their new Winchester repeating rifles. One day, "we had traveled until after dark with no signs of camp or of the command catching up, we stopped at some little spring or brook, picketed our animals, made a meal of deer meat, and slept there, wrapped in our saddle blankets." Grinnell had no qualms about camping out in Sioux country without military protection, and trusted Reynolds to make the proper decisions.

George Armstrong Custer also participated in many of those hunting side-trips. Grinnell stated: "He was very fond of hunting and a great believer in his skill as a rifle shot." It was evident, however, that Grinnell was not impressed with Custer's marksmanship. After Custer missed three consecutive shots at stationary ducks, Grinnell opined that Custer "did no shooting that was notable."

On July 24 Custer entered a resplendent valley surrounded by pines that overwhelmed everyone with its beauty and provided the botanist a virtual field day. Correspondent Samuel Barrows of the *New York Tribune* called it "an Eden in the clouds—how shall I describe it! As well try to paint the flavor of a peach or the odor of a rose." A. B. Donaldson, who collected fifty-two varieties of flowers in bloom, raved: "It is hardly possible to exaggerate in describing this flowery richness. Some said they would give a hundred dollars just to have their wives see the floral richness for even one hour."

Neither did Custer exaggerate when he chose the name "Floral Valley" for the area he described: "In no private or public park have I ever seen such a profuse display of flowers." Nearly every diary, letter home, or report contained a glowing description of this wondrous valley that teemed with wildflowers and offered a mystical serenity. Hard-bitten troopers decorated mule harnesses and hats with flowers, and preserved blossoms as a gift for wives, girlfriends, or family.

Custer noted that while seated at the mess table they could pick up "seven beautiful varieties" of flowers within reach. The column camped in Floral Valley for two days before moving on.

George Armstrong Custer, as had been his habit on previous expeditions, spent much of his free time along the way enjoying outdoor activities and indulging his curiosity of nature by exploring. He would frequently ride off with a detachment to hunt game, climb hills, or explore caves or other intriguing terrain. One notable cave shown him by a scout named Goose extended for four hundred feet, with provocative carvings and drawings on the walls and eerie shrieks and howls emanating from within its depths. He wrote to his wife: "Three days ago we reached the cave referred to by the Indian called 'Goose.' It is about four hundred feet long, its walls covered with drawings of animals, and prints of hands and feet. I cannot account for the drawings of ships."

Custer also accumulated his customary menagerie of wildlife, which was his favorite hobby. This one consisted of—among other species—a jackrabbit, an eagle, two prairie owls, several toads, rattlesnakes, and a bunch of birds. Unfortunately, two badgers had been accidentally smothered to death. These specimens as well as generous samples of flora and fossils, including a petrified tree trunk, required an ambulance detail of twelve men under Fred "Antelope" Snow for transport.

George Bird Grinnell, although hurried across the plains by the steady march of the expedition, collected numerous specimens and compiled lists of indigenous mammals that he observed, including jackrabbits, prairie dogs, mule deer, elk, mountain lion, grizzly bear, and bighorn sheep.

The predominant animal on the open plains was the pronghorn antelope, which became the object of Grinnell's fascination. "In proportion to size," he wrote, "and from its astonishing speed it is often enabled to escape even after having received a wound that would have brought a deer or an elk immediately to the ground." He was amazed to observe an antelope with two broken legs easily outdistance Charley Reynolds on horseback for more than two miles. Grinnell was also taken by watching a jackrabbit racing across the short grass with Custer's wolfhounds chasing it for over two miles before it was caught. He noted that the kit fox could outrun the hounds for a good half a mile before being snatched up in those jaws.

Grinnell observed black-tailed prairie dogs as they squatted on the mounds that surrounded their holes. Most waterways were home to muskrats, and beaver could be found in the larger ones. He was disappointed to learn that there were no bison in the region, although he never gave up hope of seeing one or even a herd. His only evidence of bison were the chalk-white bones that dotted the prairie, and a group of skulls that had been arranged ceremonially by an unknown Indian tribe—all painted red and blue and set in five parallel groups of twelve, every one of them facing toward the east.

Coyotes had been plentiful on the plains, but Grinnell would observe none of them within the Black Hills proper. He did see wolves at the higher elevations, "sneaking along the mountain sides or crossing the narrow valleys." Birds were plentiful and easy to spot. By the end of the expedition, he would have a list of 110 species of birds that he had observed.

Although Custer, a noted teetotaler, assured his wife in a letter that there were no incidences of intoxication on the march, just the opposite was true. The sutler's wagon carried an ample supply of liquor, which was freely consumed by those who so desired. It has been reported that Fred Grant "was drunk nearly all the time," which sounds like an exaggeration—except that Custer did at one point place Grant under arrest for drunkenness.

Despite these moments of indiscretion, there can be no doubt that the march through the Black Hills was as pleasant as any ever experienced by the participants—especially for the officers and dignitaries, if not enlisted, who were often assigned undesirable duty. Lieutenant Jimmy Calhoun perhaps summed up the sentiments of his peers when he wrote:

> *The air is serene and the sun is shining in all its glory. The birds are singing sweetly, warbling their sweet notes as they soar aloft. Nature seems to smile on our movement. Everything seems to encourage us onward.*

The Sioux had thus far chosen not to interfere with this—to them—insulting invasion of troops but indicated with a series of distant smoke signals that they were aware that there had been an intrusion upon their land.

On July 28, however, the column happened upon a small hunting party of five lodges and twenty-seven occupants under Oglala Sioux Chief One Stab (or Stabber) in Castle Creek Valley. According to one account, the wife of One Stab was the daughter of Chief Red Cloud. These people from the Red Cloud and Spotted Tail Agencies apparently had not noticed the smoke signals and were quite surprised to encounter the soldiers. Custer, under a flag of truce, smoked the peace pipe with One Stab, and graciously invited the chief and several of his people to visit the army camp for coffee, sugar, and bacon, a courtesy that was gratefully accepted.

The Indian scouts that had remained with the column were not as hospitable as their commander and wanted to kill their traditional enemy. Due to the threat of hostilities, Custer assigned a detail of fifteen troopers to escort his Sioux guests back to their lodges and protect them through the night. Despite that precaution, the wary Sioux abruptly galloped away with the soldiers and scouts in hot pursuit. During the chase—although Custer had ordered no violence—one of the Sioux warriors was shot by one of the Santee scouts. The troops arrived at the Indian camp to find that it had been abandoned.

Custer, however, had detained Chief One Stab, either as a hostage or guest. Custer wrote, perhaps with tongue in cheek: "I have effected arrangements by which the Chief One Stab remains with us as a guide." Whatever the circumstances, the chief was greatly distressed by his captivity, but guided the expedition into the Southern hills. During this time, rumors spread throughout the reservations that One Stab had been killed by the invading army.

At Castle Butte, Grinnell discovered what he described as "the crushed and flattened leg bone of some enormous animal and a few fragmentary turtle bones, all so fragile and weathered that we were unable to transport them to camp." That one large fossil measured about four feet long and a foot in diameter and had likely belonged to an animal at least as large as an elephant, although Grinnell was of the opinion that it came from a mastodon. He would consult Marsh about this impressive find after returning to Yale. Otherwise, most of the fossils consisted of marine specimens, mainly shells from ancient seas, including two new species.

On July 30, about one hundred miles into their reconnaissance, the column camped in a glade that Custer modestly named "Custer Park," which was near the site of present-day Custer City, South Dakota. While the troops passed the time playing cards, writing letters, catching up on their sleep, or exploring their new surroundings, miners Horatio Ross and William McKay were on the trail of "color" along the upper part of French Creek. The two miners were covertly watched by everyone in the command as they crouched along the waterway with their shovels and pans, digging, testing, and analyzing their finds.

Gold was known to run with black iron granules in creek bottoms, embedded in rocks and crevices. The prospector's method was simple—after scooping a panful of sand or gravel, it was covered with water and the pan was swirled around by hand to wash away the mud. The pan was then raised from the water while continuing the circular motion accompanied by small jerks in and out of the water to wash away the cloudy water and lighter sediment, leaving behind only gold-carrying residue. The prospector would finally separate the gold particles from the iron granules and rejoice if there was color in quantity. Ross and McKay practiced this technique, as well as seeking gold-bearing quartz from which any gold would need to be chipped.

After a day of combing French Creek, miner Horatio Ross approached George Grinnell and Lute North in camp, and said, "Well now, boys, don't say anything about this, but look here."

Grinnell wrote: "[Ross] drew from his pocket a little vial which he passed over to me and which we both examined. It was full of small grains of yellow metal which we of course knew must be gold dust. Some of it was fine, but occasionally there would be nuggets as large as the head of a pin and a few as large as half a grain of rice. We turned the bottle round and round and by the light of the fire looked at the shining yellow mass which did not much more than cover the bottom of the vial."

"'That's gold I suppose,' said North, as he handed it back to the miner.

"'Yes,' said Ross, 'that's gold, and found right on the surface, and where there is as much as that, there's bound to be lots more when we get down a little lower. I haven't shown this to anybody but Charley. If the boys knew we had got this, they'd throw away their rifles and begin to dig. Of course I'll have to report it to the General, but he'll keep it quiet until we get out of the hills.'"

Grinnell, always placing events in historical perspective, sadly realized that the discovery of gold would likely mean war with the Sioux and Cheyenne. He and North had discussed the matter at length, and both had dreaded the success of the miners. Once the genie was out of the bottle there was no telling what lengths greedy and desperate prospectors—or the government—would go to keep the dream of riches alive. Both men could imagine those pristine Black Hills being overrun with the vices of civilization created by boom towns.

Which one of the miners actually was the first to recognize gold has been a matter of speculation. Ross generally receives credit for the discovery. McKay, however, noted in an undated journal entry: "In the evening I took a pan, pick and shovel, and went out prospecting. The first panful was taken from the gravel and sand obtained in the bed of the creek; and on washing was found to contain from one and a half to two cents, which was the first gold found in the Black Hills."

Regardless of who struck color first, the two miners wrapped the few specks of gold in a piece of paper and together presented their findings to Lieutenant Colonel Custer that night. Ross and McKay were skeptical about the prospects of a big strike but vowed to continue panning in the morning.

At dawn, the miners returned to French Creek, while Custer and an escort commanded by Lieutenant Charles Varnum rode to 7,two-hundred-foot Harney's Peak, the highest point in the Black Hills. Custer, along with Forsyth, Ludlow, Donaldson, Winchell, and topographer W. W. Wood, climbed to the summit and pointed out two other distinctive peaks that he named for General Terry and himself. The climbing party wrote their names and the date on a piece of paper that was rolled up, inserted into a copper cartridge casing, and slipped into a crevice. The casing was found sixty years later, but the message was missing.

During Custer's absence, the troops engaged in a rousing game of base ball—the Actives of Fort Lincoln defeated the Athletes of

Fort Rice 11-6 in a disputed game. The umpire identified as "Mr. Tenpenny, Vetinary Surgeon" allegedly favored the Fort Lincoln team. The game was followed by a champagne dinner for some of the officers hosted by the acting commanding officer, Major Joseph G. Tilford. The diners were serenaded by the Company E glee club. The previous year, Seventh Cavalry enlisted men had established the "Benteen Base Ball Club," an athletic organization consisting of fifty-four men that would play competitive base ball against both civilian and military teams in Dakota Territory between 1873 and 1876.

On August 1, Custer moved the camp three miles away to a better grazing area, and named the site Agnes Park after Agnes Bates, a friend of wife Libbie Custer. The miners tested the loose soil around the creek and were impressed with the results. They speculated that under the right conditions a miner could expect to reap perhaps as much as $150 a day.

French Creek was soon lined with ambitious soldiers who sought their fortunes digging with shovels, picks, knives, pothooks, plates, cups, and any other implement that could penetrate dirt. Twenty troopers later staked a claim under the name "Custer Park Mining Company." One of the more enthusiastic prospectors was a black woman named Sarah Campbell, who was employed as a cook by sutler John Smith. The men had nicknamed her "Aunt Sally," and, for whatever reason, she called herself "the only white woman that ever saw the Black Hills."

On August 2 Custer decided that his superiors should be notified of this gold discovery. He prepared a dispatch to General Phil Sheridan, which read in part that "gold has been found in several places, and it is the belief of those who are giving their attention to this subject that it will be found in paying quantities. I have upon my table 40 or 50 small particles of pure gold, in size averaging that of a small pinhead, and most of it obtained today from one panful of earth."

This message was entrusted to scout Charley Reynolds, who had been engaged for such a purpose. Reynolds would travel alone ninety miles through hostile territory to deliver Custer's dispatch to Fort Laramie. Custer provided Reynolds with a canvas mailbag that had been inscribed: "Black Hills Express. Charley Reynolds, Manager. Connecting with all points East, West, North, South. Cheap rates. Quick transit. Safe passage. We are protected by the Seventh cavalry." Reynolds galloped away from the safety of the column with the awareness that his route would intersect several trails frequented by Native Americans and there was a distinct possibility that he would be discovered by hostiles.

A most stirring account of his dangerous ride was provided by Libbie Custer in her book *Boots and Saddles* published in 1885: "During the day he hid as well as he could in the underbrush, and lay down in the long grass. In spite of these precautions he was sometimes so exposed that he could hear voices of Indians passing near. The last nights of his march he was compelled to walk, as his horse was exhausted and he found no water for hours. His lips became so parched and his throat so swollen that he could not close his mouth. In this condition he reached Fort Laramie and delivered his dispatches."

Reynolds fulfilled his mission in four days. When his swollen throat healed, he gave an interview to the *Sioux City Journal*. Although he said that he personally had not found any gold, he admitted to having seen specks of the mineral washed from surface dirt that would likely yield two or three cents a pan. He then departed for his home base at Fort Lincoln, leaving behind the spark that helped ignite a gold rush in the Black Hills.

Custer's expedition did not linger over those "gold fields" but moved onward, following its old trail in a northerly direction.

On August 7, Custer attained what he considered his greatest feat as a hunter. He shot and killed a grizzly bear. The animal was seventy five yards away, sighted first by scout Bloody Knife. Custer aimed his .50-caliber Remington sporting rifle and fired a round that struck the eight-hundred-pound grizzly in the thigh. The animal spun around and quickly received several more shots from the rifles of Custer, Ludlow, and Bloody Knife.

George Bird Grinnell, diarist Theodore Ewert, and even Bloody Knife, remarked that this particular grizzly was less than fearsome, being an old male with teeth reduced to mere stumps, many incisors missing, and claws severely worn down. Despite any criticism, Custer proudly posed with his kill—along with Ludlow, Bloody

Knife, and an orderly—and photographer Illingworth snapped a photo that would soon become the most popular item sold in stationery shops back east.

Custer split up the command for a brief reconnaissance of the south fork of the Cheyenne. After returning to camp, Custer gave Sioux Chief One Stab his horse and rifle, along with rations for a week, and released him from "protective custody." The chief did not look back as he spurred his mount to freedom. The release of One Stab averted a possible attack by warriors who had planned retaliation for the surmised death of their chief.

Instead of marching back to Fort Lincoln along known trails and wagon roads, Custer—much to the disappointment of the troops—chose to map unexplored country. It was speculated that Custer decided on this route in an attempt to provoke Sitting Bull into attacking them. However, the ride proved to be uneventful.

On August 8, the expedition was engulfed in fog and compelled to make camp. On that day, after the sun broke through, the soldiers went out and killed one hundred white-tailed deer. Two days later, the Arikara scouts killed their first elk, which resulted in a celebration. Professor A. B. Donaldson, who was not impressed, wrote: "In the evening they had an Elk Feast and Dance…Whole sides of the elk were set up to roast, on long pins stuck in the ground. While the meat was roasting, they danced to the music of sticks beat on frying pans and tin wash basins. It was perfect in time, but lacked everything else to charm…they make no vocal symphonies, but grunt and whoop-howl and groan. Uneducated pigs or orangutans [sic] could excel them."

On August 14 Lieutenant Colonel Custer chose Bear Butte, an isolated granite laccolith rising 1,two-hundred feet above the prairie on the northern fringe of the Black Hills, as the location to halt his column and prepare his official report. Ironically, Bear Butte was a special place to the Lakota Sioux Nation, where they had for a century gathered to trade, share news, and participate in religious ceremonies.

The column marched east from Bear Butte through the hot, dusty plains, with Custer pushing the troopers hard. With the band striking up "Garry Owen," the regimental anthem, the column triumphantly paraded into Fort Abraham Lincoln on August 30, after a march of sixty days and 883 miles.

The news of gold in the Black Hills spread like a wind-whipped prairie wildfire. Despite government warnings to the contrary, by the summer of 1875, almost a thousand prospectors had invaded the Black Hills to seek their fortune. This provoked the Sioux, led by Sitting Bull and Crazy Horse, to retaliate by attacking these trespassers and raiding wagon trains, mail routes, and settlements. Soon, the miners were demanding that the government protect them from Indian attacks.

General George Crook was dispatched to uphold the provisions of the Fort Laramie Treaty of 1868 and chase off the miners. Late in July, Crook held a meeting with the miners and in his folksy manner, diplomatically suggested that the prospectors would be allowed in the Hills when the area was opened in the near future but for the present they must leave. Most of the miners were impressed with the general's forthrightness and agreed to comply.

Nevertheless, newspapers, especially those from nearby Dakota towns, ignored the ban on mining and jumped on the golden band-wagon, promoting themselves as the ideal place to outfit and enter the Black Hills.

There remained skepticism in some circles, however, over the validity of Custer's discovery, especially when high-profile people like geologist Newton Winchell and Fred Grant, the president's son, had claimed not to have personally observed any gold. The government therefore authorized another expedition into the Black Hills in the summer of 1875 to confirm Custer's conclusions.

This expedition was headed by New York School of Mines geologist Walter P. Jenny, with escort provided by six cavalry and two infantry companies under Lieutenant Colonel Richard I. Dodge. Although Jenny reported that it would be difficult for individual miners to extract enough gold with primitive pan and rocker to make it worth their while, he confirmed that the Black Hills did indeed hold rich minerals deposits that could be profitable if sophisticated mining equipment was utilized. Jenny's guarded opinion meant little to the public. Gold had been confirmed, and the rush to strike it rich commenced in earnest.

Red Cloud, Spotted Tail, and other chiefs were invited to Washington, DC, in that summer of 1875, believing that the meeting would pertain to agency business. To their surprise, the government requested that they sign over title to the Black Hills. The chiefs refused, saying they lacked authority to make such a decision.

The government, however, promised to reward the Lakota well should they sell the Black Hills. Spotted Tail was asked to estimate the worth of the region, which he subsequently set at between seven and forty million dollars and enough provisions to provide for seven generations of Sioux.

The tribe was split over that proposal to sell the Black Hills to the US government. Those members who resided on the reservation approved of the idea, thinking only of the rewards that they would receive. Another faction, led by Sitting Bull and Crazy Horse, vowed that this sacred land would be sold only over their dead bodies.

The Allison Commission, named for its chairman, Iowa senator William B. Allison, convened near Red Cloud Agency in September 1875 to discuss the sale. The commission members were greeted with a show of hostility from the younger warriors, who disrupted the proceedings and threatened severe reprisals against any chief who dared sign a treaty giving away the Black Hills. Senator Allison proposed that the Sioux accept $400,000 a year for mining rights, or the US would buy the Black Hills for $6,000,000. The offer was declined. The commission returned to Washington empty-handed, and recommended that Congress simply offer whatever value they judged was fair. If the Lakota refused to sell at that price, rations and other provisions should be terminated.

Ultimatums did not set well with the Sioux. Those chiefs who had witnessed the unscrupulous actions of the US government in the past believed that war was at hand. And they would be correct. President Ulysses S. Grant would become frustrated with the situation and turn the disposal of the Black Hills and those Sioux and Cheyenne who remained off the reservations to the US Army. And the army was itching for a fight.

Meanwhile, George Bird Grinnell submitted his report on paleontology for the Black Hills Expedition, made as Professor O. C.

Marsh's representative. He also wrote on the birds and mammals of the region, at the request of Colonel William Ludlow, the chief engineer of the Department of the Dakota. For many years this monograph attached to the *Annual Report of the Chief of Engineers for 1875* remained the definitive work on the Black Hills and vicinity. The section on mammals would prove particularly valuable to future researchers, since some of the subspecies described are now extinct.

Grinnell wrote in his cover letter: "The rapidity with which the command traveled admitted but a very hasty and incomplete survey of the region. The time allowed for collections was short, and only such animals were observed as could be most readily found."

Still, it would be hard to imagine that anyone could compiled a more complete or descriptive list. His description of the mammals and birds he viewed were usually brief but authoritative. Each species contained a number on his list—in no particular order—its scientific classification (genus), and its common name. For example:

4. Canis Occidentalus *var.* Griseo-Albus, Rich.
Grey Wolf; Timber Wolf.

I found the timber wolf one of the most common animals in the Black Hills, and hardly a day passed without my seeing several individuals of this species. They were generally observed singly or by twos and threes, sneaking along the mountains sides or crossing the narrow valleys. They were quite shy, and lost no time plunging into the dense woods as soon as they perceived us. Their howlings were often heard at night; and on one occasion I heard the doleful sound at midday—a bad omen, if we may trust the Indians.

50. Melapfsner Erythrocelhalus, Swain.
Red-headed Woodpecker

All through Montana, wherever there was timber, I saw the red-headed woodpecker, and in the Black Hills it was especially abundant. It seemed to me the most common species there, and its harsh cries resounded through the forest from morning till night. When the nest is approached, the parent birds give themselves little concern about the result. At first they would give a few short cries, expressive of displeasure, and then, flying off into the woods, would not be seen again.

Ludlow himself stated in his annual report that the Black Hills region was "admirably adapted to settlement," but he qualified that statement by saying, "It is probable that the best use to be made of the Black Hills for the next fifty years would be as the permanent reservation for the Sioux." It was his opinion that the area was cherished by the tribe, and that any occupation by whites would be met with aggression. He admitted that gold had been discovered but deferred to the scientists to predict whether prospectors would locate it in paying quantities.

George Bird Grinnell returned to New Haven from his latest exploration to resume life as a graduate student at Yale's Sheffield Scientific School. He also assisted Marsh at the Peabody Museum, and spent his weekends collecting birds at his father's farm in Milford, Connecticut. His notes detailing these local specimens were handed over to C. Hart Merriam and would become the basis for Merriam's important 1877 work, *A Review of the Birds of Connecticut*.

Grinnell's reputation as a naturalist was growing, and this success only heightened his curiosity to learn more about the mysterious ways of the animal kingdom, both past and present.

In time, however, he longed to once again travel through those verdant valleys and grassy ridges that sloped up into the Rocky Mountains, where drooping willows and majestic cottonwoods lined meandering, unspoiled streams, and the winds blew wild along the craggy foothills. Besides that, there were copious numbers of mammals, birds, and fossils out there that could not be found and studied back East.

To his delight, that opportunity presented itself when he received a prestigious invitation from a former member of the Black Hills Expedition. There would be more adventure in store for him, this time in Yellowstone country.

CHAPTER FIVE:
YELLOWSTONE COUNTRY

The idea of wilderness needs no defense, it needs defenders.
—EDWARD ABBEY

GEORGE GRINNELL'S ENTHUSIASM AND ABILITY TO ACCURATELY record the zoology and paleontology of the Black Hills had greatly impressed chief engineer William Ludlow. In the spring of 1875, Colonel Ludlow asked Grinnell to serve as the naturalist on an expedition that he would lead to explore and survey the Yellowstone region of Montana and Wyoming. In 1872 Congress had set aside this area as the nation's first "national park," with the idea that it was a "museum" of "curiosities" and "wonders," but it was not yet a national park as defined by modern standards.

Grinnell recalled that William Ludlow "could pay me nothing, nor even furnish railroad transportation, but he would subsist me in the field." With the blessing of Professor O. C. Marsh at Yale, Grinnell accepted the invitation.

Grinnell held a mutual respect for the man who would lead this expedition and was honored to have been selected for the position. Best of all, he would be returning to the West again and was thrilled by the prospects of yet another expedition into relatively uncharted territory with Ludlow. As chief engineer of the Department of Dakota, Ludlow had journeyed through the Yellowstone region the previous summer while on a road reconnaissance. Resourceful and perceptive, he was regarded as an exceptional man by all who knew him.

Thirty-one-year-old William Ludlow had been born on Long Island, the son of the distinguished Civil War general, William H. Ludlow. It was only natural that young William would attend the US Military Academy at West Point. He graduated in 1864, and was appointed chief engineer, XX Army Corps. Contrary to its name as a military academy, West Point graduates received degrees in engineering rather than military disciplines, and Ludlow had excelled at his studies. He also made a military name for himself during battles in Georgia and the Carolinas during the Civil War. In less than a year, Ludlow had been brevetted up to the rank of lieutenant colonel, quite a remarkable feat for a young man.

After the war, Ludlow married Genevieve Almira Sprigg of Saint Louis. The couple would have one daughter. In March 1867, he was commissioned a captain of regulars and served as assistant to the chief of engineers, stationed at Staten Island and Charleston., South Carolina. In late 1872, he had become chief engineer of the Department of the Dakotas. Ludlow had already explored the Yellowstone region on a survey expedition during the year before accompanying Custer through the Black Hills.

Now, William Ludlow was being called upon to make a more detailed survey of the Yellowstone, and regarded the talents of observation and analysis of George Bird Grinnell as an important factor to his overall success. Yellowstone had been visited on numerous occasions in recent years, but remained a land of mystery and intrigue, and it was not known if all of its hidden treasures had as yet been found.

Without question, Grinnell prepared for the trip by researching and studying all the information—rumor, myth, and fact—presently available about the region. It could only stir up his anticipation to imagine that he was about to witness one of the most unusual and sensational spectacles in the country, a place where the ground could tremble like the sound of a herd of galloping horses; and geysers could spout hot water up into the air seventy feet high at regular intervals while making a terrific hissing noise; and sparkling waterfalls could leap and thunder down high precipices to gather in clear pools below. He was anxious to see this natural wonder before the pristine wilderness had fallen victim to civilization, which has a way of ruining those special places.

Grinnell learned that archaeological evidence in the form of obsidian projectile points of Clovis origin indicated that there had been a human presence in the Yellowstone region for more than eleven thousand years when Paleo-Indians began to hunt and fish in its forests and waterways. The Wind River Shoshone were believed to have arrived in about the year 1400, and were followed by other tribes that hunted, traded, and conducted religious ceremonies in the area.

The first person of European ancestry believed to have ventured into the Yellowstone region was American trapper and explorer John Colter, who had visited after serving with the Lewis and Clark Expedition. Colter had joined that expedition in 1803 after leaving the family farm in Staunton, Virginia and intercepting Lewis at present-day Maysville, Kentucky. Lewis was impressed with Colter's résumé of outdoor skills and offered him the rank of private at five dollars per month. Colter, who would come to be regarded as one of the rowdier of the group, nonetheless became a valuable member of the expedition, known for his hunting skills, his instincts at locating passages through rough terrain, and his ability to barter with the various Indian tribes. He had been given several noteworthy missions along the way, all of which he carried out to the satisfaction of his superiors.

In August 1806, John Colter was honorably discharged from the Corps of Discovery and immediately set off with two trappers to reenter the wilderness. The three men began trapping in Montana, but soon had a falling out and went their own ways. Colter, who was on his way back to civilization in Saint Louis, happened upon Manuel Lisa and his Missouri Fur Trading Company, which included former members of the Lewis and Clark Expedition. Colter decided to head into the wilderness to trap once again.

At the confluence of the Bighorn and Yellowstone rivers, Colter and his party constructed Fort Raymond, a crude but serviceable base of operations. But soon Lisa had a special assignment for

Colter. In October 1807, with winter threatening, he was asked to travel five hundred miles alone, some of it by snowshoe where the temperature could drop to minus-thirty, and attempt to establish trade relations with the Crow Indians and other tribes that he might encounter. Colter set off carrying a thirty-five-pound pack, his rifle, and plenty of ammunition.

In the spring of 1808, Colter returned to the fort. He had not only survived the brutal winter but had some fascinating—actually, unbelievable—stories to tell. The places that he claimed to have passed through on his trek were so fantastic that he was widely ridiculed and not believed. Colter described a place of "fire and brimstone," an assertion that most people dismissed and subsequently nicknamed as an imaginary place called "Colter's Hell."

In fact, John Colter may have been the first white man to travel through Jackson Hole and into the steaming, bubbling, erupting landscape of present-day Yellowstone National Park. Unfortunately, Colter did not write about his experiences during this journey in that winter of 1807–08, and his exact route remains one of history's most-debated questions.

Regardless, Colter left behind a legacy that had a profound impact on furthering the romance of the frontier, as that of the reclusive pathfinder who braved any danger to see what was over the next hill. Famed writer Washington Irving, among others, recognized these traits, and forever preserved the image of the mountain man who shunned polite society in favor of the wilderness.

In 1827, the first published account of the region was written by Daniel Potts in a letter to his brother that vividly described Yellowstone Lake and the West Thumb Geyser Basin. This letter was printed in a Philadelphia newspaper, but was dismissed as pure fantasy.

Over the next forty years, reports from mountain men and trappers told of petrified trees, boiling and bubbling mud, and rivers with steam rising from them, but these accounts were thought to be little more than tall tales. After an 1856 exploration, legendary mountain man Jim Bridger reported observing boiling springs, spouting water, and a mountain of glass and yellow rock. His reports were largely ignored because Bridger was a known "spinner of yarns." In 1859, a US Army survey of the area was thwarted by heavy spring snows, which prevented them from entering the Yellowstone region. Official explorations were then put on hold due to the outbreak of the Civil War.

In 1869, the first detailed expedition to the Yellowstone area was conducted by three privately funded explorers—Charles Cook, William Peterson, and David Folsom. The Folsom party explored the area for thirty-six days, following the Yellowstone River to Yellowstone Lake. The members of the party kept a journal and documented all the famous tourist spots favored by today's visitors. Folsom spoke about a geyser that "shot into the air at least eighty feet," and was roundly ridiculed. They attempted to get an article published in a popular magazine or large city newspaper, but, after reading the journals kept by the men, every publication politely declined. Apparently, anyone who visited the Yellowstone region was treated with skepticism, as if some pixilation had rendered them foolish.

In 1870 and 1871, Nathaniel Pitt Langford, a former Montana tax collector who was on the payroll of Jay Cooke's Northern Pacific Railroad, led two expeditions into the Yellowstone region. Langford was a fearless man who had once formed a vigilante group in Montana and hanged a gang of thieves, which had included the town sheriff. Langford confirmed the tales of boiling sulfur springs and stunning scenery and became the primary promoter of the area by writing magazine articles and lecturing around the East Coast. He had his sights on the day when the railroad would bring tourists to the territory. Evidently, if wealthy and influential Jay Cooke approved of an idea, it was treated with credibility by the national press. No one suggested that Langford was telling tale tales because he was sponsored by Cooke, although there did remain skeptics.

In 1871, Ferdinand V. Hayden, head of the US Geological Survey of the Territories, decided to lead a scientific expedition to the Yellowstone region to confirm or refute all the rumors. He brought along a mineralogist, zoologist, botanist, and other experts who collected data about the terrain. His findings excited the public and became the final piece of the puzzle for those associated with the railroad. A railroad lobbyist encouraged Hayden to petition

Congress to preserve the place as a public park. Hayden, who could not be labeled a crackpot, added great credibility to these heretofore unknown wonders of the region. His influence would be critical, especially when another prominent man added his endorsement—Jay Cooke.

Proposals for the federal government to protect the Yellowstone region picked up a powerful voice in Jay Cooke, who recognized the full potential of Yellowstone as a tourist destination for his Northern Pacific Railway Company to pursue. Breathtaking images of the area had made their way back East, compliments of paintings by Thomas Moran, who had been funded by Cooke, as well as photographs by William Henry Jackson.

In December 1871, William Clagett from Montana introduced a bill in the US House of Representatives that would establish the Yellowstone region as a "public park or pleasuring ground for the benefit and enjoyment of people." Two months later, Congress became convinced of the benefits of this region, and acted to pass a bill authorizing the creation of Yellowstone National Park—more than two million acres of remote, mountainous terrain—which was signed into law by President Ulysses S. Grant on March 1, 1872. Congress, however, did not authorize any funds for park management or protection.

Nathaniel Langford accepted the position of unpaid superintendent. He believed that when Cooke's railroad reached Yellowstone that thousands of tourists would arrive, and he could collect money from franchising out concessions. His plans went awry with the Panic of 1973—the tracks stopped more than five hundred miles away from the park. The only mode of travel to the area was by horseback or aboard a stagecoach over dusty, rutted trails. Langford welcomed only three hundred tourists that first year.

Many of those who did visit the park vandalized the natural wonders to take away free souvenirs, chipping off pieces of geysers and other formations. The park's elk herd was decimated by hunters, as was other game. And there was no one there to protect these natural resources. Superintendent Langford had virtually abandoned the park, deciding to wait until the railroad arrived to return, when he could profit from his grand schemes.

George Grinnell likely had heard firsthand accounts of the Yellowstone region as he sat around the campfire with the Seventh Cavalry officers on the Black Hills Expedition. These stories would have made mention of violent encounters with Crazy Horse and his Sioux warriors, and, of course, the embellished intrepid acts of the heroic cavalrymen in those brief battles.

In 1873, George Armstrong Custer and his men had been part of an expedition led by Colonel David Stanley that had the mission of protecting surveyors on Jay Cooke's Northern Pacific Railroad from hostile Indians. Track was being laid east of the Missouri River, but to the west there remained the work of staking the route to be followed. Most of the trip was uneventful, but on two occasions in August, the Seventh Cavalry was attacked by bands of hostile Sioux. In those two battles, Custer lost three men killed, and four wounded; Sioux casualties were estimated at forty killed. The surveying went on as scheduled, and the Sioux remained distant after that.

Custer may have personally told Grinnell about his memories of the wildlife in that region during their long evening dinners together in the Black Hills. The lieutenant colonel had led hunting parties nearly every day, bagging deer, elk, pronghorn antelope, buffalo, geese, ducks, prairie chickens, and sage hens, which had kept the messes in fresh meat. He had also shot two white wolves and a red fox. Custer had written to wife, Libbie: "Such hunting I have never seen." Other wildlife had been captured, including rattlesnakes, a badger, a wildcat, two marsh hawks, a jackrabbit, and a porcupine, which were later donated to the Central Park Zoo. Custer also collected fossils and practiced taxidermy along the way, working late into the night most nights mounting a complete bull elk.

It would not be hard to imagine the gregarious Custer entertaining Grinnell and Charley Reynolds in his headquarters tent, with the three men relating their encounters with wild game, fossils, and unmatched scenery. And now, Grinnell would be witnessing all these wonders on his own and could make his own impressions of what he saw and have his own hunting and collecting stories to tell about the Yellowstone region the next time he accompanied Custer on an expedition.

Twenty-six-year-old George Grinnell would be joined by Edward S. Dana, a friend and instructor at Yale who had never been to the West. Dana's father was a longtime Yale professor and the country's leading geology expert. Dana would follow in his father's footsteps and report on the geology of the country they passed over. Grinnell had been mildly unsettled by Dana's mother, however, who had said to him, "'Goodbye, Mr. Grinnell; take good care of my boy.' I felt, therefore, that I must constantly look after him, to see that he did not...get into...trouble."

In the middle of June, the two men traveled to St. Paul, where they met up with William Ludlow and Ludlow's brother, Ned, and then moved on to Bismarck, Dakota Territory. Grinnell called on George Armstrong Custer at nearby Fort Abraham Lincoln, but the lieutenant colonel was absent. He had traveled to Washington to serve as a witness in a scandal over the sale of post traderships by President Grant's brother, Orville. Ludlow did receive permission, however, for Seventh Cavalry scout Charley Reynolds to accompany the expedition, which certainly pleased Grinnell.

Unfortunately, the party was delayed as they traveled upriver on the Missouri River aboard the steamer *Josephine*, when Ned Ludlow became ill. Ludlow and his brother left the steamer at Fort Buford to visit the hospital there, while Grinnell and the remainder of the men continued on through the unspoiled wilderness. They would wait at their stepping-off point for the return of Ludlow. Grinnell was thrilled to spot a grizzly bear on the shoreline when he and Reynolds were conversing on the steamer's deck. Reynolds then pointed out two black bears feeding nearby.

After traveling a distance of 640 miles, they reached a small outpost consisting of two trading stores and a dozen log cabins near Carroll, Montana, to await Ludlow. The little town had been raided by Indians on the previous night, and the hostiles had stolen every horse there. Grinnell's party had brought along their own transportation, so the raid did not affect them—other than fraying their nerves.

The party moved to a campsite on Crooked Creek, a few miles away, and Grinnell and Dana went out hunting and exploring. One soldier wrote in his diary: "Scientific parties make their daily explorations after fossils, etc. Professor Grinnell and Mr. Dana are constantly in the saddle, busy providing matter for their respective reports."

During one of these forays into country that was regarded as hostile to whites, Grinnell and Dana were investigating an outcropping of rock on a hill when they looked up to notice a dozen or so riders heading toward them. Grinnell believed that these strangers were Native Americans, and the two men prepared to put up a fight. Grinnell told Dana "to dismount and stand behind his horse and to do what he saw me do. I dismounted, and when the riders were 400 or five-hundred yards off, I pointed my gun at them."

This obvious and threatening act encouraged a reaction from the riders. One man took off his hat and waved it in the air. Grinnell and Dana recognized that the group was likely white men and allowed them to approach. Grinnell soon realized that he and Dana had encountered a ragtag party that included legendary fur trapper John "Liver Eating" Johnson.

> *Johnson announced he had left a sick man at camp and was looking to find someone who had some liquor for him. Of course we had none. As a matter of fact, I presume that Johnson, who was notoriously a practical joker, had ridden toward us with the idea that we might be stampeded and perhaps chased into our camp, which he would have greatly enjoyed. I afterward learned that Johnson had been camped for some weeks with the Crows. If these had been Indians, as I had feared, they might have killed both Dana and myself.*

After exchanging strained pleasantries, the trappers went their own way.

Back at camp, Charley Reynolds was impressed by the way Grinnell had handled this dangerous situation. Any minor incident out here involving men of questionable character could take a turn for the worse at any moment, and Grinnell had passed this test with flying colors.

William Ludlow and his brother soon arrived, and the expedition moved on toward Yellowstone. The park was about three hundred miles distant through territory that Ludlow called "a sort of debatable ground roamed over by half a dozen tribes of Indians all at war among themselves and most of them with the whites." He believed that they were "not much in excess of one hundred miles from the hostile camps of Sitting Bull on the Yellowstone."

Ludlow led his expedition toward Camp Lewis on the Big Spring Fork of the Judith River, where a small military detachment was garrisoned. They were low on supplies, and there was a trading post located there.

The men had been anxious about running into hostiles and breathed a sigh of relief when finally they reached army protection. In addition, the cold stream near the camp was very attractive to them after a long dry and dusty day's ride. But, no sooner had they arrived when the captain in command told them, as repeated by Grinnell: "The evening before, three of them [soldiers] had gone out fishing in the stream, and while thus engaged, sixteen Sioux Indians had swept down out of a ravine, killed the three men, driven off the horses and mules belonging to the camp, and disappeared into the hills."

The captain had called on the Crow tribe—bitter enemies of the Sioux—who were camped a mile and a half below Camp Lewis to exact revenge for the army. Over one hundred Crow warriors had readied themselves for battle and started off on the trail of the Sioux. Their women and children moved closer to the fort for safety. Nothing had been heard from that war party yet.

Regardless of this danger, Grinnell wrote: "As I say, we were hot, tired and dusty, and I proposed to Charley Reynolds that while supper was being cooked, we should go down to the stream and take a swim. He agreed and we started. The best and deepest pool seemed to be the one about which were the graves of the three recruits killed the night before, for the soldiers had buried them just where they had fallen."

Before long, the two men heard a shot, and then another, and then more shots. They scrambled to shore to grab their clothes and their rifles. Within moments, they observed three naked mounted Indians singing loudly in triumph. One of them carried a pole with a scalp waving from the top. Evidently, the Crow had been successful in their raid on the Sioux. Grinnell and Reynolds watched as additional warriors appeared, all of them singing and shooting off their rifles in celebration.

It was not all joy that night in the Crow camp, however. There was mourning and wailing when it was learned that the Crow had lost one man in the battle—their chief, Long Horse. Grinnell watched as a funeral procession passed, with a mule carrying a bundle done up in a green blanket followed by an elderly man, a woman, and a young man. He was shocked by what he saw next. "When they reached the sutler's store the old woman dismounted from her horse, and walking over to the building, she drew her butcher knife, placed her little finger on the wagon wheel, and by a quick stroke cut off the finger. She then gashed the top of her head three or four times with the point of the knife, so that blood streamed down over her face. 'There,' said Charley to me, 'you see that these people are really sorry for their loss.'"

This remark by Reynolds could be construed as being flippant or even cynical, but that would not have been his intention. The scout believed that his role in life also included that of frontier educator, and he was obliged to pass on his knowledge to any receptive person, in this case George Grinnell. The prevailing national perception of the Indian was that they—man, woman, and child—were simply savages, incapable of human emotions. Longtime scouts like Charley Reynolds had witnessed many "humanizing" events in the lives of these tribes—with their emotions mirroring that of whites, although their reactions could be extreme. And, despite their warring ways, they reacted to births, marriages, and deaths with joy, pride, and grief—such as the woman, who may have been his wife, cutting herself over the loss of Chief Long Horse.

Grinnell had likely already known plenty about this subject from his time spent with Lute North and the Pawnees. But it was moments such as these that were imprinted in his mind that, as time passed, would compel him to become an advocate for Native American rights and a promoter for their acceptance into white society.

Just before Ludlow's party moved on in the morning, Grinnell and Reynolds visited the trading post to purchase some last-minute items. It was there that they happened upon another well-known scout and explorer—Luther S. "Yellowstone" Kelly. The three men spoke briefly, likely about the trail conditions ahead, and then Grinnell was on his way to Yellowstone once again.

With guide Charley Reynolds leading the way, the party pushed through virgin wilderness, at times dodging Indian war parties. The Ludlow Expedition of 1875 finally reached the Park area by the middle of August.

Grinnell was overwhelmed by the natural wonders of the region. He commenced cataloging everything he saw as they passed through forests of lodgepole pine, and Douglas firs, and whitebark pine, and aspens, and along the waterways, where cottonwoods and willows dominated the banks. And he was observant as they traipsed through meadows blooming with hundreds of varieties of wildflowers and flowering plants, where the pleasant fragrance could be overpowering.

Grinnell noted those larger mammals that he observed—elk, buffalo, mule deer, pronghorn antelope, moose, black bears, coyotes, lynx, and mountain lions. And listed the smaller mammals—beaver, badgers, river otters, weasels, marten, hares, bats, and a variety of rodents. In total, he would catalog over forty mammals. He would also frequently come upon a venomous prairie rattlesnake, the only poisonous reptile species found there.

Swimming within the clear, clean rivers, lakes, streams, and tributaries could be found cutthroat trout, with its characteristic red markings under the jaw; and grayling, with its large dorsal fin with the silver-spotted, iridescent purple sheen; and whitefish, with its bulbous nose hanging over their lower jaws, among other lesser species.

Songbirds were virtually everywhere, singing, warning, flitting about in plain view. Permanent residents included nuthatches, ravens, jays, chickadees, woodpeckers, and the waterfowl—geese, sandhill cranes, loons, and trumpeter swans. Grinnell watched as overhead soared the predators—ospreys, falcons, hawks, and bald eagles. Grinnell would personally count and catalog no fewer than 139 bird species.

The party also watched in awe as the park's hydrothermal features were revealed. They stared in wonder at the distinctive colors found in such features as Norris Geyser Basin and Mammoth

Hot Springs, including Old Faithful, Mud Volcano along the Yellowstone River, Midway Geyser Basin, and Roaring Mountain.

The expedition would have been an uplifting, perhaps even idyllic, experience for everyone involved had it not been for one disturbing factor. George Grinnell, an avid hunter, experienced anguish at observing groups of skin hunters, who were slaughtering great quantities of game in the systematic fashion demanded by the processing factories. The transcontinental railroad had made the area accessible, and, armed with modern weapons, the hide hunters had descended upon the park in great numbers. Everywhere Grinnell went in the park he encountered the wanton destruction of not only game but other resources by timber thieves and souvenir collectors. He witnessed people cutting up geyserite and carting it off by the wagonload.

The expedition members endured the sight of a whisky peddler set up in a tent at Old Faithful geyser and watched as what Colonel Ludlow would describe as tourists who "prowled about with shovel and ax, chopping and hacking and prying up great pieces of the most ornamental work they could find; women and men alike joining in the barbarous pastime. We had additional evidence of the brutality of the average visitors, several of whom were busily chopping and prying out the most characteristic and conspicuous ornamental work. An earnest remonstrance was followed by a sulky suspension of hostilities, which were, however, no doubt renewed as soon as we were out of sight."

This commercial exploitation of the region's natural resources aroused in Grinnell a concern for the future of Yellowstone Park. He found a kindred soul in William Ludlow when it came to this despoiling of the environment. Ludlow had stood against the mistreatment of the Sioux by opening the Black Hills to whites, and now he had indicated his opposition to the destroyers of the country's natural resources. Both of those issues were on the mind of George Grinnell as well. He wrote that he "had a very great admiration" for the colonel.

After departing Yellowstone Park, the party separated. James Dana accompanied Colonel Ludlow into the Little Rocky Mountains, where Dana shot a buffalo and an antelope. Grinnell and Charley

Reynolds ventured into the valley of the Judith River, where reports of dinosaur remains and invertebrate fossils were located.

Several days later, a messenger arrived to inform them that the last boat on the Missouri would be leaving soon. On the morning of September 16, Ned Ludlow, Charley Reynolds, and George Grinnell loaded their possessions onto a Mackinaw boat and started downriver.

Along the way, Grinnell became fascinated with stories Charley Reynolds related about mountain sheep. The guide mentioned that the animal was not necessarily a high-country resident but was commonly found in open country as well. In fact, mountain sheep could be found feeding with antelope out on the barren prairie. These revelations were contrary to Grinnell's preconceived notions, but, as luck would have it, this theory was confirmed on the second day of their downstream journey.

In a scene that would be forever embedded as a fond memory, Grinnell wrote that as they floated down the river "the sun just topping the high Bad Lands bluffs to the east, a splendid ram stepped out upon a point far above the water, and stood there outlined against the sky. Motionless, his head thrown back, and in an attitude of attention, he calmly inspected the vessel floating along below him; so beautiful an object amid his wild surroundings, and with his background of brilliant sky, that no hand was stretched out for the rifle, and the boat floated quietly on past him, and out of sight."

They remained two days on the river, sleeping on land at night, constantly on the lookout for roving war parties. There was no doubt about whose opinion mattered when it came to survival in this wilderness. Grinnell, just as with Lute North, believed that he was in good hands with Charley Reynolds in charge. He recalled an episode one night on the march that spoke volumes for Reynolds, who ordered that they sleep that night without a fire. When Ned Ludlow objected, Reynolds said, "I don't mind getting killed, but I should hate to have somebody come along next year and kick my head in the sand and say, 'I wonder what fool this was, who built a fire in this country and then slept by it.'" Ludlow backed off.

Grinnell said goodbye to Reynolds at Bismarck and boarded a train for the East. Alas, it would be the last time he would see his frontiersman friend.

On the way home, and for weeks and months afterward, Grinnell had some serious thinking to do. He loved hunting. He had hunted since he was a boy. His favorite stories as a boy were written about hunting. He was an editor for a magazine in which hunting was a popular subject of the readers. But the kind of hunting he had witnessed in Yellowstone Park had sickened him. He simply could not justify this systematic destruction of game with those responsible people like him who hunted for sport—food or a trophy—harvesting only what was necessary. And then there was the mass destruction of the unique natural formations, pillaged for souvenirs or profit. The more he thought about the park the more disheartened he became. It was with great deliberation and concern that he compiled his final report to submit to William Ludlow.

Evidently, Colonel William Ludlow had been thinking along the same lines as Grinnell. His report was released and began by chronicling a day-by-day account of the expedition's travel through the park. In addition, there were two references that stood out with respect to the dangers facing the park. The first was the summary that Ludlow had written at the end of his report concerning his impressions of the area: "The region is, for its area, the most interesting in the world. It is situated at the very heart of the continent, where the hidden pulses can, as it were, be seen and felt to beat, and the closely written geological pages constitute a book which, being interpreted, will expose many of the mysterious operations of nature. My own interest in this land of wonder is so keen as to lead me to hope that it will be protected from the vandalism from which it has already suffered."

Ludlow went on to write: "The treasures of art and beauty, cunningly contrived by the hand of nature, are in process of removal to territorial homesteads, and the proportion of material destroyed to that carried off is as ten to one. Hunters have for years devoted themselves to the slaughter of the game, until within the limits of the park it is hardly to be found. A continuance of this wholesale and wasteful butchery can have but one effect, viz, the extermination of the animal, and that, too, from the very region where he has a right to expect protection, and where his frequent inoffensive presence would give the greatest pleasure to the greatest number."

Ludlow wrote about his concern for the natural formations:

The only blemish on this artistic handiwork had been occasioned by the rude hand of man. The ornamental work about the crater and pools had been broken and defaced in the most prominent places by visitors, and the pebbles were inscribed in pencil with the names of great numbers of the most unimportant persons. Such practices should be stopped at once. The geysers are more than worthy of preservation. It is not only that they constitute a superb spectacle in themselves; they are likewise unique, both in performance and design. Nature, abandoning for the time all thoughts of utility, seems to have been amusing herself in this far-off and long-hidden corner of the world by devoting some of her grandest and most mysterious powers to the production of forms of majesty and beauty such as man may not hope to rival.

The cure for these unlawful practices and undoubted evils can only be found in a thorough mounted police of the park. In the absence of any legislative provision for this, recourse can most readily be had to the already existing facilities afforded by the presence of troops in the vicinity and by the transfer of the park to the control of the War Department. Troops should be stationed to act as guards at the lake, the Mammoth Springs, and especially in the Geyser Basin.

George Bird Grinnell's reports detailing the natural history and wildlife of the region were for many years the standard reference works. His descriptions of birds, animals, and habitat, as well as other natural resources, were vivid and accurate, and displayed those detailed characteristics that could only be observed by the careful eye of a professional scientist. As significant as his scientific observations of nature were regarding the mammals and birds that he found during the expedition, his additional "Letter of Transmittal," served to confirm and reinforce Ludlow's dire warnings. Grinnell addressed this letter to Ludlow, and it accompanied his final report, which was published as part of the expedition papers by the Government Printing Office.

He wrote:

It may not be out of place here to call your attention to the terrible destruction of large game, for the hides alone, which is constantly going on in those portions of Montana and Wyoming through which we passed. Buffalo, elk, mule deer, and antelope are being slaughtered by thousands each year, without regard to age or sex, and at all seasons. Of the vast majority of animals killed, the hide only is taken. Females of all these species are as eagerly pursued in the spring, when just about to bring forth their young, as at any other time.

It is estimated that during the winter of 1874-75 not less than 3,000 elk were killed for their hides alone. Buffalo and mule deer suffer even more severely than the elk, and antelope nearly as much. The Territories referred to have game laws, but, of course, they are imperfect and cannot, in the present condition of the country, be enforced. Much, however, might be done to prevent the reckless destruction of the animals to which I have referred by the officers stationed on the frontier, and a little exertion in this direction would be well repaid by the increase of large game in the vicinity of the posts where it was not unnecessarily and wantonly destroyed. The general feeling of the better class of frontiersmen, guides, hunters, and settlers is strongly against those who are engaged in this work of butchering, and all, I think, would be glad to have this wholesale and short-sighted slaughter put to a stop. But it is needless to enlarge upon this abuse. The facts concerning it are well known to most Army officers and to all inhabitants. It is certain that, unless in some way the destruction of these animals can be checked, the large game still so abundant in some localities will ere long be exterminated.

Grinnell's letter was the first official protest of its kind by a professional scientist, and, along with William Ludlow's statements in his report, must have raised more than a few eyebrows and perhaps enlightened many people back east. Both men had written their impressions independently, but there can be no question that each of them had related their feelings in discussions around blazing campfires during the march. They had been charmed by the beauty, wealth, and potential of the region, and that was the motivation for their concern about its future.

Ludlow had written his account from the perspective of a military officer solving the problem with force by the presence of troops.

Grinnell had approached the issue from the sophisticated academic disciplines of paleontology and zoology to emphasize the need for some sort of resolution within the law.

Both men hoped that by exposing these facts that had nagged their consciences, they would initiate a new concern for the natural world that would make more people aware, especially those in power, that a movement for conservation and laws to regulate hunting were vital to the future of not only Yellowstone Park but all of the country's natural resources.

Now, the task at hand for George Bird Grinnell became finding a way to initiate such a conservation movement and place it in front of the public as well as government officials. Unbeknownst to even himself, he was on the threshold of a radical—for its time—form of advocacy.

CHAPTER SIX:
TRAVELING, COLLECTING, AND WRITING

Keep close to nature's heart and break clear away, once in a while, and climb a mountain or spend a week in the woods. Wash your spirit clean.
—JOHN MUIR

IN EARLY *1876* GEORGE GRINNELL RECEIVED AN URGENT MESSAGE from his mother, who was visiting Santa Barbara, California. His father, she wrote, was not in the best of health. Could he come out there and visit them to cheer up his father?

The Peabody Museum at that time was extremely busy with new material and Grinnell was neck deep in work. The staff was feverishly laboring to examine and classify all the material that Professor Marsh was receiving almost daily from all over the country. Grinnell relished his role as a hunter for science, collecting and preserving specimens that would be packed in cabinets for posterity and future examination or displayed in educational museum exhibits for the public to appreciate.

However, Grinnell obediently dropped his work in favor of his family and traveled across the country by rail, finally arriving in San Francisco. The trip, however, held an added mission for him.

"Before starting out, Marsh had commissioned me to dig, if possible, in some old Indian villages formerly occupied by the almost extinct Coast Indians. After meeting my family, seeing the local sights, and eating February strawberries, which, of course, were a surprise to me, I began to make inquiries about those ancient village sites and learned something as to their location. I went out to a place called *Cienigitas* [sic]. There, for several days I dug in the old village mounds and took out many prehistoric artifacts which I finally sent back to the Peabody Museum, where they were exhibited to many years."

Grinnell had not totally neglected his family and was pleased to know that when he departed to return home his father was doing much better. The family would return home to Milford, Connecticut in the spring.

In May 1876, Grinnell received a telegram from George Armstrong Custer asking him to accompany Custer on the Little Bighorn Campaign, on which the seventh Cavalry would be chasing hostile Sioux and Cheyenne through Montana. Custer was known to cast his excursions into the field like a producer would cast a play—inviting his favorite traveling companions to accompany him, both family and friends.

Grinnell, however, was way behind with his duties at the Peabody because of his trip to the West Coast. Marsh also offered the opinion that there would be little time to collect fossils on a military campaign. A campaign differed from an expedition in that it was designed specifically for military action, and a battle or a series of battles was likely. Therefore, Grinnell politely—and likely reluctantly—declined Custer's invitation while wishing him well. There would be future expeditions that would permit him time on the march to do his job as a paleontologist and naturalist.

The Little Bighorn Campaign had come about due to an edict by the government over its frustration with the Black Hills stalemate and raids by Native Americans in the territory. President Ulysses S. Grant had issued an order on December 6, 1875 stating that all Native Americans must report to the reservation by January 31, 1876. Otherwise, failure to comply would result in measures taken by the United States Army, which, because of noncompliance, became necessary. The army would march against those they deemed renegades.

The strategy for the Campaign, designed by Generals Alfred Terry and George Crook, called for three columns to converge on the Sioux and Cheyenne and catch them within this three-pronged movement. General Crook would command one column, and march north from Fort Fetterman, Wyoming. A Montana column would be led by Colonel John Gibbon, and march east down the Yellowstone from Fort Ellis. The third column, which was commanded by General Terry and included Custer's Seventh Cavalry, would march west from Fort Abraham Lincoln.

General George Crook's battalion was the first to fight, engaging in a skirmish at the Powder River and then fighting the Sioux to a draw in the Battle of the Rosebud. Crook, without informing his superiors, then retreated to Wyoming to lick his wounds. At the same time, Colonel Gibbon's column was some distance away on the march toward the Valley of the Little Bighorn. Only one column was actively searching for hostiles—Custer and the Seventh Cavalry.

On June 25 George Armstrong Custer, commanding the battalion in the field, located a huge Sioux village populated by medicine man Sitting Bull's people and was compelled by events to immediately attack. Contrary to popular myth, Custer had devised a brilliant battle plan that could have, would have, and should have succeeded—if not for the actions of one man.

Major Marcus Reno had been ordered to lead a battalion of about140 horsemen on a surprise charge of the village across a barren prairie. This order, according to the military's strict Articles of War, carried no discretion and the punishment for disobedience was death. Custer led his men to the high ridges across the Little Bighorn River from the village, planning to dispatch units down the coulees and enter the village at intervals after Reno attacked. At the same time, Reno and his troopers were thundering across the prairie on a collision course with the village.

About a quarter of a mile from the village, however, Major Reno inexplicably aborted his charge. He had not taken any casualties, and the Sioux were caught off guard and had not been able to mount a counteroffensive, yet Reno halted his men and formed a skirmisher line across the prairie. In fact, the Sioux later stated that they were frantically packing up to run away—until Reno halted his charge. The major had blatantly disobeyed Custer's order by not charging into the Sioux village.

When Reno received small arms fire from a ravine along the river, he made a disorganized, every-man-for-himself retreat from the prairie to a stand of timber beside the river. This timber was a defensible position that Reno could have held for some time by establishing a firm perimeter. Unfortunately for the Seventh Cavalry, Reno panicked. He was standing next to Custer's favorite scout, Bloody Knife, when a bullet crashed through the scout's skull and the remains splattered onto Reno. The major leaped onto his horse and tore out of the timber in a direction that led him away from the village. His bewildered men finally realized that they had been abandoned by their commander and commenced another every-man-for-himself retreat to follow Reno.

By this time, Sioux warriors had gathered in force. With gleeful whoops, they chased after the soldiers who were racing away on a life-or-death retreat. In what the Sioux deemed comparable to a buffalo hunt, the warriors attacked with rifle fire, bows and arrows, clubs, knives, and lances. They rode alongside the fleeing troopers and picked them off one by one.

Major Marcus Reno crashed across the river at the front of his men and ended up atop a hill, with those cavalrymen who had survived the perilous ride straggling along behind. They hastily set up a defensive position and waited for an attack. The Sioux had broken contact with Reno, however, and were headed toward Custer's position.

In time, the sound of rifle fire could be heard on Reno Hill that emanated from the direction of the village, some four miles distant. Military custom called for Reno and his men to ride to the sound of the firing, but he refused to budge off that hill. Another battalion, led by Custer critic Captain Frederick Benteen, had received written orders from Custer to hurry to the field and bring the pack train with ammunition along. Benteen instead disobeyed orders and remained on the hill with Reno.

Custer, whose plan called for his two hundred men to attack a village in turmoil caused by Reno's charge, became the subject of interest for at least 1,500 Sioux warriors. There had been no charge by Reno, which left Custer and his cavalrymen exposed and in danger of annihilation. When one part of a battle plan was not properly executed, it threatened to sabotage the entire strategy.

Custer tactically pulled back to the high ground to make a stand and wait for reinforcements and the pack train containing the precious ammo. Alas, that help never arrived. Custer and his troopers eventually ran out of ammunition and were systematically killed, finally overrun on one last sweep of the ridge by warriors led by Crazy Horse and Gall. In the end, every cavalryman with Custer was killed, scalped, and mutilated.

Reno, Benteen, and the survivors of the cowardly retreat cowered on that hill four miles away from the death scene for two days before a column led by General Terry and Colonel Gibbon arrived to rescue them. By then, the Sioux and Cheyenne had scattered into small groups and disappeared into the mountainous wilderness.

The nation was predictably outraged and horrified by Custer's defeat. George Grinnell heard the terrible news while visiting his father's farm in Milford and mourned the loss of the many friends that he had made on the Black Hills Expedition. His first thought was: "Had I gone with Custer I should in all probability have been mixed up in the Custer battle, for I should have been either with Custer's command, or with that of Reno, and would have been right on the ground when the Seventh Cavalry was wiped out."

Dead were George Armstrong Custer and members of the "Custer royal family"—brothers Tom and Boston, brother-in-law Jimmy Calhoun, and friends George Yates, and Algernon Smith. Other officers who were killed with whom Grinnell had shared time included: Thomas McDougall, Henry Harrington, Donald "Tosh" McIntosh, Benjamin Hodgson, among others, along with over two hundred enlisted men.

The one name on the list of casualties that affected Grinnell the most was that of scout "Lonesome" Charley Reynolds, who had been killed during Reno's retreat. Grinnell was heartbroken over the loss of his good friend. The two men had spent many a pleasant day and night alone together, out under the western skies, and had formed a strong bond of friendship.

Grinnell explained: "Charley's horse had been killed at once. He shot an Indian who was charging toward him on a buckskin pony, and as the Indian did not fall off, he shot the horse, and the Indian and pony rolled over together almost at his feet. He fired again, and then again. Bullets and arrows were flying thick. Suddenly Charley seemed to be hit in half a dozen places. He fell, raised himself on his elbow and fired another shot—his last. Then he sank back." Grinnell had always ridden with Charley, and would have surely been beside the scout, if not with Custer, on that fateful day.

That thought must have had him thanking his lucky stars that he had not accompanied the campaign. He had lost many Pawnee friends at Massacre Canyon and now those lives from the Seventh Cavalry had been taken at the Little Bighorn. Yet, these two tragedies would have done nothing to quell the enthusiasm and affinity that Grinnell had for the West. He had never entertained the thought that it was civilized across the Mississippi River, and the wildness and potential danger lurking around every bend was one of the factors that appealed to him. He was certain from previous trips that the area held untold fossilized treasures and unique flora and fauna, and he was willing to risk his life to seek them.

An opportunity to enhance his résumé, as well as satisfy his desire to disseminate all the information he was learning from his studies at Yale and his trips to the West unexpectedly presented itself. *Forest and Stream, a Weekly Journal of the Rod and Gun*, was the ninth oldest magazine in the country dedicated to conservation, and billed itself as being devoted to "Angling, Shooting, the Kennel, Practical Natural History, Fish Culture, Yachting and Canoeing, and the Unculcation in Men and Women of a Healthy Interest in Outdoor Recreation and Study."

The journal had been founded in 1873 in New York City by Charles Hallock, who served as editor. The forty-two-year-old Hallock was a fellow Yale alumnus, and had previously worked as assistant editor of the *New Haven Register*, and for his father, who was the editor of the *New York Journal of Commerce*. He had been the author of four books, with titles as diverse as *The Life of Stonewall Jackson* and *The Fishing Tourist*.

A great number of issues of *Forest and Stream* are archived online and available for reading. Interestingly, the magazine does not resemble in any manner the outdoor magazines of today. This publication, a cross between a magazine and a newspaper, was laid out in columns, like a newspaper. It had delightful articles, many with detailed illustrations on how-to projects, covering just about every aspect of the outdoors. Amazingly, it was a *weekly* that burst with news, information, opinion, activism, and pages of advertisements, all of which offered more than simply a snapshot of the day. It was a wonder that a reader back then could make it through one week's paper before the next week's edition was delivered. Editing this paper was obviously an ambitious endeavor and would take much coordination between many talented people to maintain its relevance and popularity.

In the fall of 1876, Charles Hallock became dissatisfied with his natural history editor, and asked Grinnell to take the position at ten dollars a week. George accepted the offer, and, in addition to editing by mail from New York City, wrote a page or two each week, including book reviews. Grinnell, who had been writing the occasional article for Hallock, was confident in the future of the magazine and began buying its stock.

Grinnell embraced his job writing and editing for the magazine with the same enthusiasm that he had for collecting bones. Now he had a platform—albeit somewhat limited—to pass along the wonders of nature and the threats, as he saw them. The material was endless.

His winter was spent at the museum learning and analyzing as much as he could as he worked toward his PhD. In early summer 1877, he was sent by the Peabody to Massachusetts to make casts of dinosaur footprints. That field work must have stirred up an appetite for a foray to the western fields and mountains. He decided that it was time to contact his favorite western scout and go hunting in the prairie wilderness.

Grinnell traveled to the Dismal River in western Nebraska to hunt elk and antelope with his friend Lute North. Earlier that year, the North brothers and Buffalo Bill Cody had purchased a Texas longhorn ranch together, which Grinnell wrote was just "a couple of tents stuck up on the edge of the alkaline lake which was the head of the Dismal River. On this lake a pair of trumpeter swans had a nest. The sand hills roundabout abounded in antelope and deer. There was some elk in the country, and one or two little bunches of buffalo."

The ranch, sixty-five miles north of North Platte, had been initially one hundred sixty acres, but would grow in size to encompass seven thousand acres, including twenty-five-hundred acres of alfalfa and twenty-five hundred acres of corn, which would be watered by a twelve-mile-long irrigation ditch. Many cottonwoods and box-elder trees had been planted around the originally barren property. The place served as a comfortable base camp for George Grinnell's hunting adventures that summer.

Frank North managed the ranch while Cody traveled much of the time for his other endeavors. Buffalo Bill had cashed in on his fame as a dime novel hero and would scout or guide hunting parties in the summer and, at the urging of author Ned Buntline, appear on the stage each winter. He had gained additional real-life fame and adoration from the public with his actions soon after the Battle of the Little Bighorn.

On July 17, 1876—several weeks following the battle—Cody was scouting for the Fifth Cavalry when he came upon thirty Cheyenne, out of an estimated eight hundred that had left Red Cloud Agency, at Warbonnet Creek. In what was later reported as a duel to the death, Cody chased down and shot the pony out from beneath a sub-chief named Yellow Hair. He then killed and scalped the defenseless man. A reenactment of this "duel" became a popular Cody play, *The Red Hand; or Buffalo Bill's First Scalp for Custer*.

Cody enjoyed his visits to the ranch and pitched in to work while his wife, Louisa, supervised the building of a magnificent eighteen-room mansion. Cody, an expert horseman, had great admiration for the tough and talented men Frank North had hired to work their Texas Longhorn cattle. "In this cattle driving business," he wrote in his autobiography, "is exhibited some of the most magnificent horsemanship, for the 'cow-boys,' as they are called, are invariably skillful and fearless horsemen—in fact only a most expert rider could be a cow-boy, as it requires the greatest dexterity and daring in the saddle to cut a wild steer out of the herd."

Grinnell spent all his time with Lute North and was once again impressed with his friend's "extraordinary knowledge of the habits of animals of the prairie." Grinnell was amazed when Lute predicted the movements of an antelope that Grinnell finally shot and killed. "I still think the act showed extraordinary hunter's sense."

Grinnell had a decided advantage over others in his field in his study of animals due to his friendship with Lute North. Whether it was at the ranch or over a campfire out under a full moon, the conversations between the two men were always about where the wild game lived, what it would eat, when it would eat, where it would move, and every other aspect of its lifestyle and habitat. North had the instincts of a subsistence hunter, which gave Grinnell an insight few others in his field could enjoy.

It was not surprising that Grinnell felt a close affinity with Luther North. Lute was a hunter of live game. Grinnell was a hunter of fossils—extinct game—and museum specimens. Both of their endeavors were in close touch with nature, and the one was as full of the thrill of the hunt and the resultant success and failure as the other.

Grinnell reluctantly ended his hunt with Lute North and returned to Yale. There was always much to do in the museum. He pitched in cataloging and analyzing specimens, imaging their origins and how they had appeared as living, breathing things. This process encouraged him to see for himself once again the wonders of paleontology at ground zero.

The following summer, accompanied by his brother, Mort, George Grinnell explored the Jurassic exposures in the Como Bluffs near Medicine Bow, Wyoming. Professor O. C. Marsh, Grinnell's mentor now for the past eight years, had been sending parties of fossil hunters to this location for several years. The stunning discoveries had been shipped back to the Peabody Museum for study and display, so Grinnell was aware of what was waiting to be unearthed by him and the other volunteers.

Countless dinosaurs had roamed the area around that ten-mile-long and one-mile-wide ridge rising from the sagebrush prairie during the late Jurassic Period, said to be some 145-155 million years ago. During that prehistoric Mesozoic Era, oceans had flooded the landmasses to create a humid climate and lush subtropical environment, which supported a diverse array of plants and animals. Birds developed back then, some of them flightless, and flowering plants flourished, which also increased the insect population. These plants provided for an abundance of herbivorous plant-eating dinosaurs—as well as carnivores, fearsome meat-eating dinosaurs.

It was here that the world took its first steps to transform from an alien prehistoric environment into the modern world of today. In what would become known as the "Dinosaur Capitol of the World,"

the fossilized remains of countless extinct mammals, turtles, croco-
dilians, and fish were well preserved in the pastel-colored claystones
of the Morrison Formation and patiently waiting to be unearthed
by the volunteers.

Professor Marsh had not discovered Como Bluffs, but had been
the first scientific person informed in secret of this potential treasure trove by a man named William Harlow Reed, station foreman
for the Union Pacific Railroad at Como Station. Reed and the station agent, William Edward Carlin, had happened upon unusual
fossilized remains of large animals nearby, and wondered what species they might have been from. The two men shipped off samples
to Marsh, who immediately recognized the bones as belonging to
ancient dinosaurs. At the direction of Marsh, Reed began super-
vising work at Como Bluff in 1878, and became the source of the
breathtaking display of Jurassic mammals at the Peabody Museum.
His efforts unearthed valuable specimens that had been unknown to
exist before then—and Marsh was the fortunate recipient.

O. C. Marsh had become one the preeminent scientists in his
field for his descriptions of new species and his theories on the
origin of birds. This forty-six-year-old native of Lockport, New
York, had been educated at Yale, thanks to the generosity of rich
Uncle Charles Peabody. He then embarked on travels throughout
the world studying anatomy, mineralogy, and geology—and went
to Berlin, Germany, to learn about paleontology. He returned to
Yale in 1866 and was appointed professor of vertebrate paleontology. That same year, his wealthy banker uncle donated the funds to
establish Yale's Peabody Museum.

While in Berlin, Marsh had met a young man named Edward
Drinker Cope, a man with less education than Marsh but who had
published thirty-seven scientific papers compared to just two for
Marsh. The two men became friends, but that relationship soon
deteriorated when Marsh pointed out that Cope had placed the
skull of an *Elasmosaurus* at the end of its tail. The two men then
dueled with papers in scientific journals in what would be called
"Bone Wars." For years, they competed to find the greatest number
of new species of dinosaurs, with Marsh eventually winning that
competition.

Therefore, Grinnell was not simply digging for fossils; he was representing Professor Marsh in his rivalry with Cope. Yes, there was pride at stake, but there was also personal satisfaction for Grinnell in this endeavor. This was the paleontology that he loved. The sounds of the dig—the chipping, the hammering, the scooping of earth, and the crumbling of soft rock—combined to create a symphony to his ears. The sky, the earth, the rock, and the prospect of discovery were the milieu he had dreamed about since that first fossil hunting expedition eight years earlier. He was now in his element and knew that this was what he was meant to do with his life.

It must have been a humbling experience for Grinnell to realize that he was standing on the threshold of a past world and that its long-hidden mysteries were now being revealed to him. His eyes and those of the volunteers would be the first humans to see the remains of living wonders that had roamed the earth millions of years in the past. Each discovery represented an ancient time when that barren land was lush and green and abundant with living, breathing things.

All the volunteers were outfitted with a standard geological hammer, along with a chisel to more precisely bore into the matrix, a trowel, and a thick-bristled brush used in the removal process, as well as a hand lens with a magnification of twenty times. The wooden-handled hammer had on one side of its metal head a flat, hard surface that was used to pound a chisel against the rock and on the other side a pick to break up the rock. This indispensable bone hunting tool with its heavy, unbalanced head was not easy to wield, and required some practice to learn how to control the direction and the impact of the hammer's blow.

The volunteers also were taught how to gauge the direction of the rock's line of weakness, the amount of force required to split off flakes, and how and when to employ the chisel to break away stubborn material. They would begin with a light stroke and gradually increase strength as required so as not to penetrate too deep and risk destroying a specimen hidden in the rock. That way, they would remove the sediment of millenniums and hopefully uncover a treasure trove of fossils.

And George Grinnell did not disappoint his mentor, or himself.

His party unearthed the remains of several rare dinosaurs there at Como Bluff that were returned to the Peabody Museum for study.

Interestingly, George Grinnell came to the defense of his mentor in an article that appeared in the September 1878 issue of *Popular Science Monthly*—and it had nothing to do with the Cope rivalry.

Marsh had traveled to the Black Hills in 1874 to hunt for fossils and was confronted by none other than Chief Red Cloud, the Sioux leader who had forced the US Army to surrender back in 1868. The chief was under the impression that Marsh was there to search for gold deposits. Marsh was able to pacify Red Cloud and convince the chief that his was a scientific expedition. Red Cloud permitted Marsh to remain—on one condition. Red Cloud's people on the reservation had not received their proper annuities from the government, and what they had received was spoiled rotten. The chief requested that Marsh carry this message to the Secretary of the Interior, Columbus Delano.

Marsh passed on Red Cloud's complaint, but was rebuffed by Delano, which compelled the professor to investigate. Marsh uncovered frauds that had victimized the Native Americans, and the scandal that followed cost Columbus Delano his job. A grateful Red Cloud regarded Marsh as the only white man who had ever kept his promise to the Sioux. In fact, the chief made the trip to New Haven and was a guest in the professor's home.

Grinnell, in sticking up for Marsh's decision to expose the fraud, ended his article by writing: "This is perhaps the only instance in which a private citizen has successfully fought a department of Government in his efforts to expose wrong-doing."

Grinnell's willingness to take the side of the Native Americans on behalf of Marsh was another example of his continuing growth as an advocate for these downtrodden people. Not much positive was being presented about these people, and the public cared little about the suffering of the race, the western tribes in particular. Grinnell believed that they had their place on the frontier, just as did the buffalo, the elk, the wolf, men like Charley Reynolds and Lute North, and the sun and the moon. As he had previously written, the Native American was pure nature.

Grinnell had taken a side-trip on his way home from Como Bluffs to visit Lute North at the ranch on Dismal River. The hunting visit had been thoroughly enjoyable, as usual, but the aftereffects were unexpected and alarming. During his return home he developed fever, chills, and delirium, and barely survived the trip. He had contracted Rocky Mountain spotted fever, a serious and potentially life-threatening infectious illness.

Grinnell probably could not recall the exact moment when he had been bitten by an infected tick, but the incubation period for this disease also known as "black measles" could be as long as two weeks. The disease had been recognized in the early 1800s and became common in the later part of that century—and the mortality rate was high. It had only been a decade earlier, in 1866, when a doctor in Montana noticed a tick embedded in the skin of one of his patients and believed that the insect was the carrier of the illness. Further research confirmed the doctor's belief, and tick-borne Rocky Mountain spotted fever now had a culprit to blame.

"I reached home barely able to totter, was met by my father at the bridge at Naugatuck Junction, and went to bed, where I remained for seven long weeks. For a good part of the time I was out of my head and my delirium always took one form. I imagined myself riding about the cattle, saw great banks of clouds coming up in the west with thunder and lightening, and then the cattle would break away, and of course we would all ride after them as hard as we could."

Grinnell suffered from fever, nausea, vomiting, severe headache, muscle pain, lack of appetite, rash, and perhaps worst of all for a man with his intellect, a wandering mind and forgetfulness. Needless to say, his illness was severe and could take his life. There were few cures, other than rest and prayer. His father took him home to Milford, Connecticut, the coastal town known for shipbuilding, farming, oystering, and as a beach resort for residents of New Haven and the surrounding area.

George Bird Grinnell, demonstrating the same strong will that he had displayed as an active adventurer, gradually regained his physical and mental strength over the winter months. "At length I began to eat the slops usually fed to sick people and gradually got up and started to walk about with a cane. Little by little, I began to go over to New Haven for an hour or two a day and finally recovered." No doubt his visits to the museum had played a major role in his recovery.

In 1879 Grinnell embarked on a hunting trip to Colorado, traveling mainly in the vicinity of the Continental Divide in what would become Rocky Mountain National Park. People had been visiting this area of valleys and mountains for over eleven thousand years, beginning with Paleo-Indians. Remains of spearheads with Clovis and Folsom projectile points used to kill mighty mammoths found along ancient trails indicated that early Native people roamed those green valleys, tundra meadows, and crystal lakes. By the 1700s, the Ute people dominated the area, but other tribes—the Cheyenne, the Arapaho, Sioux, Shoshone, and Comanche tribes—all passed through at one time or another to hunt game.

Spanish explorers, French fur trappers, and even Stephen H. Long on his 1820 expedition had avoided venturing deep into this rugged, forbidding landscape. The first known account of the area was written in 1846 by newspaper editor and publisher and political activist Rufus Sage, and was called *Rocky Mountain Life, or Startling Scenes and Perilous Adventures in the Far West During an Expedition of Three Years.*

The Pikes Peak gold rush in 1859, however, lured prospectors and settlements to the region and transformed the surrounding landscape. This influx of miners started a housing boom that was tempered only by the harsh winters. Arctic conditions were prevalent during the winter, with sudden blizzards, high winds, and deep snowpack.

By the time Grinnell arrived, this mountainous landscape was known as a tourist destination, with the people who resided there involved in lodging, mining, and the lumber industry. Another visitor at that time was the famed painter Albert Bierstadt, who had been commissioned by the Earl of Dunraven to paint Long's Peak and Estes Park.

The Native American tribes had been relocated to reservations, which left the dark forests, lush meadows, and rocky mountainsides to be populated by game that any hunter would dream of having in his rifle sights—elk, bighorn sheep, antelope, mule deer, moose, and black bear. Grinnell may have also encountered those predators that helped maintain the natural rhythm and balance—the mountain lion, gray wolf, lynx, coyote, and bobcat. The area boasted one of the most diverse plant and animal environments in the United

States, partially due to the dramatic temperature differences arising from varying elevation levels and topography. Grinnell could have documented about seventy species of mammals, almost three hundred of birds, and viewed a variety of game fish that lurked in the dark shadows of the waterways and lakes that they shared with beaver, mink, muskrat, and otter.

When Grinnell put on his paleontologist's hat, he would note formations that had been created during the Paleogene and Cretaceous periods, about seventy million years ago. Back then, the region had been covered by a deep sea, which deposited massive amounts of shale and embedded marine life fossils. Skeletons of fish and marine reptiles, such as mosasaurs, plesiosaurs, extinct sea turtles, along with dinosaurs and birds, could be dug out of the layers of rock.

The trip was pleasant with only one exception. His party was warned that the Ute tribe was in a "restless" mood. No one took this news lightly—and with good reason. A few days after Grinnell and his party had departed the North Park area, the Ute bolted from the reservation and ambushed a 160-man army column. The warriors killed the commander and thirteen troopers. But Grinnell and his party had a successful hunt and lived to tell about it.

George Grinnell wrote about his experiences on the Rocky Mountain trip in *Forest and Stream*, adopting for the first time the pseudonym "Yo" for a nine-part series that ran in the September and October issues.

Rather than writing simply a factual account of his hunting and exploring adventures, his tone of voice in the articles had a twinge of disappointment and warned of dark clouds on the horizon. The West was changing—the Native American tribes had been removed to reservations, Crazy Horse had been murdered by his own people, Chief Joseph had attempted one last futile effort for freedom, and the settlers and ranchers and mining operations had moved in to claim the land. In less than a decade since he had first traveled into the western wilderness with Marsh's expedition, he was shocked by the rapidity of change.

Grinnell wrote:

As I look back on the past ten years and see what changes have taken place in these glorious mountains since I first knew them, I can form some idea of the transformations which time to come to work in the appearance of the country, its fauna, and its flora. The enormous mineral wealth contained in the rock-ribbed hills will be every year more fully developed. Fire, air, and water working upon earth, will reveal more and more of the precious metals. Towns will spring up and flourish, and the pure, thin air of the mountains will be blackened and polluted by the smoke vomited from the chimneys of a thousand smelting furnaces; the game, once so plentiful, will have disappeared with the Indian; railroads will climb the steep sides of mountains and wind through their narrow passes, carrying huge loads of provisions to the mining towns, and the returning trains will be freighted with ore just dug from the bowels of the earth; the valleys will be filled with fattening cattle, as profitable to their owners as the mines to theirs; all arable land will be taken up and cultivated, and finally the mountains will be stripped of their timber and will become simply bald and rocky hills. The day when all this shall have taken place is distant no doubt, and will not be seen by the present generation; but it will come.

Grinnell's prophecies were not exactly Orwellian, but every aspect of damage he mentioned has been a matter of contention at one time or another in the West right up to the present day.

In 1880, not long after his return to New York, Grinnell was awarded his PhD in osteology and vertebrate paleontology from Yale. The subject of his dissertation was "The Osteology of Geococcyx Californicus (the Greater Roadrunner)."

Why Grinnell chose the roadrunner, a bird found in the southwestern United States, for his dissertation is anyone's guess. His general interest in bird bone structure might have led him to this unusual member of the species, which sported four toes on each foot—two facing forward and two facing backward. Or perhaps Grinnell became compelled to investigate the roadrunner after hearing about it from various Indian tribes. They believed that the bird protected them from evil spirits, and led lost people to trails, and even thought that, like a stork, the roadrunner brought babies.

Another theory may be that the subconscious, or possibly even the conscious mind, of George Grinnell had accepted a theory brought forth in the 1860s by Thomas Henry Huxley. This comparative anatomist noticed similarities between the body parts of birds and extinct dinosaurs. Although Huxley never claimed that birds descended from dinosaurs, a belief now embraced by most modern paleontologists, he found little support for his radical idea. But, taking into consideration that Grinnell was first and foremost a "bird man" who had come upon dinosaur bones later, there was no better specimen in the bird world than the Greater Roadrunner to demonstrate the traits and bone structure of a bird-dinosaur.

Although capable of limited flight with its 17-24-inch wingspan, the roadrunner spent most of its time on the ground where it could run at speeds up to twenty miles per hour. The bird would run down its prey, which consisted of an assortment of insects, venomous spiders, mice, small birds, and lizards and snakes. It would capture its prey in its bill and then slam it against the earth until it was dead. The roadrunner was monogamous and formed lifetime pair bonds. A mate became useful in capturing its favorite meal, the rattlesnake. One roadrunner would distract the rattler while the other one would sneak up behind it and grab it. The habits of the roadrunner could conceivably be compared to those of an extinct predatory raptor.

Regardless of reasons for his choice of a dissertation subject, Grinnell now had the paper credentials, along with extensive field experience, to prove that he was a serious and capable paleontologist and naturalist. The world in which he now traversed was decidedly different from that of a Wall Street stockbroker. Hopefully, his father was proud of the choice that George had made when he closed Geo. Grinnell and Company to pursue scientific endeavors. One thing was certain: Lucy Audubon would have been thrilled that the wide-eyed boy she had tutored about feathered creatures and the wonders of nature had demonstrated the willpower and knowledge to achieve that lofty scholarly level.

Late in 1879, although *Forest and Stream* magazine was highly popular and turning a profit, editor Charles Hallock came under fire from within his own offices. Grinnell was approached by Edward R. Wilbur, the company treasurer, and informed: "Mr. Hallock, President of the company, has become more and more eccentric, drinking heavily and neglecting his duties to the paper." The future of the magazine was at stake.

Not surprisingly, the board of *Forest and Stream* took action in May 1880 by voting out Hallock. The founder of the magazine would move on to experiment in sunflower culture, raise sheep on Indian reservations, and among other economic schemes, establish a reservation for sportsmen in Minnesota. Grinnell had respected Hallock, almost as if the man had been a hero for his work on behalf of nature, and was sorry to see him go. But he understood that his removal was for the good of the magazine—a magazine that was not only dear to his heart but dear to his pocketbook.

Grinnell wrote, "During the two-or three-years past, I had from time to time purchased a few shares of *Forest and Stream* stock, and my father at one time had purchased something over one-third of the capital stock, so that practically we had control."

It was a given that the new president and editor of *Forest and Stream* magazine would be thirty-one-year-old George Bird Grinnell. He regretfully resigned his position at the Peabody Museum and moved back to Audubon Park to run the magazine. "I left New Haven with keen regret, for I had hoped to work for a long time in the museum."

George noted that *Forest and Stream* "printed a good paper, had a large circulation, and began almost at once to make plenty of money." More important to him than the financial aspects were that the small platform he had been using as a writer to relate his observations and tell his tales of western adventure—and his concerns for its future survival—had now become a booming brass band and he was the conductor. The magazine could now function more as a tool for protest and activism to rally support for causes and still maintain its balance as an entertaining guide for outdoor activities.

In fact, one of his first editorials in the magazine took umbrage with the on-going Gilded Age, where he wrote: "The mighty dollar is the controlling agency in every branch of social and public life." He immediately challenged the New York State Association for the Protection of Game, an early conversation organization, and chastised it for not being more aggressive in its purpose. He was not above currying favor, either, as demonstrated by an editorial where he pointed out the large number of hunters and fishermen in the

Congress. This group, he asserted, was "evidence of the constantly increasing popularity of field sports."

Grinnell could have sat back and satisfied readers who merely wanted hunting, fishing, and camping articles without the politics. Instead, he chose to stick out his neck and put forth his critical observations from his travels to the West on the pages of the magazine—and it was likely that some readers were either uninterested or held opposing views. It was a time, however, when few East Coast people had visited the West, and this mysterious land that they had envisioned as one of romance was now being presented by Grinnell as a place that was changing and being destroyed by greed.

Only a man who cared deeply about the future of the wildlife and resources in the region would have taken such a chance that the public would accept his protests and not cancel their subscriptions en masse. But the sincerity—not to mention the persuasiveness—of George Grinnell came through in the articles he wrote and those of others he chose for publication, and the magazine flourished. He made certain that the articles he published were accurate and the facts were substantiated. He made a concerted effort to increase the natural history section of the magazine to the point that it gained the respect of zoologists of other scientists, not a small feat for a weekly whose main audience was common people.

Although *Forest and Stream* had taken on controversial problems in the past, such as commercial hunting, and advocated for the sportsman in various disputes, these issues had been concentrated on the relatively civilized East Coast, where law enforcement already existed. Grinnell was preparing to carry the torch of conservation to places where it had never been before.

To further his causes, Grinnell handpicked those writers that he trusted to uphold high journalistic standards with an attitude of change for the betterment of nature and for those people who enjoyed roaming the forests, waters, and fields of America. He believed that his magazine needed the voices of people who actually spent time in nature, as opposed to trained academics who studied specimens under a microscope.

Contributors to *Forest and Stream* in those days formed a "Who's Who" of the American conservation movement of the time. The magazine was an invaluable source for every aspect of the outdoor hobbies of the day but never forgot to add responsibility to nature in its presentation. The most famous contributors included future president Theodore Roosevelt; photographer Edward S. Curtis; master fisherman Fred Mather; dog expert Franklin Satterwaite; and hunting guru Josiah Whitley.

But in their time, several other writers became quite popular with the public, and household names in the sportsman's world for their practical outdoor advice.

One of the more prolific and respected writers for *Forest and Stream* during that period was George Washington Sears, who wrote under the pen name "Nessmuk." Sears wrote about technology and art, nature and life through subjects such as canoe camping in the Adirondack Mountains. He had invented and introduced an ultra-light single canoe. Before then, canoeing had been accomplished solely in heavy guide canoes. He had been compelled to write about this alternative manner of canoeing when he became ill and weak with acute pulmonary tuberculosis and could not carry a heavy canoe during portages. He retired to the Adirondacks, and had a light one-man canoe built for him—and the rest is history. Perhaps the most famous contribution to outdoor lore by Sears, however, was his book, *Woodcraft*, which was published in 1884 and remains in print today. Sears himself was an interesting man—a commercial fisherman and sailor, bullwhacker, Colorado miner, Texas cowboy, shoemaker, Civil War soldier, poet, worldwide hunter and fisherman, and above all, an environmentalist before that word had been invented.

Sears is the subject of one of the best books ever written about the Adirondack Mountains: *An Adirondack Passage: The Cruise of the Canoe Sairy Gamp*, written by Christine Jerome in 1994. The book features a 180-mile modern-day canoe trip that traces the wilderness route of George Washington Sears and the ultra-light canoe that he invented and named the *Sairy Gamp* and includes fascinating history of the area and its characters in addition to relevant quotes from Nessmuck.

Another popular columnist was Pennsylvanian Horace Kephart, who had worked as a librarian at Yale University. Kephart campaigned for the establishment of a park in the Great Smoky

Mountains and was named one of the fathers of that national park when Congress finally passed the law. He also helped plot the route of the Appalachian Trail through the Smokies. Kephart wrote about his practical outdoor experiences in articles for *Forest and Stream*, which were collected into his classic guide *Camping and Woodcraft*, first published in 1906.

In his day, Theodore Gordon was called the "father of the American school of fly fishing." He was a consumptive hermit who had taught himself to tie fishing flies and wrote about his experiences in numerous articles in *Forest and Stream*. Most of his stories were based in the Catskill Region of New York State and occasionally written under the pen name "Badger Hackle."

George Grinnell's responsibilities running *Forest and Stream* prevented him from traveling West again until 1881. That summer, the president of the Northern Pacific Railroad invited Grinnell to journey through the West by rail. He traveled to the Pacific Ocean, visiting Portland and San Francisco, and then catching a steamer to Vancouver Island, where at Burrard Inlet he saw his first mountain goat in the wild.

Grinnell, however, soon found himself at odds with the Northern Pacific. The railroad had reached Yellowstone National Park and obtained 640 acres of land at prominent points of interest and natural wonders and commenced building on it. Grinnell, through *Forest and Stream*, opposed this effort to monopolize public property for private gain and initiated a campaign to maintain the integrity of the park.

"Up to within a few years," he wrote in *Forest and Stream*, "the valley of the Yellowstone River has been a magnificent hunting ground. The progress of the Northern Pacific Railroad, however, has changed all this. The Indians have been run out and the white men have had a chance to do what they could toward killing off the game." He went on to point out that "there is nowhere in the world such systematic, business-like and relentless killing as on the buffalo plains."

Grinnell had always been an enthusiastic hunter but realized that there must be laws and regulations in order to preserve and protect game. People would not be capable of policing themselves when the dollar was there to tempt them. One of his initial targets was the Yellowstone Valley Hunting Club. He had traveled through that magnificent park and written definitively about its wildlife and resources. It was a place that was embedded in his heart, and it was painful for him to see any threat to its integrity and beauty.

When the president of that Yellowstone organization claimed that "the game is so abundant that it cannot be exterminated," Grinnell took action. In a front-page editorial, he wrote:

Let us tell the president that he is wrong. It is but eight years since we could see along the Platte River and thence south to the Republican, and beyond through Kansas, the Nation and Texas, buffalo by the thousands and hundreds of thousands. Where are they now? The buffalo will disappear from the valley of the Yellowstone, unless steps are taken to protect it there.

Grinnell did not hesitate to demand action from those who had the power to stop the madness, and he was not the only one who recognized the danger facing the buffalo. He printed letters in *Forest and Stream* from readers in the West who were witnessing the mass extermination. One Montanan wrote: "I do hope Congress will pass a law to protect our buffalo and other large game, now being slaughtered by wholesale. It is reported that one man on our border killed 2,000 buffalo this winter for their hides only. At that rate how long can it last?"

The West was a virtual slaughterhouse for hunters of the buffalo. An army lieutenant reported on a herd of 75,000 animals that were fleeing their normal range and attempting to cross the Yellowstone River and head north, away from the carnage. Alas, the carnage followed them. The lieutenant stated that "Indians, pot-hunters, and white butchers" shot the vulnerable animals as they emerged from the river. Then, these assassins followed the straggling herd to wipe them out one by one. And this was not an isolated incident but was happening across the West.

In one case, the Indian Agent at Standing Rock reservation in Dakota Territory allowed one thousand warriors, led by Sitting Bull, to hunt a herd of buffalo to supplement their government rations. White hunters were also aware of the herd, and the hunt turned into a competition to see which ones, red or white, could kill the most animals. In what would be called "the last Indian buffalo chase," this herd was decimated. According to a participant, "there was not a hoof left."

In 1882, more than two-hundred,000 buffalo hides were loaded onto seven hundred boxcars and were shipped on the Northern Pacific Railroad to processors back east. The next year, that number had fallen to forty thousand, and, by the year after that, only one boxcar was needed. That was the last shipment of buffalo hides ever made by the Northern Pacific Railroad.

No doubt George Grinnell anguished over this tragedy that he had predicted, but as yet he was unable to persuade Congress to act. Those state and territorial governments that passed laws against commercially harvesting these animals were thwarted by the impossibility of enforcing their laws due to the vastness of the country.

In 1883 Grinnell, who had been visiting the various Plains tribes for years now during each summer, decided to find a suitable permanent getaway and a base of operations in the West that he could use for rest and recuperation, as well as for personal writing, away from the daily rigors of running a magazine. To that end, he purchased a 1,one hundred-acre sheep ranch in the Shirley Basin, near Como, Wyoming, and hired William Reed, the Como Bluff discoverer, to run it for him.

The ranch, which would eventually abandon sheep in favor of raising cattle and horses, proved to be a financial failure, perhaps due to Grinnell's lack of attention, not to mention the blizzard of 1886–87—known as "the Big Die-up"—that had a devastating effect on livestock throughout the Rocky Mountain West.

On November 16, 1886, an arctic wind blew in, lowering temperatures to twenty below, and at least six inches of snow fell to blanket Wyoming and Montana. Three weeks later another blizzard struck, and then a third on January 9, 1887. Snow came down at a rate of an inch an hour, and temperatures plummeted to as low as sixty-eight degrees below zero throughout the region. Then, on January 28, heavy snow fell for seventy-two hours straight. Never before had anyone in the area endured such low temperatures combined with the constant, driving snows. Ranchers were aware that something dramatic was happening; still, they hoped for the best when the skies turned blue and they could ride out and investigate the damage.

By the end of February, a Chinook finally arrived with its warm, dry wind that pushed out the cold and thawed the snow. Within a week the ranchers had their answer—and no one was prepared for what was revealed.

The open range was littered with tens of thousands of dead or dying cattle, horses, and sheep, their bloated carcasses dotting the landscape for miles and miles. Snowdrifts had piled up to heights of more than one hundred feet in many areas. Some ranch houses, barns, and outbuildings were completely buried under the snow. In addition to bodies of the livestock, searchers encountered more macabre scenes—corpses of cowboys, sheepherders, and Native Americans who had frozen to death. An estimated ninety percent of range stock in Wyoming and Montana had perished in the snow and cold.

The Great Blizzard of 1886–87 had been the final straw for George Grinnell. He was never suited for ranching anyway and found that he preferred to explore regions where solitude or freedom were his companions, such as wilderness areas and Indian camps, and rarely visited the ranch again. Reed went back to fossil hunting as an independent contractor before becoming curator of the museum at the University of Wyoming. The property would finally be sold in 1903.

Grinnell's position as owner and editor of *Forest and Stream* magazine had provided a national platform from which he could affect people's consciences and inspire action on subjects that were dear to his heart. Now, he was done merely writing about an issue and *asking* for action—he was about to elevate the cause of conservation to the level of a holy war.

CHAPTER SEVEN:
CRUSADING EDITOR

The more clearly we can focus our attention on the wonders and realities of the universe about us, the less taste we have for destruction.
—RACHEL CARSON

FOREST AND STREAM *MAGAZINE HAD A PROUD TRADITION* of advocacy even before George Bird Grinnell first came onboard as editor of the natural history page. In the first issue of the paper, founder Charles Hallock expressed his intention to take his publication to a different level than had been the standard policy in outdoor journals. "It is not sufficient that a man should be able to knock over his birds right and left, or cast an inimitable fly. A practical knowledge of natural history must of necessity underlie all attainments which combine to make a thorough sportsman." He made it clear that "for the preservation of our rapidly diminishing forests, we shall continually do battle."

One of Hallock's first targets was a minister, the Reverend William H. H. Murray, a Bostonian who had visited the Adirondack Mountains in 1867 and hunted and fished out of season. Not only did this man of the cloth break the closed-season laws, but he wrote a book that boasted about his devious deeds. Hallock penned an editorial under the heading of: "Killing Game Out of Season." He wrote:

Among all true sportsmen there is a bond of sympathy, one touch of which makes the fraternity akin, and within this charmed circle, Mr. Murray has not yet been admitted, and never will be, so long as he continues to slaughter game out of season. Against waste, we shall wage a constant war.

Hallock had in effect unofficially banned the reverend from being part of that exclusive club of sportsmen who prided themselves in their responsible hunting practices, and he further called for the shunning of the man. No doubt Hallock's condemnation of the illegal hunter, a reverend no less, caused more than a few readers to question their own outdoor ethics. The line between poaching and hunting was not always properly defined, and more than a few unwitting sportsmen crossed it without thinking twice about consequences.

Reverend Murray, however, was not in the least bit affected by Hallock's righteous attack. Murray wrote the book *Adventures in the Wilderness; Or, Camp-life in the Adirondacks*, which chronicled his Adirondack Mountains experiences, and he became an instant celebrity—and the public rushed to enjoy the Adirondacks. The book was so successful that Murray not only became the leading expert on all things Adirondack but forever after proudly wore the nickname "Adirondack." He was much sought after as a lecturer and advisor and can be credited with the popularization of the area.

Although Murray was one abuser who got away with it, Hallock continued to point out those people and businesses that threatened nature. Therefore, it was only natural that Grinnell would keep the torch of advocacy aflame on his watch. The people who had influenced him the most in his life—Grandma Audubon and Professor O. C. Marsh, not to mention the ethical example of his father—had served as a mentor to mold him into a virtuous man of strong opinion with a clear vision of right and wrong. Add to that his love for all things in the natural world—both extinct and present—and he had all the makings of an activist for conservation matters.

He was certainly aware of the power that he could now wield to promote his ideas and to call attention to abuses in the natural balance. Unlike some critics who complained and then sat back satisfied that they had done their part, however, Grinnell offered solutions to the issues he presented. He was not about to shirk his moral duties, no matter how ingrained the problem or how powerful the commercial industry that he must battle against. Although the paper thrived financially, there can be no question that *Forest and Stream* lost advertising revenue from offended businesses throughout the tenure of Grinnell as its owner and editor.

One major difference between Grinnell's advocacy and that of Charles Hallock was that his predecessor only occasionally stepped into the national arena, preferring to point out regional and local abuses. Whereas, Grinnell embraced a wider vision for the paper and set out to change issues on a national level.

As a male of the human species, George Grinnell must have known that to meddle with women's fashion could result in a swift and curt reaction for him to butt out and mind his own business. But for some period of time there had been discussions about the fashion trend—or obsession—of women wearing hats made from real bird plumage. And, in his mind, this practice had become a subject that called for action.

Plumage on hats had been a tradition in many societies throughout recorded history. Roman god Mercury wore wings in his helmet; Native Americans decorated headdresses with the finest feathers available, especially eagle plumage; English noblemen preferred peacock and ostrich feathers for ornamentation; officers in the French and English military wore fancy plumed headgear; even Marie Antoinette started a fad when she went out wearing ostrich feathers in her hair. And in the late nineteenth century, bird plumage hats were the sign of a refined lady, and those of every class strived to be recognized as fashionable. Rich or poor, the proper style of hat made the woman.

European and American milliners fueled this fashion necessity of women by offering for sale ordinary hats with songbird feathering. The fanciest plumes were stripped from the backs of the rare birds, and then whole birds, or halved birds, and occasionally a half dozen birds were clumped together to resemble a nest—right on top of a hat. The rarer the bird, the more valuable the feathers, and the more it was coveted by the fashion-conscious wearer.

The well-dressed woman simply could not present herself in public without the proper feathered millinery. Magazines, such as *Harper's Bazar* (later *Harper's Bazaar*), a tabloid-size weekly newspaper catering to middle- and upper-class women, advertised the latest fashions in hats from around the world, and women responded. The current styles from Germany or France quickly became the rage in the United States—and every one of those hats sported feathers or stuffed birds.

It was not unusual to notice on the sidewalks of fashionable New York City, women adorned with hats accessorized with the feathers plucked from woodpeckers, herring gulls, mourning doves, egrets, great blue herons, common terns, robins, or owls. There were feathers and bodies of songbirds, shore birds, and game birds— every species that bird hunters could kill and supply to the milliners.

In fact, by the late 1800s, birds of all species were being killed at an annual rate of an astounding five million—some say the number was up to twenty million—mainly for plumes used to decorate hats. That fashionable application, and the mass killing of birds that were considered to be pests by farmers—which in truth were vital to regulating the pest population—was devastating to the natural balance of nature and threatened to reach into every facet of American life. Birds of every species were a vital part of the eco-system, and they could not reproduce as fast as they were being exterminated.

Strangely enough, people could wear a hat decorated with a dead bird while watching, feeding, and appreciating live birds in their own backyards. It can be argued that the love of nature compelled women to embrace the fashion of bird-feather hats. It would be difficult, however, to understand the appreciation for the heads of dead birds, with blank, staring eyes, to be attached to a hat and proudly worn. True, taxidermy was popular, but a stuffed bird on display in a museum or on a fireplace mantle was not on the same level as walking around with a nest full of poultry on your head.

Although there had been the random article appearing now and then for years pointing out this horrific practice, no one had brought forth any concrete answers to the problem. George Grinnell's first encounters with nature had been with the birds around Audubon Park, and birds had fascinated him his entire life. The Audubon family influence was deeply ingrained within him. He decided that it was time for him to speak up against this mindless slaughter and explain the consequences of the extermination of birds. But, as was his common methodology, he would also propose a logical solution.

Grinnell wrote an editorial in the February 11, 1886 issue of his *Forest and Stream* magazine under the heading "The Audubon Society."

Very slowly the public are awakening to see that the fashion of wearing the feathers and skins of birds is abominable. There is, we think, no doubt, that when the facts about this fashion are known, it will be frowned upon and cease to exist. Legislation of itself can do little against this barbarous practice, but if public sentiment can be aroused against it, it will die a speedy death.

The reform in America, as elsewhere, must be inaugurated by women, and if the subject is properly called to their notice, their tender hearts will be quick to respond. While individual effort may accomplish much, it will work but slowly, and the spread of the movement will be gradual. Something more than this is needed. Men, women and children all over our land should take the matter in hand, and urge its importance upon those with whom they are brought in contact. A general effort of this kind will not fail to awaken public interest, and information given to a right-thinking public will set the ball of reform in motion. Our beautiful birds give to many people a great deal of pleasure and add much to the delights of the country. These birds are slaughtered in vast numbers for gain. If the demand for their skins can be caused to fall off, it will no longer repay the bird butchers to ply their trade and the birds will be saved.

The birds of the fields, the birds of the woods, the birds of the marshes, and those of the sea, all suffer alike. It is needless to repeat the oft-told story of destruction. How can we best go to work to combat this great and growing evil, what means can we best employ to awaken at once popular feeling against it?

We desire to enlist in this work everyone who is interested in our birds, and we urge all such to take hold and assist us.

In the first half of this century there lived a man who did more to teach Americans about birds of their own land than any other who ever lived. His beautiful and spirited paintings and his charming and tender accounts of the habits of his favorites have made him immortal, and have inspired his countrymen with an ardent love for birds. The land which produced the popular naturalist, John James Audubon, will not willingly see the beautiful forms he loved so well exterminated.

We propose the formation of an association for the protection of wild birds and their eggs, which shall be called the Audubon Society. Its membership is to be free to every one who is willing to lend a helping hand in forwarding the objects for which it is formed. These objects shall be to prevent, so far as possible (1), the killing of any bird not used for food; (2), the destruction of nests or eggs of any wild bird, and (3), the wearing of feathers as ornaments or trimming for dress.

To bring this matter properly before the public at large, we shall employ every means in our power to defuse information on the subject over the whole country. Those who are willing to aid us in our labors are urged to establish local societies for work in their own neighborhood. To such branch societies we will send without charge circulars and printed information for distribution among their neighbors. A little effort in this direction will do much good. As soon as the association shall have a membership and shall be in position to organize and shall have attained an existence, we will hand the books and any funds which it may have, over to its members, who will thereafter take charge of it.

Those who desire to join the Audubon Society, established on the basis and for the purpose above set forth, should send their names at once to the Forest and Stream, *40 Park Row, New York.*

There was an immediate, overwhelming response from a public anxious to sign the pledge to save the birds and be a part of this new society. Letters of support poured in from such notables as abolitionist minister Henry Ward Beecher, poet John Greenleaf

Whittier, naturalist John Burroughs, and jurist Oliver Wendell Holmes, each of whom endorsed the proposed organization on the pages of *Forest and Stream*. Writer Charles Dudley Warner was bluntly insulting when he wrote of his support: "A dead bird does not help the appearance of an ugly woman." Even *Harper's Bazar*, which was not involved in environmental reform and was the main source for advertisements of the latest feathered creations, published in its "Personal" section: "A society taking its name after the great naturalist J. J. Audubon has been established for the purpose of fostering an interest in the protection of wild birds from destruction for millinery and other commercial purposes."

Within three months almost forty thousand people had joined the Audubon Society—a number that increased to over fifty thousand by the fall of 1888. The organization soon became too burdensome for the magazine to maintain and was discontinued in 1889. But that was not the end of it by any means.

Just as George Grinnell had suggested in his initial editorial, he expected local neighborhood organizations to be established and to come together in a combined effort—and that was what saved the society and its mission. Various states filled the void by forming Audubon Societies that were eventually incorporated into the "National Association of Audubon Societies for the Protection of Wild Birds and Animals," the organization that exists to this day— with some five-hundred local chapters. Grinnell would serve on its board of directors for twenty-six years.

It can be reasoned that Grinnell named the society as much in the memory of Lucy "Grandma" Audubon as he had for her husband. He had never known John James Audubon, except from his work and from what Lucy might have related, but he believed that she was responsible for her undisciplined husband's success. He wrote:

The great lesson of his [Audubon's] life lies in our recognition that he triumphed in the strength of another, who moulded his character, shaped his aims, gave substance to his dreams, and finally, by exercise of that self-denial which he was incapable of as a long-sustaining effort, won for him the public recognition and reward of his splendid talents.

Birds were his first love, and he had done what he could to motivate people to help protect them—successfully, it might be added. He was encouraged by the support for that cause, and slowly but surely women moved on to wear hats without bird feathers. Untold millions of birds—and entire species—were saved for future generations by one man's vision and willingness to stand up and present a reasonable solution that would stop the wanton slaughter.

Now, George Grinnell turned his attention to another subject dear to his heart—the American West. The issues affecting Yellowstone Park had never been far from his mind. Grinnell lived in an age when no federal laws protected America's national parks, and he was continually nagged by the abuses that he had witnessed years before.

In those early days of Yellowstone National Park, the land and animals had been treated poorly—geysers were rammed and closed up, vandals marred trees, hunters slaughtered animal populations, timber was cut and not replanted, and tourists littered and trashed the most popular spots.

Grinnell had for years engaged in an ongoing battle to preserve the integrity of Yellowstone National Park on the pages of *Forest and Stream*. As early as 1883 he had taken on a powerful New York City firm calling itself the Yellowstone Park Improvement Company, which desired to build hotels and make the park tourist friendly. The Northern Pacific Railroad was finally completed and brought tourists in droves to the edge of the Park, and work had begun by commercial industry to accommodate them.

Grinnell was not so sure that this company's intentions were all that honorable. Under the title "Park Grab," he wrote an editorial in his January 3, 1883, issue of *Forest and Stream* that pointed out that this "improvement company" would actually pay a fee of two dollars an acre, and in turn receive a section of land, 640 acres, around the seven most popular tourist attractions, re-channel some of the hot springs, and have a monopoly with respect to all creature comforts, from transportation to commercial interests. In addition, these alleged land poachers would be able to cut down as much timber as they desired for its own private use. By the time Grinnell wrote his editorial, the company was already in the process of surrounding the Park and had commenced exploiting its resources.

Once again, Grinnell not only called attention to a potential fraud being committed but offered a solution to the problem. He followed that initial editorial with a series of articles, beginning in January 18 under the headline "The People's Park," that attacked this effort to commercialize the Park. He called on Congress to stand up and protect the "interest of the people." He wrote:

> *Every citizen shares with all the others the ownership in the wonders of our National Pleasure ground, and when its natural features are defaced, its forests destroyed, and its game butchered, each one is injured by being robbed of so much that belongs to him.*

He went on to state that "the Park is for rich and poor alike, and every one should have an equal interest in it."

Grinnell and his outraged readers put as much heat as possible on the Department of the Interior to act and deny this commercial company a lease for Park land. Toward the end of January, Secretary of the Interior Henry Teller finally saw the light, and wrote to Senator George Vest of Missouri, who had taken up Grinnell's cause. Teller promised that he would "take no action in the matter of the lease" for the Yellowstone Park Improvement Company, which effectively postponed if not ended that company's attempted land grab. Not only that, but Teller also issued a regulation that closed a loophole that had allowed killing game in the park "for purposes of recreation, or to supply food for visitors or actual residents." The senseless slaughter was now prohibited—any killing would be regarded as illegal poaching.

George Grinnell, as might be expected, was thrilled. His headline, "The Park Saved," in his January 25 issue stated that "This ends the fight." Through his heroic efforts, Grinnell had spearheaded his activist readers to mobilize and facilitate real change. But the fight was far from over. That change would depend upon people obeying the law, which would be a challenge given the tempting resources found in Yellowstone Park. Wherever there was profit to be made, there were those people who would break any law and cross any boundary, especially in a place where enforcement was almost nonexistent. It would not be easy to find a way to patrol Yellowstone's over two million acres and put a halt to the illegal activities.

He believed that there should be effective game wardens to protect habitat and prevent the killing of younger animals and animals out of season, and that licenses should be issued seasonally—and strict laws needed to be passed to bring this about.

Alas, wildlife continued to be killed in great numbers in the park. Deer, elk, and bears were easy targets for commercial hunters, who could receive six dollars for each elk hide. One dead buffalo was worth hundreds of dollars to the poacher. In addition, Yellowstone lakes were under siege from fisherman utilizing everything from nets to dynamite to capture fish and sell them for profit.

The voice of preservation once again prevailed when the Department of the Interior allocated the hiring of ten people at a salary of $900 a year to police the Park. George Grinnell, however, warned that these men must be from the West and not easterners who knew little but what they had heard about the flora and fauna of Yellowstone. Contrary to Grinnell's wishes, the jobs went to political appointees, men who were ignorant about the ways of poachers or the game that they illegally hunted. These tenderfeet were outwardly ridiculed by the locals as well as those who flaunted the laws and continued to wreak havoc on the park's wildlife.

Even Grinnell's ally in Congress, Senator Vest, was unable to push through legislation that would "prevent trespassers or intruders from entering the park for the purpose of destroying the game or objects of curiosity therein." Every bill that he presented was defeated. Grinnell was disappointed by this failure but understood exactly what he was up against—money. "It is very evident, as it has been from the first, the monopolists have a strong lobby," he wrote in the February 22 issue of *Forest and Stream*. Just as the case today and throughout history, those influence peddlers with money to spread around usually prevailed with a Congress more interested in preserving their careers than preserving the people's interests.

Grinnell had his own opinion of lobbying. He wrote to Lute North: "I would rather break bronchos for a living than talk to Congressmen about a bill. It makes me feel like a detested pickpocket to do it." He regarded his necessary lobbying efforts to be "the meanest work I ever did."

The following year, an attempt by President Chester A. Arthur to silence the growing number of voices protesting the destruction of Yellowstone came when he appointed a new superintendent for the park, Robert E. Carpenter. The new man immediately removed the squatters that had overrun portions of the park. Grinnell took notice and wrote an editorial in the March 12, 1885, issue of *Forest and Stream*: "The new superintendent of the Park will have an opportunity during the season that is coming to show what stuff he is made of. If he does his duty he will be applauded, but if he fails it will soon be known."

Carpenter was closely watched, and his actions became anything but effective in preserving the Park. He was eventually removed from office after it was learned that he was conspiring with the persistent Yellowstone Park Improvement Company to commercialize Yellowstone for private use.

In 1882, Civil War hero General Philip Sheridan had led an army expedition that entered and explored the Park. Sheridan had witnessed the mass destruction of wildlife, and called for an expansion of the Park, which would account for the seasonal migrations. Politics once again prevailed—Congress quickly scuttled the idea, claiming that the Park was already too big.

Four years later, Sheridan took matters into his own hands. He dispatched troops to take control of Yellowstone, with intentions of protecting it from poachers and souvenir hunters. But once again, it was impossible to patrol two million acres on horseback, and the destruction by hunters and vandals continued. When violators were caught, there was little the soldiers could do except issue a warning. There were no laws in place to charge anyone with a crime, but at least the presence of the military was some small measure of a deterrent in itself.

Every capture and subsequent release of a poacher in the Park was publicized in the columns of *Forest and Stream* by George Bird Grinnell with stinging editorials. He also dispatched news releases to newspapers throughout the country along with printed circulars, all of which were put into the hands of senators and congressmen. He believed that at some point these lawmakers would follow their consciences and protect the Park. The competition for the hearts and minds of the congressmen, however, was fierce. Grinnell was offering nothing but a chance to do the right thing; other lobbyists, especially those paid by the railroads, were offering cold, hard campaign cash and other material benefits.

While the army attempted to protect the natural resources of the Park, Grinnell and his allies in Congress continued to fight hard to maintain Yellowstone as a National Park and to prohibit railroad, mining, and real estate interests—known collectively as "The Railroad Gang"—from exploiting the resources. Various solutions had been presented by the lawmakers, and, for one reason or another, each failed to produce legislation. One popular idea was to surrender and sacrifice a portion of the Park to railroad interests. It would be prudent to either shrink the park or allow railroad tracks to be laid running through it.

That proposal, termed "segregation," was totally unacceptable to Grinnell. Proponents of the railroad pressed hard for a boundary readjustment that would restore the northern part of the Park to the public domain and allow access to Cooke City without going through the Park. The merchants in that city were poised to profit from such a change and commenced preparing for it. In addition, the Northern Pacific Railway Company had already extended a branch line all the way to the northern entrance of the Park. The various bills proposed to accomplish this dismemberment were collectively known as "segregation bills," and were vigorously opposed by friends of the Park.

Grinnell could sense that support from the Congress was weakening, but he was not about to give up the fight. His columns in *Forest and Stream* denounced those who advocated the reduction of the Park. In a most ambitious and effective series of articles, he commenced a furious lobbying effort against the idea and appealed to his readers by writing that the Park should be preserved for their children and their children's children. He maintained that the proposed boundary change would exclude from the Park its most attractive portions, and destroy the winter range of the elk, antelope, and mountain sheep, which would lead to the destruction of half the game in the area. In addition, he distributed throughout the country a pamphlet outlining his opinions entitled, "A Standing Menace; Cooke City vs. the National Park."

Grinnell—believing that the pen was mightier than the sword—was an excellent lobbyist, although he hated the title and the work itself, but he was able to temporarily delay any legislation that was detrimental to the Park. He was unwavering in his belief that harsh penalties should be put in place for offenses by poachers, including jail time.

At one point, Grinnell managed to obtain from an anonymous source a damning telegraph from railroad lobbyist B. J. Barr to the Speaker of the House that implied a backroom deal for a quick vote approving Park changes was in the works. Grinnell published the contents on the front page of *Forest and Stream*. Having this behind-the-scenes maneuvering exposed, the Speaker and Congress held off on any decisions about the Park for the remainder of the session. With the railroad lobbyists stymied for the present, Grinnell and his fellow advocates of conservation and preservation directed their energies to the long-standing campaign of achieving legal protection for the Park and its resources.

In 1893 Grinnell devised a plan in private that he believed would have the impact necessary to compel Congress to act once and for all—if he only could get his hands on something, anything tangible that would swing the pendulum firmly in his direction. He secretly assigned an undercover correspondent to investigate game poaching and other misuses at Yellowstone National Park—a lawyer and author named Emerson Hough.

Hough, a native Iowan, was better known for his western stories and historical novels but was also a committed conservationist. Hough served in the position of western editor for *Forest and Stream*, editing the "Chicago and the West" column, and counted among his friends Sheriff Pat Garrett, the man who had shot and killed the notorious outlaw William "Billy the Kid" Bonney.

Hough's initial covert project was to tally the buffalo that survived in Yellowstone National Park. Grinnell wanted proof to show that the herd was disappearing—and he found it. Hough and his escort thought that they would find at least five hundred buffalo, but were hard pressed to count even one hundred, which compelled him to report that poachers were running rampant in the park and decimating its wildlife. This investigation resulted in an expose about the slaughtering of animals written by Hough that Grinnell published in *Forest and Stream*.

While writing his editorials and editing Hough's articles, Grinnell must have thought back to that summer day in 1870 when he had accompanied Professor Marsh on the paleontology expedition and they had sat idly aboard the train for three full hours before the last buffalo had crossed the tracks. The sight of all those huge, shaggy creatures parading in front of them en masse would have made an impression to last a lifetime. And to a man with Grinnell's appreciation for wildlife, the thought that such an event would never again happen must have been agonizing. But he chose his words carefully, wisely believing that he could strike more of blow with reason than with rage.

The lack of buffalo in the Park was not only disappointing but disastrous, largely because Grinnell knew that evidence had been found to prove that the buffalo had been victims of poaching and not natural selection. Greedy people with rifles were responsible for the diminishing herd, and these human enemies of nature needed to somehow be brought to justice. And the surviving buffalo must be saved from extinction.

As if fate had stepped into the picture, an unexpected incident occurred while Emerson Hough remained investigating Yellowstone. And it would turn the tide in both the public arena and, more importantly, within the halls of Congress.

The most notorious poacher in the Park was a man from Cooke City named Edgar Howell. He was well-known to everyone in the vicinity, both civilian and military. He was said to be a man of more than ordinary intelligence with a fair education, stoutly built, with dark hair, bluish-gray eyes, and a heavy blond mustache. With a dog that served as a keen lookout and a shelter set up in the woods, Howell was killing buffalo and elk at will and selling their parts. His plans were simple: he would kill as many buffalo as possible, remove the heads and hang them in trees, and return in the spring with packhorses to retrieve the heads and then sell them for as much as $300 apiece. And he always escaped before he could be caught in the act. Edgar Howell was without question number one on the US Army's most-wanted list of poachers.

And, yes, that list of poachers was a long one. Countless numbers of park moose and bison were being killed, not for food but for the profit gained from selling the heads, tongues, hides, and antlers. Local taxidermists regularly mounted bison heads from animals that had been killed illegally and would become prized possessions for display in eastern offices, dens, and taverns. Worse yet, these poachers would often lace the carcasses they left behind with strychnine that would kill wolves, wolverines, and other scavengers that sought to dine on the rotting remains. This act would stop the predators from killing off game that the poachers wanted for themselves.

General Sheridan's troops were frustrated at every turn in their attempt to maintain the Park's integrity. The man presently assigned by the army to head up the cavalry unit charged with stopping poachers in Yellowstone was forty-four-year-old Captain George Anderson. This tough-minded West Point graduate was a veteran of Indian campaigns across the West, mainly against the wily Apache tribe. Anderson had served in a variety of capacities in his career, both stateside and abroad, and was said to be politically connected. Anderson was determined to stop the poaching, and dispatched patrols throughout the frozen wilderness to search for violators.

George Grinnell would eventually publish in *Forest and Stream* an account that outlined the modus operandi employed by the poachers to elude the army—from the most notorious poacher, Edgar Howell. "It is the simplest thing in the world. When the snow begins to fall in September and October, we wait until a nice snowstorm has set in, and then taking a saddle horse and two or more pack horses, we start for the Park and travel fast. After reaching the ground we have previously selected to hunt over, we make a long detour and cross our tracks perhaps ten miles from camp so as to ascertain whether the soldiers are following our trail or not. If no other tracks are seen we go back to camp feeling safe, for we know that the new snow will obliterate all tracks before dawn. We then secure enough elk to load our pack horses and are soon on our way out of the Park and to the railroad. The railroad companies are glad to haul freight and we have no trouble there in getting our spoils to market."

But Captain George Anderson was not without his own tactics in an attempt to outwit his adversaries. He ordered his soldiers to veer off main roads and trails and patrol those less-traveled pathways and look for tracks or other sign, in their quest to thwart poachers.

Civilian scout Felix Burgess, another veteran of the Indian wars against the Apache, had recently replaced Edward Wilson, Captain Anderson's most trusted scout. Wilson had allegedly committed suicide while on patrol in the Park. The new scout, Burgess, walked with a limp due to an incident during his time in the Southwest when he had been captured and tortured. Native Americans had taken pleasure in slicing off two of his toes and damaging his great toe so badly that it would turn black and become painful in the cold weather. Nevertheless, Burgess was an excellent tracker and did not allow his disability to interfere with his work out on the trail.

Burgess and a detachment of soldiers were on a winter patrol in Yellowstone's backcountry when they came upon a faint sign of runners forming a sledge trail that appeared to run from Cooke City to Astringent Creek in Pelican Valley. This was an area that Captain Anderson had targeted as a likely place for poachers. Earlier, a patrol led by Anderson had located what he called "old signs of bisons" in the area. Several excursions into this area found nothing more than one faint snowshoe track, but it was evidence that someone had passed through there and would require further investigation.

On March 12, 1894, scout Felix Burgess and a Sergeant Troike headed out into a severe storm with the mission of exploring the area where the snowshoe tracks had been observed. The terrain in this Yellowstone backcountry was not conducive to easy travel, to say the least, even on skis or snowshoes. This was a place where the high temperature might reach twenty below zero and over five feet of snow could fall in one month alone. The two men would have likely taken turns breaking trail and finding a way to wind through the various natural obstacles as they pressed onward. They camped that first night, and the following morning started out early. Before long, not far from camp, they were startled by a most macabre sight.

Captain Anderson later wrote in his report:

On the 12th inst. in a terrific storm, Burgess and the Sergt. started across to the Pelican country and camped. Next A.M. he found, near his camp, a cache of 6 buffalo scalps and skulls, 3 good skins and 3 more that the hair had been partially taken off. The trail was there—but dim—of the poacher and it was soon lost. However Burgess kept on and about noon of that day he ran into a fresh trail which he followed to a lodge, erected near the mouth of Astringent Creek. While there he heard several shots & soon saw the culprit down in the middle of the Pelican Valley. Here he performed an act of bravery that deserves especial mention and recognition. The poacher [Edgar Howell] was undoubtedly armed with a repeating rifle; it was equally certain that he was a desperate character & would resist arrest even to the point of taking life. The only arms Burgess and the Sergt. carried was a single Army revolver. Notwithstanding the serious risk, they boldly started forward over the 400 yards of open valley. The poacher was so occupied in skinning his buffalo that he did not see Burgess until he was within 15 or 20 feet of him. He then started for his rifle, but on order from Burgess stopped and surrendered. Near him were the bodies of 5 buffalo, freshly killed.

The shocked and angry poacher "stood stupid like," according to Burgess, and assured his captors that they would not have taken him if he had seen them coming or his dog had warned him. He punctuated his sincerity by trying to kill his derelict dog—until Burgess stopped him.

The bravery and determination displayed by Felix Burgess in traversing those four hundred yards all by himself to surprise the poacher cannot be overstated. Howell's rifle, according to the scout "was leaning against a dead buffalo, about fifteen feet away from him." That powerful rifle could bring down at buffalo at two hundred yards. Burgess carried only a .38-caliber army revolver, which had an effective range of perhaps fifteen to twenty yards at the most. In addition, Howell's dog, a sharp-nosed shepherd, was lying nearby. But, to the luck of Burgess, the strong wind was blowing into his own face and not toward the dog.

Burgess glided those four hundred yards undetected toward Howell on his silent snowshoes but was suddenly confronted by an obstacle. "Right square across the way I found a ditch about ten feet wide, and you know how hard it is to make a jump with snowshoes." Somehow, he made it up the slope and across. "I ran up to within fifteen feet of Howell, between him and his gun, before I called to him to throw up his hands, and that was the first he knew of anyone but him being anywhere in that country." Howell was immediately placed under arrest.

Felix Burgess, with his prisoner in tow, arrived back at the camp in bad shape. He had been limping severely; his great toe had swollen to four times its normal size. Burgess was taken to the post surgeon who immediately amputated that toe, which saved the scout from dying from gangrene.

Two things set the arrest of Edgar Howell apart from the previous arrests of poachers in the Park. First of all, this was the first time a poacher had been caught in the act of killing and skinning game and his guilt undeniably established by the presence of still warm bodies. Secondly, this arrest was about to become national news with an urgent call for action to prevent future butchery.

With poacher Edgar Howell in custody on the return trip to the guardhouse at Fort Yellowstone, the patrol happened upon Emerson Hough, the field correspondent for *Forest and Stream* magazine. Hough, who was still exploring Yellowstone as part of the magazine-sponsored "Yellowstone National Park Game Expedition," was incensed by the story of Howell's devious bison killing.

Hough wrote a dispatch about Howell's poaching for the soldiers to telegraph to George Grinnell in New York City when they got back to Fort Yellowstone. Hough wrote: "Scout Burgess captured Howell, the notorious Cooke City poacher with ten fresh buffalo skins, on Astringent Creek near Pelican." Grinnell published the wire from Hough in the March 24 edition of *Forest and Stream*, along with a scathing editorial he penned under the headline "A Premium in Crime." Grinnell again challenged Congress to act on this issue of poaching, calling Howell's capture "unquestionably the most important that has ever been made in the national park."

Grinnell implored his readers to write to their representatives and complain that laws were needed to punish poachers in the Park. He advised his readers that the last remnants of the once numerous bison would surely be slaughtered if action was not taken immediately. Under the existing laws, the only punishment that fort commander Captain George Anderson could administer to Edgar Howell—or any other poacher for that matter—was confiscation of the bison and his equipment, and expulsion from the Park.

Not only did Grinnell's readers respond to his plea for help, but the national press picked up the story and spread it far and wide. Congress was inundated with letters from an indignant public that learned for the first time that no law existed to punish poachers. Grinnell had also circulated petitions across the country, with the result being that "thousands upon thousands of these, fully signed, came into Congress from all quarters."

The morning after the capture of Edgar Howell, correspondent Emerson Hough, and E. Jay Haines, a noted photographer, accompanied the soldiers on a trip back to the Pelican Creek site of Howell's bloody killing grounds. The soldiers would collect evidence; Haines would take photographs that would stun and outrage the world with their scenes of brutality. One particularly grisly photo showed a group of soldiers kneeling behind the severed heads of six buffalo.

Meanwhile, poacher Edgar Howell had been confined to the guardhouse at Fort Yellowstone where he taunted and ridiculed his guards. He bragged about how much money he had made in a season selling buffalo heads, which was at least ten times more than the annual salary of an army private. He also ate more than his share, consuming at one breakfast twenty-four pancakes. Apparently, Howell was in high spirits, which soared even higher when his cause was taken up by the Secretary of the Interior. Little did Howell know, however, but this government official, an enemy of the railroad lobby who favored protecting the Park, ordered that Howell be released to heighten the political drama of the incident. The poacher was escorted to the Park boundary, expelled, and told never to return. Grinnell made certain in *Forest and Stream* that the public would be outraged by the setting free of this man who had participated in such despicable acts.

While Emerson Hough was visiting Pelican Creek, George Bird Grinnell boarded a train headed for Washington. He would strike while the iron was hot. He was aware of the impact that the capture of Howell and the damning photographs had on the public conscience and hoped to convert that anger into a political advantage. His first stop was to visit Senator George Vest, his trusted ally, but was pleased when another congressman came forward to voice his concern and promise action.

Congressman John F. Lacy of Iowa, the chairman of the House Committee on Public Lands, was personally familiar with Yellowstone's lawlessness. Back in 1888, Lacy had been visiting Yellowstone when armed robbers had held up the stagecoach in which he was riding and stole some money from him. The thieves had been caught, but to Lacy's dismay they had received a light sentence due to issues regarding the legal status of the Park. Now, six years later, he had the power with which to change that legal status.

Just two weeks after Edgar Howell's capture, John Lacey introduced to Congress the Yellowstone Park Protection Bill: "An Act to protect the birds and animals in Yellowstone National Park, and to punish crimes in said park, and for other purposes." The bill affirmed that Yellowstone National Park was under the "sole and exclusive jurisdiction" of the United States and placed it in the Judicial District of Wyoming. The Secretary of the Interior was directed to protect,

...all timber, mineral deposits, natural curiosities, or wonderful objects within said park and to protect the birds and animals of the park from harassment and destruction.

Any person found guilty of violating any of the provisions of this Act or any rule or regulation that may be promulgated by the Secretary of the Interior with reference to the management and care of the Park, or for the protection of the property therein, for the preservation from injury or spoliation of timber, mineral deposits, natural curiosities or wonderful objects within said park, shall be deemed guilty of a misdemeanor, and shall be subjected to a fine of not more than one thousand dollars or imprisonment not exceeding two years, or both, and be adjudged to pay all costs of the proceedings.

The bill mandated that a magistrate be appointed to hear complaints for violation of the Act, to issue warrants, and to determine whether people charged with felonies should be held for trial in District Court. The Secretary of the Interior would build a jail and an office for the magistrate. The penalty for violating the Act included forfeiture of all equipment, including firearms and means of transportation, used during the crime.

The Yellowstone Park Protection Act of 1894—a keystone of park legislation— was signed into law on May 7 by President Grover Cleveland. The act established penalties and law-enforcement authority to protect animals and other natural resources— measures that had not been, but should have been, provided by the legislation creating the Park. The act also called for strict punishment for those who were caught defacing geysers or rock formations, extracting minerals, and harvesting timber.

This must have been a red-letter day, a day of both celebration and relief, for Grinnell, as well as Congressman George Vest and their allies. They had hit stumbling block after stumbling block but had never wavered, had never given up on their quest to protect the resources of Yellowstone for future generations. It had taken years, but now the precedence had been set for every future park. All the wildlife and birds in every national park would have a chance to flourish in their natural settings without danger from men with rifles, traps, or axes—or from railroad tracks.

This incredible effort by Grinnell and his allies cannot be understated. Although Texas rancher Charlie Goodnight would capture a small herd of buffalo and raise them much like cattle, the herd in Yellowstone was the only wild buffalo that remained alive in the West. These wild buffalo had been saved at the last moment from extinction by the power of public pressure on Congress, a tactic that should be employed any time a species faces a catastrophe. Grinnell, who had witnessed buffalo when the great herds covered the Plains, could finally rest assured that the survival of this majestic beast was now a probability.

In a sobering thought, however, it can only be speculated about how many animals could have been saved had this momentous act been passed years earlier when Grinnell and others first pointed out their concerns and pressed for legislation. The toll had been devastating, especially for buffalo, but at least those animals that survived could now multiply and replenish their numbers. Much of this blame for the wanton destruction can be placed squarely on the shoulders of the railroad lobby, which now had lost in their disregard for anything except profits and would be compelled to find other sources of fresh revenue. Hunters would no longer be traveling by rail to Yellowstone.

This new law was a major turning point in policing Yellowstone by military authorities. Poaching was not completely stopped with the passage of the Act, but it was substantially reduced. Vigilance by the army was still maintained, and patrols continued to search the back country and places where animals were known to winter. Once in a while, a hunter or trapper was apprehended, and those headlines served as a warning for others to avoid illegal activities in the Park.

Ironically, the first man to be arrested and tried under the new law was Edgar Howell. The poacher had been told to never return to Yellowstone. But Howell did return to the Park the following summer. He was arrested and charged with violating the order of expulsion. Howell was found guilty, fined fifty dollars—a hefty sum in those days—and sentenced to thirty days in jail under the provisions of the Lacey Act.

Howell appealed his conviction to the United States District Court and was subsequently released from jail. It was determined that he could not be prosecuted criminally for returning to the Park after having been banished because such an act did not "constitute a criminal offense under any statute of the United States." And Howell could not be tried for killing buffalo because "there was no statute in force at that time."

Oddly enough, in 1887 Edgar Howell was employed by the Acting Superintendent of Yellowstone as a scout with the duty of apprehending poachers—a case of "using a thief to catch a thief."

However, Howell had served his purpose as a rallying point for George Grinnell and his allies to exploit for the good of conservation. Grinnell with his constant editorials in *Forest and Stream* had once again proven that if the collective voice of the people shouted loud enough it would eventually be heard. His concerns had made national news and thereby educated the public about the abuses. He was correct in his assumption that the masses would respond if only they were made aware of a grievous situation. Publicity was the key to action by stirring the hearts of a sensible populace, a majority of whom would always choose preservation over corporate profit.

George Bird Grinnell was not by any means alone in waging his holy war against the railway and the poachers. In his battle to protect Yellowstone, he had enlisted the help of many notable people, including a rising political star who had drafted petitions and testified before committees to influence key legislators to pass the act. This man would eventually ascend to the highest office in the land, and with advice from mentors like his friend George Grinnell would forge a legacy as the conservation president—his name was Theodore Roosevelt.

CHAPTER EIGHT:
A PRESIDENTIAL FRIENDSHIP

Wildland will remain wild only as a result of deliberate human choice.
—RODERICK F. NASH

THE INITIAL MEETING BETWEEN GEORGE BIRD GRINNELL and Theodore Roosevelt in 1885 commenced in contentious fashion, to say the least. Grinnell, in his role as editor of *Forest and Stream*, had written a review of Roosevelt's just published first book, *Hunting Trips of a Ranchman* in the July 2 edition of the magazine. The twenty-six-year-old Roosevelt had written the book at his Dakota ranch where he had taken refuge after his wife and mother had died on the same day. Writing this manuscript could be viewed as part of his healing process and a labor of love for the heartbroken man. And, as any author will attest, that first published book is a special occasion, and any criticism is painful. Other reviewers without exception had raved about the book, but Grinnell was less than excited about it and explained why to his readers.

Grinnell first praised Roosevelt for his "freshness, spontaneity, and enthusiasm," but the review pointed out that the author had generalized too often about certain species when he should have taken more time studying and analyzing before making observations that were incorrect. He added: "Mr. Roosevelt is not well known as a sportsman, and his experience of the western Country is quite limited, but this very fact in one way lends an added charm to the book. He has not become accustomed to all the various sights and sounds of the plains and the mountains, and for him all the difference which exits between the East and the West is sharply defined. We are sorry to see that a number of hunting myths are given as fact, but it was after all scarcely to be expected that with the author's limited experience he could sift the wheat from the shaft and distinguish the true from the false."

Roosevelt, who prided himself on his scientific research when describing the habits and habitat of wildlife, took umbrage with Grinnell's review that had basically called the author a tenderfoot or a greenhorn. Just one year earlier, Grinnell had paid tribute to Roosevelt's activism in the New York State Assembly when he had worked to stop dams on streams that fed the Hudson River. Grinnell wrote: "It is satisfying to see, now and then, in our legislative halls, a man whom neither money, nor influences, nor politics can induce to turn from what he believes to be right to what he knows to be wrong."

Theodore Roosevelt was incensed that Grinnell had turned on him with that damning review of his first book. He arrived outraged and unannounced at the Broadway offices of *Forest and Stream* magazine and insisted that the editor who had insulted him with the bad review meet him face to face. George Grinnell, always the gracious host, welcomed Roosevelt into his office.

Roosevelt was furious and demanded to know what Grinnell knew about western hunting. The soft-spoken Grinnell, nine years older than Roosevelt, proceeded to calmly tell his guest about his countless hunting and exploring trips to the West, not to mention the fact that he was a professional naturalist with a PhD from Yale. Roosevelt was most impressed when he learned that Grinnell had lived with various Native American tribes for months at a time and had studied—and participated in—their Native hunting tactics.

The two men then discussed *Hunting Trips of a Ranchman* point by point and practically page by page. Grinnell observed that they "talked freely about the book, and took up at length some of its statements." Roosevelt almost immediately was aware that this learned, well-traveled man was obviously far more knowledgeable than he was on the subject of western wildlife and hunting. He had no other option but to swallow his pride and agree with Grinnell on every point. As the hours they spent together that day passed, the animosity seeped from Roosevelt like air from a leaking balloon. His outrage turned to a glowing respect for George Bird Grinnell.

The conversation eventually turned to abuses that were affecting the West that were dear to Grinnell's heart. "I told him something about game destruction in Montana for the hides, which, so far as small game was concerned, had begun in the West only a few years before that, although the slaughter of the buffalo for their skins had been going on much longer and by this time the last of the big herds had disappeared." Roosevelt agreed that something must be done to preserve and protect that wildlife.

The subject would be discussed at some length during future conversations in an attempt to seek a solution to this wanton abuse. Grinnell would write: "No doubt it [the discussions] had some influence to making him the ardent game protector that he later became, just as my own experiences had started me along the same road."

This initial encounter established a warm friendship between the two men based on a mutual interest in hunting, natural history, and conservation. Roosevelt conceded that Grinnell, by virtue of his position as editor of a sportsman's magazine and his firsthand experiences, was always well ahead of him in conservation matters. He accepted the older man as his mentor, and frequently called on Grinnell with questions or just to chat.

Grinnell would write about their budding relationship: "Though chiefly interested in big game and its hunting, and telling interestingly of events that had occurred on his own hunting trips, Roosevelt enjoyed hearing of the birds, the small mammals, the Indians, and the incidents of travel of early expeditions on which I had gone. He was always fond of natural history, having begun, as so many boys have done, with birds; but as he saw more and more outdoor life his interest in the subject broadened and later it became a passion with him."

George Grinnell became a sage-like advisor to Roosevelt, never telling him what to do but casually and intentionally putting ideas into his friend's head. He understood how desperately Roosevelt wanted to be known as a competent naturalist, in addition to his hunting skills, and stoked the fires within the younger man with stories that the awestruck Roosevelt would take to heart about the vanishing west, its wildlife, and its Native peoples.

Grinnell and Roosevelt were both raised in wealthy, socially well-connected families, but that was where their boyhood similarities ended. Whereas Grinnell was an active youngster, traipsing through the woods and exploring nature around Audubon Park, Roosevelt was a frail, sickly child who suffered from asthma and weak eyesight and was relegated for the most part to the indoors.

Theodore Roosevelt (he disliked the nickname "Teddy" bestowed upon him by the country after he became president) was born on October 27, 1858, on East Twentieth Street in New York City, the second of four children born to Theodore Roosevelt, Sr. and the former Martha Bullock. His father was a wealthy businessman and philanthropist, and his mother had come from a slave-owning plantation family in Georgia.

Young Theodore's health was cause for great concern in those days because asthma was a mysterious condition without a known cure. The boy suffered from constant headaches, coughs, fevers, and stomach problems—not terribly unlike his mother who was also frail and complained of chronic fatigue. Martha was obsessive in her hygiene and made certain the house was kept spotless, but she was said to have been a cold and distant mother to her children.

The family was so concerned about Theodore's health that he was educated by tutors and only briefly attended school. He remained inside the house during the day, and, despite his weak eyesight, could usually be found in his father's library where he devoured books on every subject imaginable. He displayed a wide-ranging intellectual curiosity, but his favorite books were *Missionary Travels and Researches in South Africa* by David Livingstone (yes, that Dr. Livingstone, I presume), and the author that George Bird Grinnell had also favored as a youngster, Captain Mayne Reid. Roosevelt was captivated by Reid's books about hunting and animals, and especially by the scientific and travel aspects of the novels.

Like Grinnell, Roosevelt envisioned himself as a hunter-naturalist, following the lead of those fictional boys in Captain Reid's books. No doubt Roosevelt patterned himself after those characters and imagined himself out exploring the wilds of the world while confined to the house. And perhaps that ambition to act out those roles in real life was part of the motivation for him to adopt what he called a "strenuous life" to overcome his childhood maladies through exercise. He was constantly working to strengthen his body with the goal in mind of becoming healthy and as active as any boy his age.

In the meantime, he studied natural history, and began collecting specimens of birds and animals. At the age of nine, he wrote an essay titled "The Natural History of Insects." Following instructions in Captain Reid's novels, he learned how to preserve skins and bones by practicing taxidermy. After seeing a dead seal at a local market and obtaining the head, he became a voracious collector. He even recruited his brothers, sisters, and cousins to keep on the lookout for skulls and other such treasures found around the neighborhood.

In fact, Theodore was so serious about preserving nature that he founded what he called "The Roosevelt Museum of Natural History." This museum, which was located in his bedroom, soon grew to contain hundreds of dead rodents and birds. The museum ran into problems, however, when the housekeepers protested its filthy existence—the smell alone had to be disgusting. Theodore feared that his father would demand that he dispose of his innate menagerie but was relieved when he was told that he could keep his collection as long as he moved it to a back hallway. He would say about his father, "My father, Theodore Roosevelt, was the best man I ever knew. He combined strength with courage and gentleness, tenderness, and great unselfishness. He would not tolerate in us children selfishness or cruelty, or idleness, cowardice, or untruthfulness."

Over time, he was able to condition his body to not only tolerate his asthma, but he became healthy enough to maintain a serious regimen of exercise, which paid off in allowing him to pursue his outdoor interests. No longer would he be home schooled—in September 1876, he went off to Harvard, with this advice from his father: "Take care of your morals first, your health next, and finally your studies."

Roosevelt took his father's advice to heart. He worked out

regularly at school, growing to his full-grown height of 5'9" and weighing between 123 and 135 pounds. He neither drank nor smoked, and he taught Sunday school at the Cambridge Episcopal Church. He was a member of the Porcellian Club, the most exclusive social club at the school, as well as Alpha Delta Phi, Hasty Pudding, and the National History Society. Theodore excelled in German, rhetoric, and, of course, natural history. He had continued his treks into the woods to learn as much as he could on his own about everything associated with nature. Roosevelt graduated from Harvard magna cum laude in 1880, and briefly attended Columbia law school but dropped out to seek a career in politics.

That same year, on his birthday, he married Alice Hathaway Lee. He had been visiting a friend's home in Chestnut Hill, Massachusetts, two years earlier when first he saw her—a tall, 5'7" fair-skinned young lady with her honey-colored hair fashioned in curls. Roosevelt claimed that "he loved her as soon as he saw her sweet, young face."

Roosevelt had planned to become a naturalist after graduating but claimed that his studies at Harvard had discouraged him from that notion. He wrote that the school "treated biology as purely a science of the laboratory." Apparently, Harvard ignored the idea of an outdoor naturalist in favor of a scientist spending his days peering through a microscope. Roosevelt believed that a true naturalist needed to get mud on his boots and dirt on his hands.

Roosevelt turned to politics and was elected to the New York State Assembly in 1881 at age twenty-three. He quickly became known as an enemy of corrupt politicians and businessmen who had an attitude of entitlement and money to spread around under the table. He stood in the way of the wealthy financier Jay Gould who made an underhanded attempt at lowering his taxes and exposed the corruption that was rampant in the state capital. He was reelected three more times, and in his final term wrote more bills than any other legislator.

The year 1884 was a time of tragedy for Theodore Roosevelt. The couple welcomed a daughter, Alice Lee, on February 12th, but Theodore's wife died two days later from what was then known as Bright's disease, or kidney failure. Roosevelt wrote in his diary:

"The light has gone out of my life." Not only was his wife's death a blow to him, but eleven hours earlier—in the same house where his wife had given birth—his mother had died of typhoid fever.

Roosevelt would ask his sister to care for the baby while he mourned by pouring himself into his political work. He would assume custody of the child when she was three years old. Meanwhile, he resumed his attacks on state corruption, which gained him the admiration of the public. His efforts as a delegate to the 1884 Presidential Convention in Chicago, however, was not as successful, although he did accept an invitation to speak to an audience of ten thousand, the largest crowd he had ever addressed. But his candidates were all voted down, and he decided to retire from politics for the time being and retreat to his ranch in the Dakotas. He had been traveling West since the previous year and was quickly falling in love with this land teeming with wilderness, wildlife, and hardy people.

It was at the badlands ranch that he had named Elkhorn located near Medora, North Dakota, that he tried to come to terms with the events of the past year. He found solace in writing, and hunting, and raising cattle, and practicing all the riding and roping skills of a cowboy out there near the Little Missouri River. He was a passable cowhand, according to observers, but not up to par with the real cowboys who rode for him or the neighboring ranches. He became known as a man of action, once leading a posse to chase armed thieves who had stolen his rowboat. Roosevelt favored wearing outfits made of buckskin to emulate those trailblazing frontiersmen of yesteryear that he so admired. It was at his ranch, while he healed as best he could from the loss of his wife and mother, that he wrote his first book, *Hunting Trips of a Ranchman*, based on his hunts and adventures around that area.

And that book led to a chance meeting with George Bird Grinnell that would evolve into a warm and fruitful relationship for many years to come.

Roosevelt returned to New York City after the harsh winter of 1886–87 had wiped out his cattle herd. On December 2, 1886, he married Edith Kermit Carow, although his sisters had been opposed to him marrying so soon after the death of his first wife.

Consequently, Theodore and Edith, whom he had known since childhood, were married in London, England. The couple would have five children—Theodore III (1887); Kermit (1889); Ethel (1891); Archibald (1894); and Quintin (1897). Roosevelt's first daughter, Alice, was also part of the household but was said to have not gotten along with her stepmother.

The family settled in at their home, Sagamore Hill, in Oyster Bay on Long Island, New York, and Roosevelt resumed his literary career. Just as Grinnell had done, he thrilled readers with his tales of the rugged western life. His stories, first published in *Century* magazine, were compiled into a book, *Ranch Life and the Hunting Trail*.

Grinnell and Roosevelt would engage in long talks at the *Forest and Stream* offices or socialize now and then, sharing their stories of hunts and treks into the wilderness, and discuss and analyze the nature of things. The subject, however, would usually turn to a sad reality—game was being wantonly slaughtered all over the country, but mainly in the West where there were few laws against it and no one to enforce them if there were. Grinnell was becoming obsessed and haunted by the bleaching buffalo bones and the carcasses that lay rotting on the Great Plains—all that remained of the millions of animals that needlessly perished. There had to be an answer, and soon, before more species were exterminated in the same manner.

Grinnell, who had witnessed the cruel slaughter of so many western animals—the buffalo in particular—convinced Roosevelt of the need for strong measures to protect all game species from further destruction and eventual extinction. And when Grinnell featured the killing of over three thousand buffalo in Yellowstone in his September 1886 issue of *Forest and Stream*, Roosevelt was moved into action.

Theodore Roosevelt eventually came up with a master plan, and asked Grinnell to be part of it as co-founder of an exclusive sportsman's club. Grinnell had been successful in creating the Audubon Society, which was one reason Roosevelt had recruited him, and now it was time for another crusade to rally people around an idea that could change hunting forever. They would create a new organization comprised of serious hunters with the mission to do everything possible to bring about sensible hunting laws and to protect wildlife habitat across the country.

Why would membership be limited to just hunters *and* not hunters and non-hunter nature and animal lovers? Grinnell had always professed that hunters made the best naturalists, and that they would be vital in any effort to preserve wildlife. Hunters had a stake in making sure that game would be there not just for future hunts but for future generations. With the extermination of millions upon millions of buffalo fresh in their minds, there was no telling what species might capture the fancy of the commercial killers next. Habitats must be preserved so that the indigenous wildlife could thrive, and they must be protected from over-hunting and possible extermination.

Grinnell held to the opinion that the United States was one of the only countries in the world where anyone who owned a gun could go out and hunt and keep whatever he or she shot. In most places only the wealthiest of society were able to hunt. The practice in this country was democratically sound, but it posed a danger. The lack of accepted ethics or laws to control hunters, who believed they could kill as many animals as they pleased, would eventually lead to the extinction of many species. These sportsmen must be educated to understand that over-hunting—as well as damaging the habitat—would eventually lead to no hunting at all when the game disappeared. Grinnell had been promoting this idea on the pages of *Forest and Stream* for years.

Not surprisingly, Roosevelt enthusiastically adopted Grinnell's philosophy as the primary mission of the club. Not killing as much game as they liked would be a new and disagreeable experience for the average hunter, but laws against reckless slaughter must be implemented if wildlife preservation was to work.

Perhaps the initial epiphany to organize a formal club came during a discussion when the two men shared their childhood fascination with the stories written by Captain Mayne Reid. They would endeavor to fashion this organization after a grown-up version of Reid's "hunter-naturalist" philosophy for boys that would have made the late captain proud.

Grinnell, who preferred to remain behind the scenes, let Roosevelt take the lead in forming this elite hunting club. Roosevelt named the club after his two favorite trailblazers—Daniel Boone and David Crockett—and the "Boone and Crockett Club" came into being. He believed that these two frontiersmen were the epitome of hunter-naturalists with strong ethics and proper hunting protocol, and they were certainly household names as American icons. They would be ideal role models to represent this new organization.

In December 1887 Roosevelt invited a number of prominent men who happened to be avid hunters to a dinner party at his Manhattan home. He outlined his plans for this new club and selected twelve men to be founders. This list of founders was a virtual "Who's Who" of New York elite, including his brother, Elliott, and cousin J. West Roosevelt, who had been collectors for Theodore's childhood nature museum; J. Coleman Drayton, the brother-in-law of John Jacob Astor; investor and yachtsman E. P. Rogers; Thomas Paton, a wealthy socialite; real estate investor Rutherford Stuyvesant; and the rear admiral of the New York Yacht Club, Archibald Rogers— and, of course, George Bird Grinnell.

The twelve chosen men met next at Pinnards Restaurant in Manhattan in early January 1888 for the first official meeting of the Boone and Crockett Club. At this time, ideas were exchanged, enthusiasm increased, and bylaws were introduced. The men agreed that they were all committed to balancing human needs with wildlife needs, as well as conserving wildlands and wildlife and the proper management of natural resources. They would have a permanent membership of one hundred, with up to fifty associate members. The associate ranks were filled by industrialists, businessmen, investors, and politicians, painters, novelists, and counted among its members army generals Philip H. Sheridan and William T. Sherman; artist Albert Bierstadt; the author of the classic western novel *The Virginian*, Owen Wister; and Senators George Vest and Henry Cabot Lodge.

This elite hunting club now included among its members many of the patrician sportsmen in New York and Washington, which gave it an element of clout right from the start. The organization's constitution, authored by Roosevelt but with unmistakable Grinnell-like themes, reads in part:

The Boone and Crockett Club is an association of men living for the most part in New York, but also in other parts of the country, who are interested in big-game hunting, in big-game and forestry preservation, and generally in manly out-door sports, and in travel and exploration in little-known regions. The objects of the club, as set forth in its constitution, are:

1. To promote manly sport with the rifle.
2. To promote travel and exploration in the wild and unknown or but partially known portions of the country.
3. To work for the preservation of the large game of this country, and, as far as possible, to further legislation for that purpose, and to assist in enforcing the existing laws.
4. To promote inquiry into and to record observations on the habits and natural history of the various wild animals.
5. To bring about among the members the interchange of opinions and ideas on hunting, travel, and exploration, on the various kinds of hunting rifles, on the haunts of game, animals, etc.

The constitution went on to state the eligibility for membership was reserved for only those who have hunted game with a rifle, listed the species of North American game that qualify a hunter, and outlined the hunting techniques that disqualify an individual for club membership, meaning those that are not a "fair chase"— there were restrictions against hunting deer with lights, dogs, or driving them into the water and clubbing them to death.

A prospective member must have shot at least three species of North American big-game with a rifle, he must promise to never lie about a kill, and he must be that "hunter-naturalist" type of person who believed in protection and preservation of wildlife. The oath taken by these men bonded them together in a brotherhood with frontier values that would last a lifetime. They all understood that animals were in danger of being over-hunted and in some cases, such as the buffalo, exterminated. They were determined to preserve their hunting heritage by preserving the creatures they hunted. It was a cause worth undertaking, and each man vowed to do whatever he could to make a difference.

This historic meeting was the beginning of what would become the most active conservation organization of its day. George Grinnell set to work promoting the Boone and Crockett Club in

Forest and Stream, calling his magazine "the natural mouthpiece of the organization," and writing: "It would seem that an organization of this description, composed of men of intelligence and education, might wield great influence for good in matters relating to game protection." Theodore Roosevelt reached out to other publications to add his touch to the publicity.

In addition to sponsoring numerous research programs and countless symposia, the club supported the growth of America's conservation system. The club extended its reach beyond hunting, and lobbied Congress for the protection of the sequoias and Yosemite, successfully arguing that there was a legal precedent set by early American village common land management.

Politics were in Roosevelt's blood, however, and in 1889 he was appointed to the US Civil Service Commission by President Benjamin Harrison. He fought to replace the current patronage system with awarding government positions based on merit, and clashed with a number of Harrison's appointees, especially with Postmaster John Wanamaker.

In 1891, Roosevelt and Grinnell, representing the board of the Boone and Crockett Club, met with Secretary of the Interior John Noble. Grinnell spoke about the threat of deforestation now taking place, and out-of-control wildfires due to improper forest management, and how loggers cut trees with no thought of replanting. This meeting led to Congress passing and President William Henry Harrison signing the Forest Reserve Act of 1891, which gave the president the power to create forest preserves and protect the trees from logging. Under that law, Yellowstone National Park became the country's first Timberland Reserve.

After the Act was passed and signed, Grinnell and Roosevelt co-wrote an essay titled "Our Forest Reservations," which essentially called for all settlement and commercial development in the fragile protected environs of the West to be prohibited, mainly because of the problem of enforcement of the new law. They lamented the lack of game wardens to protect against corporate greed. "We now have forest reservations, refuges where the timber and its wild denizens should be safe from destruction…The mere formal declaration that they have been set aside will contribute but little toward their safety...The forest reservations are absolutely unprotected. Although set aside by presidential proclamation, they are without government and without guards. Timber thieves may strip the mountain-sides of the growing trees, and poachers may still kill game without fear of punishment."

Grinnell and Roosevelt wanted the protected land to be regarded as government property, with strict law enforcement and violators fined or even imprisoned. It would be some time before that would come to pass.

This pioneering work on behalf of game protection laws, however, was a giant leap in the right direction. The establishment of western reserves, and the expansion of the national park system made conservation history—well before Theodore Roosevelt was elected president. The National Forest, the National Park, and the National Wildlife refuge systems exist today in a large part because of the extensive efforts of this influential club.

The essential character of the Boone and Crockett Club has changed little from those early days, when Grinnell wrote: "It has not been the club's practice to announce its purposes, nor to glory in what it has accomplished, but rather to move steadfastly forward, striving constantly to do whatever fell within its province which would tend to promote the country's welfare." He would trumpet the success of the club, writing: "Those who used to boast of their slaughter are now ashamed of it, and it is becoming recognized fact that a man who wastefully destroys big game, whether for the market, or only for heads, has nothing of the true sportsman about him."

Meanwhile, there were countless conservation causes that needed attention, and Grinnell was a tireless activist. Among other pressing issues championed on the pages of *Forest and Stream* was the protection of the Adirondack Mountains, which was on the brink of wide-spread deforestation. Finally, in 1892, the same year that John Muir co-founded the Sierra Club, the state of New York recognized its value as wilderness and designated six million acres, equal to the size of Vermont, to be set aside to preserve the area's pristine waterways, lakes, mountains, and forests. Two years later, the Adirondacks became a forest preserve and was constitutionally protected as "forever wild." Although more than half of the park was privately owned land, conservation and civilization were partners in preserving the 3,000 lakes and ponds, 30,000 miles of rivers and streams, and all the other the natural wonders that keep this state park wild and primitive.

Theodore Roosevelt and his family were frequent visitors to the Adirondack Mountains, and as a youngster he even wrote self-published books about the area. His first work was "Journal of a Trip to the Adirondacks," written from field notebooks that he had kept at the ages of fifteen and sixteen. The manuscript included entries about the wildlife he had seen during his first trip to the Park at age twelve.

In 1877, at age nineteen, he paid to have a pamphlet published titled, "The Summer Birds of the Adirondacks," co-written with his friend and fellow explorer, Hal Minot. Only several hundred copies of the ornithological work were printed, but one of them happened to make its way into the hands of Clinton Hart Merriam, the prominent naturalist who was at the time the head of the US Biological Survey, associated with the Smithsonian Institution. Merriam wrote that the study by Roosevelt and Minot was one of the best he had ever read from amateur naturalists.

Roosevelt would find solace and inspiration in the Adirondack wilderness for the rest of his life—he was visiting those mountains as vice-president when he was informed that President McKinley had been gravely wounded and may not survive.

In 1895, George Bird Grinnell took on another issue—the sale of wild game. He had taken up the cause of waterfowl conservation almost as soon as he had acquired *Forest and Stream*. At the time, few people would have believed that North American ducks were in any trouble. Grinnell, however, wrote countless editorials about the significant decline in wildfowl populations, which was the result of market hunting—for example, during one five-day period two hunters on the Mississippi River sent more than five thousand mallard ducks to Chicago for sale. Grinnell began a campaign against spring shooting of waterfowl and proposed bag limits, and gradually gained support as hunters around the country began noticing a decline in the birds. Grinnell was a fellow of the American

Ornithological Union, which added its support for a new law and a ban against spring hunting of waterfowl. It would be a long, hard fight, but Grinnell dug in for the long haul.

Also, in 1895, the Boone and Crockett Club formed the New York Zoological Society (now known as the Wildlife Conservation Society). Grinnell had been involved in the initial discussions and favored soliciting more input from the membership before going forward. He believed that the club should continue to focus its efforts on pushing for stricter hunting laws, and running a zoo was not only off track but a difficult task that could take away from their primary purpose.

Roosevelt was insistent, however, and Grinnell grudgingly went along with the plan. It was decided that they would build a zoo that would not only be unique for its time but would rival any other park in the country. George Grinnell, as was his custom, once again gave Theodore Roosevelt the lead on this project, but voiced his concerns about one aspect.

Grinnell was aware that Roosevelt was anxious to bring a herd of buffalo to the East for people to marvel over, and that was a worrisome proposal. He argued—based on his knowledge and experience—that the type of grasses available in New York were entirely different from on their home range and consequently would have a negative effect on that animal's health and well-being. The impulsive Roosevelt, however, dismissed that notion, and pushed ahead, recruiting several other members to take the lead with him and charging ahead with his idea of stocking wild buffalo.

Planning for the zoo was under way, and the hierarchy of the Boone and Crockett Club set out to create a park that would be like no other before it with high hopes that it would become the prototype for all quality zoological displays of the future. George Grinnell located a piece of property in the Bronx that would be ideal. Most of that land was purchased from Fordham University for $1,000, and the design for a world-class zoological park could start to take shape.

That same year, Theodore Roosevelt became a New York City police commissioner, and started carrying a big stick to deal with local politics. But while he was reforming the police department, and while zoo animals, birds, and reptiles were being collected from all over the world and areas to house them were being readied, the attention of Grinnell and Roosevelt had also been focused on national politics.

William McKinley would be assuming the office of the presidency on March 4, 1897, having beaten William Jennings Bryant. But to the outgoing president, Grover Cleveland, waited until George Washington's birthday, February 23, ten days before his term ended, to make a startling announcement that thrilled conservationists everywhere. Cleveland designated thirteen new forest reserves totaling twenty-one million acres, much of the land in the northwest United States.

Timber barons, and ranchers, and miners exploded in protest over the act. They called Cleveland treasonous and worse, but the forests would be protected, and the government would make sure there was no trespassing. This move by Cleveland was exactly what the Boone and Crockett Club had recommended and worked hard to achieve. Roosevelt and Grinnell could rejoice in another victory.

Meanwhile, as work on the zoo continued, a threat that had been simmering ninety miles across the ocean from Florida finally exploded.

On February 12, 1898, the country was shocked when two explosions on the American battleship *Maine*, which had been anchored in the harbor at Havana, Cuba, sent two officers and 204 of her crew to the bottom of the sea. The *Maine* had been dispatched to that harbor as a show of force after the Cuban people had revolted against Spain and declared themselves an independent country. Spain had tried to stop the rebellion by sending in troops, declaring martial law, and mistreating and imprisoning Cuban citizens. The United States was concerned about the situation because American business had invested millions of dollars in the Cuban economy, especially in sugar plantations.

On April 24, the United States of America formally declared war on Spain. The country began mobilizing for what Secretary of State John Hay called a "splendid little war."

The huge outpouring of jingoism—patriotic fever—generated by the impending conflict was caught by millions, including Theodore

Roosevelt. The year before, he had been appointed assistant secretary of the Navy, and therefore was too highly ranked to engage in combat. So, against the wishes of family and friends, he resigned his position as secretary. He had valuable contacts within the War Department and managed to wrangle an appointment as lieutenant colonel and second in command to Colonel Leonard Wood of the First United States Volunteer Cavalry. When Colonel Wood departed for another command, the unit would be nicknamed "Roosevelt's Rough Riders."

The Rough Riders was comprised of mainly of working-class people from the southwestern states—cowboys, ranchers, policemen, former military men, Native Americans, and outdoorsmen, although there were a few college athletes and upscale gentlemen among the ranks. The reason these men, who were all excellent horsemen, were chosen from Arizona, Oklahoma, Texas, and New Mexico was that they would be accustomed to the heat that they would endure while fighting in Cuba. Through his connections, Roosevelt was able to procure ample supplies for the men, including Colt Single-Action Army Revolvers, Bowie knives, and Krag-Jorgansen carbines. Their uniforms were appropriate for their rough-and-tumble persona—blue flannel shirts, brown trousers, leggings, boots, a slouch hat, and a handkerchief around their necks.

These men would be facing about eight thousand troops that Spain had stationed in Cuba. The American navy, however, had established a blockade of Cuba to prevent Spain from landing any additional troops or supplies.

While Roosevelt's Rough Riders were training and learning basic military skills, the first battle of the war took place thousands of miles from their destination of Cuba. Immediately after the declaration of war, Commodore George Dewey had set sail with several American warships from Hong Kong toward the Spanish fleet in the Philippine Islands. On the morning of May 1, 1898, these American ships sailed into Manila Bay and attacked those Spanish vessels. Within a few hours' time, the ships from Spain had been defeated—without the loss of even one America life.

At the end of May, Roosevelt and his Rough Riders traveled to Tampa Bay, Florida, where they would set sail for Cuba. After several mix-ups, only eight of the twelve companies would leave for the island. The other men, as well as many horses and mules, had been left behind.

On June 23 the Rough Riders arrived at Daiquiri, Cuba, and within days were engaged in a battle to secure a Spanish outpost at Las Guasimas in which eight Americans were killed and thirty-one wounded.

It was on July 1, however, that Theodore Roosevelt became nationally famous for a charge up Kettle Hill, familiarly known as San Juan Hill, a part of San Juan Heights. While in support of the regulars, Roosevelt, who rode the only horse, led his Rough Riders on an advance up this strategic hill. The determined unit sustained heavy casualties but prevailed against their enemy.

Roosevelt later wrote: "On the day of the big fight I had to ask my men to do a deed that European military writers consider utterly impossible of performance, that is, to attack over open ground an unshaken infantry armed with the best modern repeating rifles behind a formidable system of entrenchments. The only way to get them to do it in the way it had to be done was to lead them myself."

The "splendid little war" was little indeed—in duration. Soon after American forces landed in Cuba, Spain was looking for a way out of the conflict. After negotiations lasting two weeks, an armistice was signed on August 12, less than four months after the war's beginning, and was later formalized by the Treaty of Paris. Spain granted independence to Cuba, and gave the United States possession of Puerto Rico, the island of Guam in the Pacific Ocean, and the Philippine Islands.

On September 15 the Rough Riders turned in their equipment and said goodbye to each other—and the regiment was disbanded. They had returned from Cuba a month earlier to a hero's welcome, but most had been quarantined or remained in the hospital due to malaria, or what they called "Cuban Fever." Theodore Roosevelt gave them a farewell speech, calling them true heroes and wishing them well as they returned to civilian life.

In 1898, Roosevelt ran for governor of New York State, and won by a margin of one percentage point. The new governor did not hide in his office, rather held twice-daily press conferences, which was something new. He wrestled with economic and political issues, but always remained faithful to his middle-class base. Roosevelt was a people's governor, who championed the poor, regulated railroad rates, mediated labor problems, and demanded that corporations take responsibility for their actions.

On November 8, 1899, the Boone and Crockett Club celebrated the official opening of the Bronx Zoo, a 261-acre park resplendent with forests, meadows, and with the Bronx River flowing through it. There were 843 animals and 22 exhibits on display—not in cages but, amazingly for the time ever, housed in as close a replica of their natural habitat as possible.

This zoological park was the largest in the world at that time, and quickly became a popular tourist attraction. Visitors had never before experienced being one with the animals and could watch lions and antelope roam in an authentic African terrain—fortunately for the antelope they were separated by a wide moat. There was a range for moose, rocky dens for bears, mud pits for alligators, ponds stocked with beaver, and twenty grassy acres reserved for buffalo. Its open-area concept was a model for parks of the future.

Scientists thought they had successfully bred the buffalo at the zoo, but, over time, most of the entire bison herd—the first domestically raised herd in the country—died. George Grinnell had been correct, and it was a sad and tragic "I told you so." The grass in the Bronx was radically different from that on which the bison grazed back home on the range, and the animals could not survive by eating it. Roosevelt was, of course, devastated by this loss of those animals. The zoo would forego raising buffalo in New York at that time and concentrate instead on a breeding program in the Indian Territories (present-day Oklahoma) that started with fifteen animals. But the Bronx Zoo would thrive despite a setback now and then.

In 1900, Grinnell's unceasing work that had begun five years earlier to save the waterfowl from being over-hunted began to bear fruit. Congressman John F. Lacey pushed a bill through Congress that made it illegal to transport illegally taken game across state borders—a law that remains on the books to this day. This act also prohibited trade in animals, fish, and birds that had been illegally taken. The Lacey Act bolstered state game laws at a time when wild-life law enforcement was poorly funded and lacked support from most average Americans. But on May 25, 1900, President William McKinley signed the bill, which authorized the Department of the Interior to help restore wildlife in those parts of the country where they had become extinct or rare, and regulated the introduction of species in places where they have never existed.

Theodore Roosevelt attended the 1900 Republican National Convention as a delegate and left as William McKinley's vice-presidential nominee. He was a vigorous campaigner, making 480 speeches in 23 different states in support of the platform. His main themes were attacking Democratic nominee William Jennings Bryant and praising the heroism of those who fought in the Spanish-American War. The McKinley-Roosevelt ticket easily won.

On September 5, 1901, William McKinley was attending the Pan-American Exposition in Buffalo, New York, when a gun-man shot and severely wounded the president. McKinley died on September 14, and Theodore Roosevelt was sworn in as the country's twenty-sixth president.

The relationship between George Bird Grinnell and Theodore Roosevelt remained close throughout most of Roosevelt's presidency. The older Grinnell became a trusted mentor and advisor to Roosevelt on conservation matters. Although Roosevelt consulted other notable naturalists and experts in their fields—John Burroughs, William T. Hornaday, Frank Chapman, and, of course, C. Hart Merriam—it was George Grinnell who was closest to his ear on most matters. This resulted in the passage of countless laws and regulations that benefited wildlife, natural resources, and public land—including the official establishment of Yellowstone National Park.

Roosevelt's famous environmental administrator, Gifford Pinchot, often received credit for the administration's actions and ideas—and rightfully so in many cases—but the real brain trust behind Roosevelt's policies was George Bird Grinnell. Together, they launched the country's modern conservation movement, and their successes have lasted until this day. It would be hard to imagine in what state our wilderness and parks would be in had this alliance never come about. Roosevelt depended on Grinnell because he knew that the older and much more experienced man was not only a level-headed, passionate defender of nature but he had his finger on the pulse of his readers as well as hearing advice from the experts who wrote for *Forest and Stream*.

Pinchot traveled around the country on publicity tours to promote natural resource management and rose to prominence as a national celebrity. As usual, George Grinnell preferred to remain in the background and let others carry the torch in public. Pinchot did have one major detractor in John Muir, who disagreed with Pinchot's philosophy that preservation for the sake of wilderness or scenery was a waste, and commercial interests should be allowed its fair share of natural resources. Muir never wavered from his belief that the wilderness should be free of any intrusion by commercial ventures.

Over the years, Roosevelt and Grinnell managed to accomplish much in conserving and protecting the nation's natural resources, treasured places, and wildlife during Roosevelt's presidency. With Grinnell's guidance, among others, Roosevelt became known as the "conservation president," a title that he richly deserved.

He established the United States Forest Service, five national parks—Crater Lake; Wind Cave; Sully's Hill; Platt (now Chickasaw); and Mesa Verde; and added land to Yosemite—eighteen new U. S, National Monuments, several of which became national parks—the most well-known being Devil's Tower; Petrified Forest; Chaco Canyon; and Grand Canyon—the nation's first true wildlife refuge on Pelican Island, Florida, and fifty-three more refuges to protect a host of birds around the country, four national game preserves, 121 Forest Reserves in 31 states, and 150 National Forests. He placed under protection nearly 230 million acres of valuable land.

There have been numerous books written specifically about Roosevelt's attachment to nature and his accomplishments. This brief chapter cannot do justice to the legacy of a man who came along the right time with the right ideas and the right background to make a tremendous difference. If he had ascended to the presidency from the working business sector or was simply someone who had only a passing interest in nature, this country's conservation movement may have fallen flat, and we would not be as blessed as we are to have so much land and so many animals and birds protected that we can enjoy for generations to come.

In those days when many politicians and commercial developers regarded our resources as inexhaustible, Theodore Roosevelt viewed them as treasures to protect and cherish.

He wrote:

It is also vandalism wantonly to destroy or to permit the destruction of what is beautiful in nature, whether it be a cliff, a forest, or a species of mammal or bird. Here in the United States we turn our rivers and streams into sewers and dumping-grounds, we pollute the air, we destroy forests, and exterminate fishes, birds and mammals—not to speak of vulgarizing charming landscapes with hideous advertisements. But at last it looks as if our people were awakening.

And the two people of that era who rang the alarm bell the loudest to awaken the nation about conservation matters were Theodore Roosevelt and his advisor, George Bird Grinnell.

Top, Como Bluffs, Wyoming;
Bottom left, Edward Harriman;
Bottom right, Photographer Edward Curtis

Forest and Stream Magazine, the leading sportsman's magazine of its time

George Armstrong Custer with Grizzly Bear shot in the Black Hills

*Top, George Bird Grinnell, c. 1890; bottom, George Bird Grinnell,
later years*

Top left, Grinnell standing on Grinnell's Glacier; top right, Grinnell with a Blackfoot friend, Bottom, Harriman Expedition Members at Cape Fox Village, Alaska

Top left, Naturalist John Burroughs; top right, Lucy Audubon; bottom left, Scout Luther North; bottom right, Professor O. C. Marsh

New York Times, April 12, 1938

From left: Chief Red Cloud, Buffalo Bill Cody, Chief American Horse

On Left, Scout Charley Reynolds; on right, Theodore Roosevelt and John Muir at Glacier Point, 1903

*Bottom, 6th Cavalry with buffalo heads taken from Edgar Howell
at Yellowstone, 1894*

CHAPTER NINE:
AUTHOR AND ADVOCATE FOR NATIVE AMERICA

What is life? It is the flash of a firefly in the night. It is the breath of a buffalo in the wintertime. It is the little shadow which runs across the grass and loses itself in the sunset.
—BLACKFOOT TRIBAL WISDOM

IT IS ONLY FITTING THAT GEORGE BIRD GRINNELL, THE author, would be combined with George Bird Grinnell, the advocate for Native America. His love of American Indian culture and his dedication to explain this mysterious and unknown lifestyle to the public was the basis for much of his writing, especially his best works. His advocacy for better treatment and acceptance of Native Americans by the public and the government was unwavering at a time when the race had been wrongfully demonized as being unfit for American society.

Next to conservation issues, Grinnell had no greater love than spending time with Native Americans at their villages and campsites. Like a migrating bird, he departed his eastern home summer after summer for more than forty years and, often accompanied by Lute North, traveled to areas in the West inhabited by Native American tribes. His winters were consumed with scientific work, writing, club activities, and public service, but each summer was reserved for trips into uncharted land where few white men dared to venture.

He lived for periods of time each year with the Pawnee, or the Blackfeet (also known as Piegan), or the Cheyenne, and conversed with members of these tribes about their history, culture, folk tales, and hunting skills—gradually erasing cultural differences and gaining acceptance with his sincere desire to learn about them. His notebook was always open, and he recorded the stories told him by the tribal elders and his observations of a lifestyle rarely experienced by outsiders.

He was so trusted and respected that he was adopted into various plains tribes. The Pawnee gave him the name "White Wolf"; the Blackfeet called him "Fisher Hat"; the Gros Ventres, enemies of the Blackfeet named him "Grey Clothes"; and the Cheyenne, the tribe that so inspired him and most captured his interest, referred to him as *wikis* or "Migratory bird," or simply as "Bird."

Author Stanley Vestal wrote: "His integrity, sincerity, and understanding made him welcome in every tipi. In my own research among the Northern Cheyenne in later years, I found that a letter from Grinnell opened every door. He was one of the few historians who knew how to get accurate information from Indians, and how to present things as they saw them in readable form."

Before Grinnell was forty years of age, he was not only an accomplished student of Native American culture but had learned sign language and was studying the spoken language. He once explained: "When you are talking with your Indian friend, as you sit beside him and smoke with him on the bare prairie, or at night lie at length about your lonely campfire in the mountains, you get very near to nature."

But not everyone held the same opinion of Native Americans as Grinnell, as evidenced by the attitude of the country toward these far away people. Horace Greeley, the man who said, "Go west, young man, go west," set the tone for the country with his opinion of Native Americans that endured for decades—and even to this day. Greeley went west, to Denver, expecting to find the idealized, literary "Indians" that he had imagined and read about. Instead, he viewed them as major obstacles to Western expansion.

He wrote:

[One] needs but little familiarity with the actual, palpable aborigines to convince any one that the poetic Indian—the Indian of Cooper and Longfellow—is only visible to the poet's eye.

Greeley was an advocate for abolishing slavery and welcoming African-American people into polite society, but when it came to Native Americans, he believed—as did most of America—that those savages were morally unfit and unworthy of respect or justice. Some of them, Greeley conceded, with appropriate charity could be educated and taught to live like proper humans. But one thing was clear—these Native people would have to become civilized by white standards or face extinction. They could no longer practice their pagan ceremonies, or carry out long-held traditions, and would have to abandon customs laid down for centuries. In other words, they would have to become practically white in order to gain approval from this "learned" man.

The words of Horace Greeley were carried east and went a long way in forming the impression that the public held of the free-roaming western tribes: "These people must die out—there is no help for them," Greeley professed. "God has given the earth to those who will subdue and cultivate it, and it is vain to struggle against His righteous decree." Greeley had invoked God into the equation, without God's permission, of course, but still it made for a powerful argument, especially with only a few weak voices to refute it or refine it—until George Bird Grinnell came along.

Forest and Stream and other national publications would become a forum from which George Grinnell could promote Native American rights as well as offering an understanding of the customs and culture of the various tribes, which he hoped would serve to dispel contemporary misconceptions. He wanted the country to understand them as fellow human beings, not just as those savages whose war-painted, fierce faces and hands gripping a tomahawk or a fresh scalp donned the covers of dime novels. He wished to dispel those ideas spewed by narrow-minded people like Horace Greeley who could not bring himself to accept any race that was different from his own. Grinnell embarked on a mission to halt the movement toward the destruction of the nation's Native American population, which had been brought about partially by the environmental and cultural changes that followed the taking of their land.

During his annual western trips, Grinnell studied the Plains tribes and eventually published books about their way of life and their folklore. His writings record the West and the Plains tribes just before and while they underwent radical change. Much of his work was devoted to preserving what he could before it disappeared. His articles about Native Americans, in addition to *Forest and Stream*, appeared in such publications as *The Journal of American Folklore*, *Harpers' Magazine*, *American Anthropologist*, and *Scribner's Magazine*. Grinnell introduced positive aspects of Native American culture into American homes by exposing his readership to such fascinating and previously unknown subjects as: "Pawnee Mythology," "Coup and Scalp Among the Plains Indians," "Great Mysteries of the Cheyenne," and "A Buffalo Sweatlodge." He related stories that, in his words, "showed how Indians think and feel…how they look at every-day occurrences of their life, what motives govern them, and how they reason."

In the 1880's Grinnell began relating a series of folk tales that he had heard from the Pawnee in *Forest and Stream*, and a collection of these stories were published in book form as *Pawnee Hero Stories and Folk Tales* (1889). Grinnell had visited the Pawnee Agency in Indian Territory on numerous occasions, and at last spoke to Eagle Chief, an old acquaintance: "Father," he explained, "we have come down here to ask the people about how things used to be in the olden times, to hear their stories, to get their history, and then to put all these things down in a book." The chief thought about that for a while, and then responded: "It is good and it is time. Already the old things are being lost, and those who know the secrets are many of them dead…The old men told their grandchildren, and they told their grandchildren, and so the secrets and the stories and the doings of long ago have been handed down." Stories include: "The Dun Horse," "The Bear man," "The Snake Brother," and "The Ghost Wife." Grinnell also added notes that describe the origins and migrations of the Pawnees, tribal customs, methods of warfare, and their later history.

That book was followed by *Blackfeet Lodge Tales* (1892). Grinnell was respected as a friend to the Blackfeet Nation—and honorary member—and they freely entrusted their heritage to his keeping. The first half of his book, thirty stories of the Blackfeet, were recorded just as the elders had related them to him, and chronicle the tribe's origins, social customs and culture, tales of creation and the Creator, and, of course, their many wars. Those stories are followed by the history of the Nation, their daily lifestyle and customs, tribal organization, and religion. Grinnell's attention to detail and rich narrative bring alive the adventures and primitive but satisfying lives of these people.

In *The Story of the Indian* (1895), Grinnell attempted to preserve the West that he had experienced between Sonora and Vancouver and Texas and Dakota. These human-interest stories offer the reader a seat at the campfire in various Indian villages to hear stories relating to every aspect of the primitive, fascinating, and fulfilling Native lifestyle as told by those who lived it. Grinnell attempted to humanize his subject by explaining that, although regarded as savages by white America, they are people with the same wants and needs as human beings everywhere. His attempts at bringing realism to the reader come across the pages like a heartbeat of drums and the pace of a wondrous dance of moccasins pounding the ground into dust.

The Indians of To-day (1900) is illustrated with three chromolithographic plates and fifty-five black-and-white photographic portraits of Native Americans ("Portraits of Living Indians"). The three chromolithographic plates are from the eleventh Census of the United States, with the titles: *Omaha Dance* by Walter Shirlaw; *Hunting Party of Shoshones* by Peter Moran; and *Sioux Camp* by Gilbert Gaul. This work brought the eastern reader face to face with the Plains people, whose expressions display a wide range of emotions.

The Punishment of Stingy and Other Stories (1901) has become a true classic of American Indian literature. The book features the twin themes of stinginess and generosity and is the only Grinnell work to feature collected stories from different tribes, including the Pawnee, Blackfeet, Piegan, and Chinook. Like can be found in any "good and evil" tale, these protagonists are rewarded for their generosity and punished for their greediness. Stories include "The Star Boy"; "The Girl Who Was the Ring"; "The First Medicine

Lodge"; and "Nothing Child." These tales are truly brilliant as they cover the spectrum from humor to mystery, and once again bring alive the days when tribes were free to roam the land.

Blackfeet Indian Stories (1913) are a retelling of stories passed down from the old ones to the young ones, those traditional tales that bind together a tribe. Grinnell called upon his memory and his notes to offer another classic book that depicts a lifestyle and a society that has long disappeared.

When Buffalo Ran (1920) tells the story of a young member of a Plains tribe, named Wikis. As Wikis grows up, he has encounters with wild buffalo and enemy tribes. Along the way, he is guided by his uncle, a mentor and tutor, who teaches him all the necessary skills to becoming a warrior.

Grinnell wrote about his methodology:

For many years the government of the Indians by the United States was carried on in haphazard and often dishonest fashion by officials ignorant and careless alike of the customs and ways of thought of the savages with whom they were dealing. Since the Indians could not write, the history of their wars has been set down by their enemies, and the story has been told always from the hostile point of view. White writers have lauded white courage and claimed white successes. If it has been necessary to confess defeat, they have abused those who overcame them, as the defeated always abuse the victors. Evidently there is another side to this history, and this other side is one which should be recorded.

Grinnell set about presenting and balancing the accounts by both whites and Indians, without biased comment or opinion, to provide a rich and intimate history.

His first opportunity to directly aid Native Americans came in 1895, when President Grover Cleveland appointed him to negotiate the purchase of land from the Blackfeet tribe, whose reservation was being infringed upon by prospectors. As a friend and an adopted member of the Blackfeet—they called him "Fisher's Hat," or "Pinyutoyi Istsimokon"—Grinnell managed to obtain a fair price for the tribe, which provided them with the resources necessary to reestablish home sites and hunting grounds. This topic is covered in detail in chapter 11: "Grinnell's Glacier."

George Grinnell's most important contributions to the record of Native American civilization in America and their wars are his works about the Cheyenne tribe: *The Fighting Cheyennes* (1915), a two-volume work, *The Cheyenne Indians* (1923), and *By Cheyenne Campfires* (1926). These volumes, *The Cheyenne Indians* in particular, are the foundation of any present-day research about that tribe.

He was fascinated with this tribe above all—and there was much to be fascinated about, albeit the freedom to roam came to a tragic end for this proud tribe. His opinion with respect to the character of the people he studied and with whom he became friends can be noted by his statement: "The old time Cheyennes possessed in high degree the savage virtues of honesty, trustworthiness, and bravery in the men, and of courage, devotion, and chastity in the women." He was particularly impressed by the chiefs.

He wrote:

A good chief gave his whole heart and his whole mind to the work of helping his people. Such thought for his fellows was not without its influence on the man himself; after a time the spirit of good- will which animated him became reflected in his countenance. True friends, delightful companions, wise counselors, they were men whose attitude toward their fellows we might all emulate.

Grinnell's initial contact with the Cheyenne, the tribe that he would masterfully chronicle, was in 1890, in the summer before the Sioux Wounded Knee Massacre. But it was not until five years later that he had made the proper contacts to begin his research. Grinnell wanted to hear the tribal stories from the elders and per- suaded a number of them to participate. He spoke at length with Two Moon, the battle-tested warrior who had led an assault on Fort Kearney, Wyoming, in 1866 in what became known as Red Cloud's War (not to be confused with Two Moons, his nephew who led his people into the Little Bighorn Battle).

And he met with Little Chief, known for his talent as an ora- tor and who had negotiated his band's surrender in 1877. The year after that, Little Chief had led a delegation to Washington with the request to move his tribe to their traditional homeland. This effort failed, and he and his band had been imprisoned to prevent them from joining Little Wolf when they broke from the reservation on an ill-fated flight toward their homeland in 1878. No doubt Grinnell probed this old man's heart and mind to learn the emotions and tradition behind the decision of these desperate people to risk their lives the way they had.

Grinnell was likely transfixed as warrior Brave Wolf told him about how the Little Bighorn Battle unfolded, how Custer and his detachment were wiped out. The warrior concluded his story by saying, "It was hard fighting; very hard all the time. I have been in many hard fights, but I never saw such brave men." It is nothing less than remarkable that Grinnell could sit there with a man who had participated in killing his friends Custer and Charley Reynolds, among others, and maintain his composure as an unbiased historian and journalist.

But Grinnell had been around Native Americans long enough to likely understand the frustration and hate that had built up within the hearts of these people. It was only natural to him that they would rebel and fight back against their oppressors. Custer himself had once said that if he was Native American, he would not remain a prisoner on some government reservation—he would flee. It would not be out of the question that the cavalryman had discussed the subject with Grinnell over a nighttime campfire in the Black Hills. The customs and traditions of the various Plains tribes would have been a favorite topic for Custer, Charley Reynolds, and Lute North, and each of them were quite knowledgeable. Still, it is admirable that Grinnell could separate himself from the drama in order to hear those stories and impassively put them into perspective while seated in the camp of a former enemy.

Grinnell convinced stubborn Chief Bear Coal to cooperate by casually chatting about how the Pawnees had captured the Medicine Arrows, a version that the chief had also heard. Bear Coal was impressed by Grinnell's knowledge and opened up with customs and traditions never before heard by a white man. Soon, Grinnell's notebooks were filling with the foundation for his classic books.

The Cheyenne story that Grinnell documented demonstrates how a tribe fought to maintain its identity—and existence—as rival tribes and the white man encroached on its homeland. Although Grinnell had lived through much of this history by the time he interviewed his subjects—albeit from eastern newspaper stories with varying levels of facts—he wanted to hear the story from those who had witnessed and participated in this saga, all the while knowing that it would end tragically.

Who were the Cheyenne? Where had they come from? How did they live? Why did they fight? What were their marriage ceremonies? He wanted to know everything about them.

Grinnell learned about the days before the white man came, when the villages were relatively safe and secure, and each day was a celebration of peace and contentment—almost idyllic in its retelling by the nostalgic tribal elders. The Cheyenne camp, the bleached-white, buffalo-hide lodges, or teepees, could be found arranged in a circle, broken only by an opening that faced the rising sun, with water and timber close by. And just as he had done with the trappers' camp on his first trip west with Professor Marsh in 1870, Grinnell would certainly have drifted away in his mind and imagination to fantasize about how it would have been for him if he had been living as a member of this free-roaming tribe.

At first light the Cheyenne women began their daily chores by visiting the nearby stream and filling containers with fresh water— they believed that yesterday's water was dead, and the Cheyenne would drink only living water. The water-bearers wore dresses, or smocks, that fell to midway between the knee and the ankle, with cape-like sleeves that hung loosely around the elbows. These everyday work clothes, designed with freedom of movement in mind, had been handmade from the skins of deer, elk, or antelope and were quite plain. On ceremonial occasions, however, the women adorned themselves in skin garments decorated with colorful beads, bells, dyed porcupine quills, and perhaps teeth from an elk.

When the first golden rays of the sun spread across the land, the men and the boys, with toddlers in tow, straggled to the stream and, regardless of the weather, washed away all sickness and were made hardy with a morning bath. Upon completion of this ritual, the male members of the tribe returned to their lodges and without fail pulled on their breechcloths—those scanty pieces of animal skin that covered their loins and hips. Custom dictated that a man would lose his manhood if he did not wear his precious breechcloth.

The camp was bustling with activity by the time the sun peeked fully above the horizon. Women, assisted by daughters and other female members of the extended family, attended to the morning meal, their cooking pots hanging over smoking fires, the pleasant aromas teasing the men, who chatted nearby while anxiously waiting to be fed. Boys rode out to drive the pony herd toward fresh grazing grass and selected certain mounts—usually the war horses—to be tied in front of lodges in the event they might be needed at a moment's notice.

While families settled in to eat breakfast, the Crier strolled through the camp, beginning at the opening of the circle, and announced the news of the day. In a loud voice, repeating his words as he moved along, he relayed orders from the chiefs, perhaps about how long the camp would remain in that place, or to notify everyone that a certain soldier band planned a dance for that evening, or to mention items that had been lost and found. Most anticipated were the latest tidings of a personal nature—possibly about a child having been born during the night or the previous day or a marriage that would be taking place soon.

With breakfast completed, a good number of the men readied their horses and weapons and rode out to hunt. Cheyenne men were exclusively big-game hunters, favoring buffalo, antelope, deer, elk, and wild sheep, in that order. Wolves and foxes were hunted only for their fur, and other smaller animals were usually ignored by the men. Small game, however, was hunted by the boys as a learning experience.

Those men who remained in camp gathered around lodges or shade trees to smoke and gossip while repairing a bow, fashioning a pipe, making arrows, or working on some other necessary implement. The boys would assemble in small groups to engage in spirited activities. Swimming was a favorite, as were running foot races, wrestling, practicing with bow and arrows, riding ponies, throwing sticks at targets, and other games that symbolized their status as warriors-in-training.

At some point, the women and girls ventured off into the hills to gather firewood, berries, or roots. This was a time of laughter and merriment for the women, who viewed work not as a tiresome chore but as an outing, an opportunity to discuss camp news, gossip, and engage in practical jokes. The boys would occasionally happily harass the girls as they worked, perhaps as a way of flirting in prelude to courting.

The primary responsibility of a Cheyenne man was to provide food and other material needs for his family. The men were also obliged to protect their wives and children, as well as the collective interests of the tribe from any outside threat. They were always ready for battle in case a rival tribe would come calling.

The women were accomplished in domestic relations and were expected to care for the children and perform every household duty. The women, however, contrary to the custom of some Plains tribes, were not chattel but partners with their husband, and most marriages endured for life.

By midday, as the sun beat down on the camp, most people sought refuge inside their lodges to escape the heat. Later in the afternoon, the men who had gone out hunting rode back into camp. They dismounted in front of their lodges and handed over their kill to the women for preparing and cooking. Then they relaxed, perhaps gathering here and there to boast about their hunting skills, pass along information, or speculate about the location and availability of game.

The camp came alive once more when the sun began its descent. Daily tasks were set aside in favor of leisurely and festive amusements. Preparation of the evening meal commenced, fires were ablaze, and children could be seen scurrying around the circle of lodges with invitations to guests for dinner. The boys drove the horses to a safe, fresh grazing area, while turning out other mounts for the night.

Eventually the sound of music and drumming could be heard, and people of all ages wandered around the camp to share a feast, attend a social dance, play games, court that special young lady, gamble, or simply enjoy the companionship of their fellow tribe members. Storytelling was a big part of the evening, as certain ones known for their talent to entertain with tales drew audiences to their lodges. This bustle of activity was punctuated by frequent shouts and laughter, combined with the incidental whinny of a horse, the bark of a dog, or the howl of a distant coyote, or the cry of a child. Some people might choose to seek solitude, perhaps by chanting a prayer to the spirits or playing a flute on a nearby hill. For several hours, illuminated by the comforting glow of huge bonfires, the camp celebrated the simple pleasures of a satisfying lifestyle.

One by one, the fires burned down, the music faded away, and visitors drifted back to their own lodges. The camp gradually became silent, and another harmonious day had come to an end.

And then the white man came West, and daily life for the Cheyenne people would never be the same.

In his pioneering work, *The Cheyenne Indians*, George Grinnell explored all of those topics that created a full disclosure of the life of this tribe—their marriage ceremonies; children's education and games; the way they trained their horses; their weapons and hunting techniques; sacred ceremonies for war, and their belief in the Great Spirit. Grinnell delved into the mind-set of these people to reveal the way they thought, and why they acted in a certain way, and what their hearts were like. He was impressed by the charitable acts the tribe displayed: "It often costs civilized man a struggle to carry out the precept of love his neighbor, but the Cheyenne did kindly, friendly, or charitable acts of his own free will, and took no credit for them."

After a time, he developed a kinship with the Cheyenne. "I have never been able to regard the Indian as merely an object for study—a museum specimen. A half-century rubbing shoulders with them, during which I have had a share in almost every phase of their old-time life, forbids me to think of them except as acquaintances, comrades, and friends."

Grinnell attempted to humanize Native Americans at a time when the public regarded them as wanton killers without morals or principles. "While their culture differs from ours in some respects," he wrote, "fundamentally they are like ourselves." Grinnell wanted his readers to understand that he had the highest regard for these people and that they were not any better or any worse than any other race of mankind. It was his way of letting people know that it was all right for them to change their opinions and welcome the Native American into society.

But the Cheyenne then and now are defined by the conflicts in which they participated. And the information that Grinnell collected offered a tragic view of a once-proud tribe that had been brought to near extinction for defying the wishes of the United States government.

He focused one entire book—*The Fighting Cheyennes*—on tribal warfare, primarily because it was the subject that most interested the tribal leaders, as well as white readers back east. His study did not feature warfare exclusively; however, rather he went beyond that to portray the culture and customs that had been handed down for generations. He was as much a student as he was an anthropologist on a quest for answers. "I am constantly impressed by the number of things about Indians that I do not know," he wrote.

Grinnell's work was historic because it came at a time when white Americans had only heard the US Army version of events, which, at times, were highly propagandized and embellished to favor the white man. Stories from the "enemy" side of the battlefield suddenly offered the public a complete picture of the battles waged between the Cheyenne and the soldiers. Grinnell explained it simply: "Since the Indians could not write, the history of their wars had been set down by their enemies."

At some point in the seventeenth century, this agricultural Algonquin tribe called the Cheyenne tired of constant warfare with the Sioux and Ojibway in Minnesota and began migrating to the Great Plains to become nomadic hunters. In about 1832, the tribe split into two distinct bands—the larger group became the Southern Cheyenne, and established residence along the upper Arkansas River; the Northern Cheyenne, who settled around the North Platte River in northern Nebraska, assumed a lifestyle similar to their allies, the Sioux. The tribe had seven military societies of which the Dog Soldiers was regarded as the most aggressive and feared, and constantly waged war on enemies.

There were countless skirmishes or occasions of horse stealing that led to conflict with neighboring tribes—territories overlapped, and the nomadic nature of the Plains Indian bands would cause them to cross paths. But it was not until the white man came West to seek riches and farmland that the fighting became furious and eventually futile.

In 1858, the Pike's Peak or Bust gold rush in Colorado incited violence between the Southern Cheyenne and white intruders onto their traditional land. Provisions of the Fort Wise Treaty of 1861 resulted in the removal of the tribe to western Colorado, where they were neglected and compelled to raid white settlements in order to survive.

Colorado governor John Evans responded by encouraging civilians to take up arms against the marauding Indians. In 1864, Evans decided that friendly tribes would be protected by settling at designated sites. Chief Black Kettle accepted this offer, and his six-hundred Cheyenne were settled for the winter of 1864 in a camp along Sand Creek, about forty miles from Fort Lyon. On November 29, diabolic Methodist minister and volunteer Colonel John Chivington and the seven-hundred-man Third Colorado Cavalry attacked this peaceful camp, slaughtering and committing atrocious acts on more than 150 men, women, and children. The surviving Cheyenne and their allies stepped up their raids—forcing the February 1865 abandonment and sacking of the town of Julesburg, Colorado.

In 1866, the Northern Cheyenne aligned themselves with Sioux Chief Red Cloud and participated in war with the US Army over the Bozeman Trail that resulted in a victory for the Indians and led to the Fort Laramie Treaty of 1868.

In 1867, attacks by the Southern Cheyenne on work crews from the Kansas Pacific Railway as well as white travelers along the Smoky Hill, Arkansas, and Platte roads compelled the army to form the Hancock Expedition for the purpose of punishing these hostiles. George Armstrong Custer's Seventh Cavalry pursued the Cheyenne under Tall Bull and their Sioux allies throughout Kansas, Nebraska, and Colorado, but failed to deter the raids. In hopes of peace, the Medicine Lodge Treaty of 1867, which the Cheyenne signed, provided for a reservation shared by the Cheyenne and Arapaho. The treaty provisions, however, were unworkable, and raiding by the Cheyenne to survive resumed.

In September 1868, warriors under Roman Nose attacked Major George Forsyth in what became known as the Battle of Beecher Island. Fifty-one soldiers were trapped on that island for nine days while the Indians laid siege. On the ninth day, a detachment of the

Tenth Cavalry—black Buffalo Soldiers—arrived to rescue Forsyth and his men.

In an effort to force the Cheyenne and their allies to the reservation, General Phil Sheridan launched his Winter Campaign of 1868–69. On November 27, 1868, Custer's cavalry attacked Black Kettle's village on the Washita River, and killed nearly one hundred Cheyenne, including Black Kettle. Many women and children were taken captive. The campaign continued with a sweep of the Plains, which encouraged many bands to submit to their assigned reservation.

Free-roaming Southern Cheyenne under Tall Bull were defeated by Major Eugene Carr—accompanied by Major Frank North's Pawnee Battalion—at the July 11, 1869, Battle of Summit Springs, an action that effectively ended hostilities on the Southern Plains when most of the Cheyenne and their allies submitted to the reservation at Fort Cobb. But the tribe was not satisfied with reservation life and would remain to receive annuities but roam free and often raid white farms and settlements at will much the year. Thus, the government decided to act.

The Northern Cheyenne and their Sioux allies were targeted by the US Army in what would be known as the Great Sioux War of 1876, which included the Battle of the Little Bighorn, which ended in disaster for Custer's cavalry but was more disastrous for the Indians. The public was outraged and had revenge on its mind.

Revenge came in November 1876 at the Dull Knife Fight where Colonel Ranald MacKenzie defeated Northern Cheyenne under Dull Knife and Little Wolf, and the tribe was settled on a reservation with their Southern Cheyenne brethren in Indian Territory (present-day Oklahoma), far removed from their traditional homeland in Montana. The conditions were miserable, the food lacking, people were dying, and the men could not leave the reservation boundaries to go hunting to provide for their families.

In September 1878, members of the tribe, led by Dull Knife and Little Wolf, had suffered enough. In an effort to save their people, they fled the reservation heading north toward their former Tongue River homeland. More than ten thousand soldiers and civilians pursued them in what has been called the largest manhunt in US history. The escaping Cheyenne were eventually apprehended and returned to the misery of the reservation. In the early 1880's, the Northern Cheyenne were finally granted their wish and awarded a Tongue River Agency—they could finally go home, those who were still alive, that was.

George Bird Grinnell listened and wrote down the facts as well as his impressions while the old ones told tales that no white man had ever before heard. Most of those elders and warriors with whom he spoke had lived portions of their tribal history, and could relate the action but, much more importantly, could also speak about the emotions and suffering of the people. How the women would weep when their husbands did not return home from battle. How the tribe sacrificed, and how babies died when their winter stores were burned by the army. It was a side of the story that would have remained relatively unknown if not for Grinnell having gained the trust of these tribal leaders. They were a proud people, not ones to whine, but their stories of events that led to the captivity of the tribe and reservation life must have been heart wrenching to a man like Grinnell.

Native Americans were always wary of speaking to the white man for relevant reasons—one of which was that interrupters often, accidentally or on purpose, would misinterpret their answers, or, the Native American would say what they thought the white man wanted to hear in order not to cause trouble or controversy or to curry favor. In Grinnell, they encountered not merely a sympathetic ear but a man who truly desired to tell an accurate story and offer a vivid yet unembellished portrayal of the tribe and its colorful culture. If their story did not add up in his mind, he would ask questions to clarify, to make certain that he received the accurate details.

It can only be imagined how many teepees Grinnell visited listening to a century of wars, and treaties, and disappointment for this proud tribe. In addition, his curiosity took him deeper, into the heart and soul and mind of the Cheyenne. He wanted to know all about their rituals, and ceremonies, and spiritual beliefs, along with their daily dress, activities, and relationships. And, because he was trusted by these normally wary people, Grinnell became a pipeline through which never before revealed information flowed. He recorded events, the triumphs, the sadness, the challenges, as if it was simply another ethnic culture, like the Irish, or the Germans, or the French, rather than what was perceived by America as an alien enigmatic and feared race of wild and untamed people.

Famed anthropologists Margaret Mead and Ruth Bunzel stated in their book *The Golden Age of American Anthropology*: "Of all the books written about Indians, none comes closer to their everyday life than Grinnell's classic monograph on the Cheyenne. Reading it, one can smell the buffalo grass and the wood fires, feel the heavy morning dew on the prairie."

Mari Sandoz, author of the classic Cheyenne Autumn, a fictionalized account of the 1878 effort by the Cheyenne to reach their old homeland, said of Grinnell: "His Indian writing, from the early Pawnee and Blackfeet tales to the later comprehensive body of work on the Cheyenne Indians, no one but Grinnell could have done. He had the forthrightness, the scholarly open-mindedness and training in investigation and evaluation, the firsthand knowledge and experience, the warmth of understanding and the prophetic vision."

When Theodore Roosevelt ascended to the presidency in 1901, he drew upon Grinnell's vast knowledge of Native American affairs to advise him on issues and to help shape administration policy. Roosevelt believed as Grinnell did that Native Americans should be treated fairly and demanded that his administration follow suit. In 1902 the president commissioned Grinnell to settle a dispute—a national scandal—on the Standing Rock Sioux Reservation on the border of North and South Dakota, involving a proposal to lease cattlemen large sections of reservation land.

The Dawes Act, passed in 1887, broke up the present Lakota Sioux reservation into smaller reservations, and reduced their total holdings by nine million acres. At that time, land allotments were granted to tribal individuals and those people were provided with cattle. The intention, certainly well-meaning but misguided, was that the Lakota would change their lifestyle and become agricultural. This system of individual ownership, however, was a drastic move for what had been a stable land base and a unified tribe, and it resulted in poverty and the erosion of the tribe's cultural and social structure.

Cattlemen were granted access to that freed up land in 1889, the same year that South Dakota had achieved statehood. Rumors began to swirl that the ranchers were taking advantage of the Lakota Sioux by grazing their cattle on tribal land without paying and that they were selling bulls and heifers that were diseased to the Indian Agency for distribution amongst the Sioux people.

The Indian Rights Association (IRA), founded in Philadelphia in 1882, was an activist organization whose main objective was to "bring about the complete civilization of the Indians and their admission to citizenship." The IRA contacted President Roosevelt and asked him to investigate the propriety of the leases to white cattlemen.

Roosevelt appointed his friend George Bird Grinnell to look into the situation on the Standing Rock Sioux Reservation. Grinnell's spent time carefully assessing the situation, and his final report blasted the government's unscrupulous leasing practices. Grinnell was appalled at these one-sided arrangements, but another more personal issue set his pen aflame. The commissioner had ordered that the Indians must cut off their long hair. Grinnell wrote: "Such an order was never before heard of in a free country, and the enforcement of it tends to make the Indian themselves feel like slaves."

Soon afterward, the white livestock growers settled their tensions with the tribe by paying them the annual asking price for grazing fees and dealing more honorably with the agency, and the fraud charges were forgotten. And—they could keep their long hair.

At the same time, Grinnell lobbied to increase the amount of government beef issued to the Cheyenne tribe at the Tongue River Agency. The present rations were inadequate to feed the tribe, and the prevailing thought was that the Indians could bolt the reservation to go hunting, which would cause mischief. Two months later, Grinnell's requests were approved, and the beef issue was increased.

An ally of Grinnell in this effort had been Charles Fletcher Lummis, who enlisted Grinnell in his Native American Rights organization called the "Sequoyah League." Both men were disgusted by the ignorance of the government when it came to conditions in the west that affected the various tribes. Accordingly, Grinnell ramped up his efforts in *Forest and Stream* and other publications to educate the public—and hopefully the government as well—about the care and feeding of these needy and deserving people. He wrote in an *Atlantic Monthly* article that "the task of giving help to the Indian is one worthy the best thought and effort of the country."

Another of Grinnell's complaints was that the government was trying to suppress the Indian's religious and ceremonial practices— the Blackfeet Medicine Dance in particular—believing them to be a prelude to war. Grinnell responded that this ceremony was "entirely innocent and harmless." He also assured the Secretary of the Interior E. A. Hitchcock that at his request the Blackfeet had quit the practice of insulting white people in their ceremonies and that they were not by any means orgies as some had implied.

Grinnell also served as speech writer for those parts of Roosevelt's annual messages to Congress that dealt with Native Americans. And when the President sought a new Commissioner of Indian Affairs, Grinnell recommended Francis E. Leupp, who filled that office with distinction during Roosevelt's second administration. Leupp would write several books about Native Americans after leaving office, including *The Indian and His Problem* (1910), which reflects Leupp's experience and insight into tribal affairs at that point in time.

Although best known for his volumes on Native Americans, Grinnell also wrote extensively about hunting, camping, and conservation. His *American Duck Shooting* (1901) and *American Game-bird Shooting* (1910), written for "the higher class of sportsman-naturalist," are recognized to this day as classic works.

With Theodore Roosevelt, he co-edited the highly regarded *American Big-Game Hunting* (1893), which was published during the Panic of 1893, financed by a personal check for $1,250 from Roosevelt. Grinnell recalled: "We thought that perhaps there were enough big game hunters in the country to make it possible to publish the book without too great a loss."

The stories for the book were solicited from founding members of the Boone and Crockett Club, and one of those tales led to the near expulsion of one of their own. Landscape painter Albert Bierstadt wrote a story for the book about a moose hunt that had rendered the painting *Moose Hunter's Camp*. Roosevelt had requested that the artist write the account of his hunt for this record-setting animal, and it was learned that Bierstadt had not personally shot the moose initially—his guide had pulled the trigger, which was against the "fair chase" rules of the club. Not only that, but Bierstadt wrote that he had hated to shoot the animal: "I took the rifle then and ended his misery; he reeled, staggered, and tried to lean against a smaller tree which bent over as he gently breathed his last....I have made up my mind that I don't want to kill any more moose, but to go and see them in their own haunts is a pleasure."

Roosevelt did not want to expel the famous artist from the club. He suggested that they creatively edit the story to imply that Bierstadt had indeed shot the moose and leave it at that, but the artist refused to compromise. Roosevelt then decided to wash his hands of the whole affair and set the article aside. Bierstadt's story would not be included in the book, and no action would be taken on expelling him from the club. Perhaps Roosevelt and Grinnell realized that such publicity would be damaging for the credibility of the fledgling club and could affect sales of their first published book.

The one article in the book written by George Bird Grinnell is "In Buffalo Days," which was basically a love story where the author professed his admiration for that Plains beast. Another story, "The White Goat and His Country," was written by Roosevelt's Harvard classmate Owen Wister, who lived in Philadelphia but brought the West to life in his writing. Roosevelt's contribution was "Coursing the Pronghorn," about those herds of antelope running free in his beloved badlands of the Dakotas.

Other Boone and Crockett Club books included *Hunting in Many Lands* (1895), which transported the reader out of the United States on hunting trips to such exotic locales as China, Tibet, and East Africa; *Trail and Campfire* (1897), which once again featured stories by club members—Grinnell writing "Wolves and Wolf Nature," Roosevelt adding "On the Little Missouri," and other stories that range in location from the Adirondack Mountains to Africa. Grinnell wrote and with Roosevelt edited *American Big Game in its Haunts* (1904), a book that answers questions asked by the public, such as "What is the difference between a bison and a buffalo?" The two men edited *Hunting in High Altitude* (1913), a book that spans the globe and features information about the Boone and Crockett Club. *The Wolf Hunters: A Story of the Plains* (1914), is a scholarly work written by Grinnell from his experiences. He also edited and wrote chapters for Hunting and Conservation (1925), in which he encouraged protecting wildlife and saving the Redwoods and migratory birds.

Grinnell wrote several pamphlets, including *Social Organization of the Cheyenne* (1905); *Some Cheyenne Plant Medicines* (1905); *Brief History of the Boone and Crockett Club* (1910); *Bent's Old Fort* (1923); and *Audubon Park* (1927).

Grinnell understood how important literature was to young readers, because he had been a voracious reader early in his life. With that in mind, he wrote and published seven novels under the nom de plume "Yo" in the so-called "Jack" series. The hero was an eastern boy named Jack who visited the West seeking adventure and found plenty of it. Grinnell claimed that the books had been written for his nieces and nephews, which may be partially true. Actually, it could be fairly speculated that the inspiration for these books came from those warm childhood memories of the tales written by Captain Thomas Mayne Reid that had mesmerized him as a boy. He wanted to pass along to another generation of impressionable boys the pleasure and excitement that he had derived from reading outdoor adventure stories. This series, written between 1899 and 1913, was based on his own experiences and set against a background of solid authenticity. Titles include *Jack the Young Ranchman* (1899), *Jack Among the Indians* (1900), *Jack in the Rockies* (1904), *Jack and the Young Canoeman* (1906), *Jack the Young Trapper* (1907), *Jack the Young Explorer* (1908), and *Jack the Young Cowboy* (1913),

In that same vein of accuracy were his historical studies compiled from stories he had written for *Forest and Stream*. *Trails of the Pathfinders* (1911) featured stories based on original journals and notes about early English-speaking explorers, trappers, and traders—several before Lewis and Clark—who opened up the American wilderness. *Beyond the Old Frontier* (1913) describes early frontier life and its explorers, hunters, trappers, Indians, and their adventures in the unknown lands of the West. His *Two Great Scouts and*

Their Pawnee Battalion (1928) pays tribute to brothers Luther and Frank North, who had shared their knowledge of the Plains and its inhabitants with Grinnell over the years. Lute North for all intents and purposes could be called a brother to Grinnell—they were that close—and this tribute portrays the contributions that the North brothers made to the country as army scouts and guides.

Most of the books that George Bird Grinnell wrote or co-wrote are available through bookstores to this day, and many of them remain on library shelves. In addition, there are websites where some titles can be downloaded for free. Every book offers a perspective of a period in history as seen through the eyes of an experienced scientist who paid great attention to detail.

His classic ethnographic studies, particularly those about the Cheyenne tribe, continue to be an invaluable source for researchers. Rarely would an historian write about Native Americans, especially the Cheyenne tribe, without referring to Grinnell's work. His output of books is truly amazing given the fact that he also wrote essay after essay for his weekly *Forest and Stream* magazine as well articles for many other publications.

A quote from Sherry Lynn Smith's excellent *Reimaginng Indians* perhaps best sums up the Grinnell Indian legacy:

> *Grinnell, as much as any man of his generation, worked diligently to commit Indian memories to the page and thus preserve them. He attempted to accomplish this with minimal interference and embellishment from "outsiders," including himself. Trained as a scientist, not a moralist, Grinnell wanted to log Blackfeet's, Pawnees,' and Cheyennes' words, actions, practices, history, and religious beliefs as objectively, accurately, and faithfully as possible.*

> *Grinnell's writings helped lay the foundation for a fundamental reassessment of Indians and thus contributed to an evolving perception of them as people worthy of interest and respect. Grinnell's essential message was this: Plains Indians were human beings with histories of their own, full lives, and complete cultures. If no one could stem the inevitable tale of evolutionary change ushered in by conquest, at least readers should consider and appreciate what had been destroyed.*

At a point in history when public sentiment condemned them, Native Americans had no truer friend and ally than George Bird Grinnell—as a prolific author of their culture and traditions, a tireless promoter for their acceptance by society, and an effective activist for their rights.

CHAPTER TEN:
THE HARRIMAN EXPEDITION

Look deep into nature, and then you will understand everything better.
—ALBERT EINSTEIN

AS THE TURN OF THE CENTURY APPROACHED, AMERICA WAS undergoing an era of spectacular growth with significant advances in mining, manufacturing, shipping, and fishing. The transcontinental railroad, the Brooklyn Bridge, the telephone, and westward expansion had led the way to a better life. And in New York City, construction was everywhere, with the Tower building and the Flatiron building going up, and workers busily building the city's first subway. Around the world, incredible accomplishments, such as the Suez Canal, the Panama Canal, and the Eiffel Tower were being undertaken in this time of Industrial Revolution.

One place that had captured the fancy of the American public, especially the well-to-do with money to burn, was Alaska, the new frontier. The ocean cruise lines were quick to recognize this infatuation and organized tours for hunters, fisherman, and casual sightseers. Big-game animal trophies adorned studies, libraries, and boardrooms. Those hunters who had not yet bagged their Alaskan trophy endured the boorish conversations at elegant dinner parties of their peers who had been successful. Businessmen debated the worth of the rumored resources in this vast land, and companies were formed to take advantage of those investors who wanted to speculate on future riches. No one had expected such excitement about this frozen land when it was purchased just after America's Civil War.

In 1867, this Russian territory had been bought by the United States for $7,two-hundred,000, or two cents an acre. The purchase came under immediate scrutiny and ridicule and was nicknamed "Seward's Icebox" and "Seward's Folly" in honor of Secretary of State William Seward who had negotiated the deal. The secret purchase may have sounded foolish at first, but not only was the territory rich in fish and fur but, from a national security perspective, the United States had rid itself of one more monarch from the continent.

The sparse population, which included many Native Alaskans, numbered about 63,000. These Indigenous People struggled to maintain their traditional cultures against the negative influences and often ruthless treatment from first Russia and then the United States. The discovery of gold along Canada's Klondike River in 1896 drew over one hundred,000 prospectors to north-western Alaska, especially after gold was also found near Nome. This mad rush to prospect would change Alaskan culture forever—and not for the betterment of its Natives. The prospect of quick riches had a way of transforming a society with every vice imaginable, and those permanent residents usually became victims of the transients.

Just reaching the gold fields was an immense challenge for the gold seekers. The Canadian government required that each prospector bring along a year's supply of food to prevent starvation. They would then follow either the Chilkoot or White Pass trail, both of which were physically demanding due to the mountainous terrain and the bitter cold, to the Yukon River where they would sail to the Klondike. By the time they arrived, many of them found that the best claims, those that yielded any color at all, were already being worked. Most returned home broke and disappointed, their dreams shattered, but others remained and established boom towns, such as Dawson City, to accommodate the miners' needs and wants. Stories of tragedy and triumph in the gold-fields, with appropriate embellishment, made their way around the continental United States, which added to the allure of this forbidding wilderness.

For every man who made a fortune during those gold rushes of 1897 and 1898, however, there were hundreds, perhaps thousands, who departed the territory penniless. But Alaska remained a place of mystery, and of romance, and it had captured the fascination of America—and the interest of a man named Edward H. Harriman.

By the summer of 1899, American business tycoon Edward Harriman was not only bored with his daily routine but was suffering from extreme exhaustion. His doctor advised him to take some time off from work and go on a vacation or risk seriously damaging his health. Harriman had been working steadily ever since he had left school at fourteen years old to become an errand boy on Wall Street.

Harriman had entered the world on February 20, 1848, the second son born to an Episcopal clergyman named Orlando Harriman, Sr. Edward had quit school at that young age and joined his uncle in a Wall Street investment firm. He was an ambitious and talented young man, and by the age of twenty-two he was a member of the New York Stock Exchange. In 1878, he had married Mary Williamson Averill, who would bear him six children; sadly, one would die at five years of age.

Before long, Harriman had set his sights on the railroad industry, perhaps because his father-in-law was president of the Ogdensburg and Lake Champlain Railroad Company. Harriman found his niche in that industry by purchasing bankrupt railroads—beginning with the Lake Ontario Southern Railroad—and rebuilding them to profitability. His talent at reestablishing these lines had made him a millionaire many times over.

Incidentally, Edward Harriman, as president of the Union Pacific Railroad, was remembered in railroad history well enough to be mentioned in the legendary 1969 movie *Butch Cassidy and the Sundance Kid* starring Paul Newman and Robert Redford as the railroad baron who had hired professional hunters to track down those two famous train robbers. He was also a villain that same year in the movie *The Wild Bunch*.

Over the ensuing years, Harriman had become a highly successful investor as well as a railroad mogul. Despite his wealth, however, he was considered unacceptable by the Wall Street elite due to his being an uneducated outsider and lacking the proper social graces of the aristocratic class. He had not, after all, graduated from an elite college or even attended high school. Therefore, he was always seeking ways to represent himself to the public that would enhance his social standing.

He decided in 1899 that he would follow his doctor's orders and take a family vacation and go hunting in Alaska. But Edward Harriman was not one to do anything on a small scale, and the chip on his shoulder provoked him to seek a way to publicize his trip and gain recognition. He had always been able to outsmart or outmaneuver his rivals regardless of his lack of schooling. In this instance, he would perhaps surprise himself at the brilliance of the idea that he arrived upon.

Harriman, with advice from C. Hart Merriam, Chief of the Bureau of Biological Survey, would organize and finance a scientific expedition like no other with the mission of exploring along the Alaskan coast. Twenty-five of the finest scientists in the fields of geology, botany, ornithology, and ethnology would be assembled for a two-month steamship cruise for the purpose of investigating and documenting the country's newest frontier. This proposed expedition would be the largest of its kind in history. Its progress and accomplishments would surely be splashed across the front pages of newspapers worldwide. It was a dream venture for a man hungry for acceptance by the business community and the public at large.

Harriman wrote: "Our Comfort and safety required a large vessel and crew, and preparations for the voyage were consequently on a scale disproportionate to the size of the party. We decided, therefore to include some guests who, while adding to the interest and pleasure of the expedition, would gather useful information and distribute it for the benefit of others."

Members of the invited party were carefully selected, and comprised a cast of distinguished professors, learned scholars, and noted government scientists. Invitations were sent out to renowned naturalists John Muir and Yale's William Brewer; popular nature writer John Burroughs; botanist Frederick Coville, known for his exploration of Death Valley; C. Hart Merriam, perhaps the foremost scientist of his time; former chief US forester Bernhard Fernow; hawks and owls expert A. K. Fisher; Robert Ridgeway, the first curator of birds at the National Museum; zoologist Daniel Elliot; topographical map pioneer Henry Gannett; geologist G. K. Gilbert; landscape painter Robert Swain Gifford; and others who had distinguished themselves in their fields of study.

By this point in time, Scotsman John Muir, who had come to America with his family at age eleven, was a veteran of wilderness study. He had spent many years living and working alone—once as a shepherd—in the Yosemite area and other remote locations. Muir had investigated glaciers, and plant-life, and the ecology of groves of Giant Sequoias. He had become an expert on numerous conservation topics and was respected by the scientific community for his vast knowledge. In 1892 he had co-founded the Sierra Club and served as its president, with the intention of pushing a bill through Congress that would create Yosemite National Park. He was concerned about the preservation and protection of this wilderness area that was being discovered and abused by the public. Clear-cutting by timber companies was becoming more and more prevalent in forests across the country, and Yosemite was no exception. This campaign to save Yosemite would take fourteen years to be successful. Muir was a voracious writer, whose work about nature's spiritual and transcendental qualities appeared regularly in such magazines as *Outlook*, *Harper's Weekly*, *World's Work*, *Atlantic Monthly*, and *Century*. He had visited Alaska on four previous occasions when he accepted Harriman's offer to accompany this expedition.

Naturalist John Burroughs was less scientific than his contemporary John Muir. He had a writing style that projected his own opinions and perceptions about the nature of wild things, rather than simply facts, which had become quite popular with the public. He wrote about flora and fauna but also delved into religion and philosophy and was published by the leading magazines of the day. Burroughs was living a romantic life on a farm in West Park, New York, where he entertained visitors and students from nearby Vassar College, grew celery, and wrote his essays in an Adirondack-style cabin he called "slabsides," when Harriman summoned him join the floating university to Alaska.

George Bird Grinnell had been aware of this mad rush to hunt, fish, and explore the wilds of Alaska for some time. The pages of *Forest and Stream* had dutifully recorded hunts that had taken place and offered tips for those who were preparing their trips seeking brown bears, grizzly bears, moose, or just wanting an adventure in the wilderness. Grinnell, however, had not as yet taken steps to visit on his own. That was about to change. One of those invitations sent to the foremost scientists of the day by Edward Harriman was addressed to Grinnell. He would now have the opportunity to explore Alaska in a scientific role.

He had been chosen for this prestigious sea-going laboratory not as a paleontologist or a naturalist but primarily for his expertise in Native American cultures. His formal assignment was to report whatever he observed about Alaska's Native people and on the status of the fisheries. There were plenty of capable paleontologists and naturalists available, but few white people alive, if any, had the knowledge and experience that Grinnell had accumulated in his many years of visiting Native American tribes in the West. His writings about the various facets of these people had fascinated the public, and his techniques in gathering information went a long way in gaining credibility for the science of anthropology.

Anthropology was beginning to emerge as an accepted and important discipline, having been long regarded as a minor aspect of science. Grinnell was anxious to help push anthropology to the forefront as well as being able to learn for himself the secrets held by the Natives in the north. Plainly, he loved being in the company of Native peoples. He gladly accepted this assignment from Edward Harriman.

He soon realized that he would be handicapped in being able to study the primary components of anthropology due to the ship staying for only brief periods of time at villages. He would not be able to live with his subjects or consult at length with their spokesmen, as he had with western tribes, a disadvantage that would affect most of the scientists on the expedition. There would be brief camping trips, but many reports would be reduced to mere travel logs rather than in-depth studies. On the positive side, the scientists would be provided far more opportunity to experience, observe, and study than those passengers traveling on commercial steamships.

Grinnell prepared for his role by researching as much as possible about his subject. He chose to rely in part on the writings of Franz Boaz, who has been referred to as "The Father of Anthropology." Boaz had published "The Native Peoples of the Alaska Coast Region," pertaining to the Indigenous Peoples of British Columbia, which Grinnell would use as a model and guide for his own study. Grinnell would concentrate on what he called the "ancient customs and beliefs," in order to study how these cultures had existed before the influence of nonnative people. He planned to provide detailed accounts of hunting and fishing techniques, as well as the material culture, such as canoe-building, and also delve into daily routine and ceremonies.

George Grinnell arranged with Harriman for a photographer named Edward Curtis to serve as expedition photographer. In 1898, while hiking on Washington's Mount Rainier, Grinnell and his party had become lost. They were eventually "rescued" by a fellow hiker, a photographer named Edward S. Curtis. This chance encounter would prove quite beneficial to young Mr. Curtis.

Grinnell was impressed by Curtis's photographic talent and sincere interest in Native American culture. He arranged for Curtis to accompany him to a Blackfeet reservation, where the young man learned a great deal about that tribe, even witnessing a sacred Sun Dance ceremony. By the end of his visit, and encouraged by Grinnell, Curtis was determined to begin a most ambitious project. This project would last twenty-five years and would produce the classic photographic work *The North American Indian*. But first, it was time for the two men to explore Alaska on this historic mission.

Host Edward Harriman, of course, was not blind to the commercial ventures that Alaska could provide for him in a wilderness said to be teeming with oil, copper, gold, and animal furs, not to mention an ocean abundant with fish. One of his more grandiose ideas—albeit fantastic—was to build a railroad line from Alaska to Siberia that would connect the world with tracks. He also desperately wanted to shoot a massive brown bear and be part of that trophy conversation at dinner parties. This expedition that would showcase all those respected scientists would be his ticket to credibility with those who had looked down their noses at him for so long.

Harriman was not entirely selfish in his motives for organizing what could be called a floating liberal arts conference, however. He hoped that the professionals that he invited would make ground-breaking discoveries and contribute to their own particular cultural discipline. And he wanted his family and the other passengers to gain an education from this captive assemblage of the finest minds in science. To that end, he requested that the members of the party take turns presenting their findings each evening along the way with lectures in the ship's auditorium. The trip would be casual and pleasant for the little scientific community, but they were expected to remain focused on their scholarly endeavors. Harriman also added three artists and two photographers to record their creative and spiritual experiences as a balance to the scientific findings.

The ship that would carry the elite scientific party to Alaska was the *SS George W. Elder*. This ship had been launched as an East Coast passenger/cargo ship in 1874 after being built in Chester, Pennsylvania, and assigned to the New York City to Chesapeake Bay route. Two years later, the *Elder* had moved to the West Coast via Cape Horn and placed in the San Francisco to Portland, Oregon route. She was not considered a large ship by any means, measuring only 250 feet long, with a beam of 38 feet, and was equipped with a brigantine-sail configuration and a triple-expansion steam engine rated between 900 hp and 1,000 hp. The *George W. Elder* would be captained by Peter A. Doran for the proposed 9,000-mile Harriman Expedition.

The cabins and salons of the ship had been remodeled, and the decor on board could not be called anything less than luxurious, comparable to a plush New York City hotel. A noted chef had been hired, and with his crew would prepare gourmet meals each day for the guests. The finest cigars and beverages that money could buy had been stocked. Adequate space for the scientists to work on spec-imen preservation and a laboratory for research had been provided. There was even a research library with over five-hundred books pertaining to every known aspect of Alaska. Harriman also arranged for a chaplain to be on board, as well professional hunters, guides, packers, and taxidermists who would assist him in his sacred quest to shoot a bear. His own family and his servants rounded out the total number of people aboard at 126. The passengers on the expedition ship were comprised of some the most famous and influential people in America at that time.

By the end of May, the guests, passengers, and crew had arrived in Seattle, with much fanfare provided by the press and public. John Muir wrote to his wife: "We sail from here in about two hours, and I have just time to say another good-bye. The ship is furnished in fine style, and I find that we are going just where I want to go. Yakutat, Prince William Sound, Cooke Inlet, et cetera. I am on the executive committee and of course have something to say as to routes, time to be spent at each point, et cetera. The company is very harmonious for scientists."

Shortly before 6:00 p. m. on May 31, 1899, 126 passengers and crew of the good ship *George W. Elder* sailed away from the port of Seattle as an enthusiastic crowd cheered. Newspapers all over the world featured the story on their front pages. Harriman had achieved what he had dreamed about—thus far—and basked in the glory of this trailblazing expedition. It was no easy task to put together an operation of this magnitude, but Harriman had succeeded, and the world had taken notice. They were off to explore and seek adventure in Alaska—the most romantic and mysterious place on earth at that point in time.

The ship's first stop was on Vancouver Island for a visit to the Victoria Museum. This museum, established in 1866, was an answer to European and American museums that had been appropriating irreplaceable artifacts from British Columbia, and would tell the story of the local people and their culture. And then it was on to Lowe Inlet, where the *Elder* docked, and the scientists briefly went ashore to study and document the local wildlife. They enthusiastically dove into their tasks, but the stay was short and soon the ship was on its way again.

On Sunday morning, June 4, the ship docked at New Metlakatla on Annette Island in southeast Alaska. George Grinnell was perhaps disappointed to discover that the Tsimshian Indians who lived there were under the stern control of an English-born Anglican missionary named William Duncan, who had made his charges abandon their customs and culture in favor of "the white man's way." Duncan served as a religious leader, political head, and judge, and had created this model village as an experiment.

Sixty-eight-year-old William Duncan had entered the world as an illegitimate child, born in Yorkshire, England to a teenage servant named Maria Duncan. He was raised by his mother's parents and worked as a bookkeeper and a tanner before finding religion. He was the only member of his family to attend church, which led him to the Church Missionary Society College in Islington. He was sent as a missionary by the Anglican Church to remote areas of Canada where he worked to convert the Natives to Christianity.

Duncan successfully created a strict Anglican community of Tsimshians that he called Metlakatla, at one point surviving a smallpox outbreak that killed five hundred tribal members. He was careful to avoid mentioning communion for fear that this sacrament might temp the cannibalistic tendencies of his congregation. Duncan's rules and total control over the people eventually resulted in his expulsion from the Anglican Church. Duncan decided that he could no longer remain in a place where the church had authority over him.

In 1887 he had traveled by canoe with about eight hundred Tsimshians to Alaska to set up a second community named New Metlakatla. His bitterness toward the Anglicans was demonstrated when he dispatched Natives to destroy the original community back in Canada so it would not fall into the hands of his religious enemies. This new Alaskan settlement quickly became economically and self-sufficiently a success and boasted enterprises such as a cannery and sawmill. This town, the vision of one determined man, that could be called a utopian oasis carved from the wilderness, welcomed the passengers of the *Elder* when it arrived.

George Grinnell wrote about this European-style settlement created by William Duncan:

The town is laid out with straight, broad streets, and wide broad sidewalks. Each house and its garden is surrounded by a fence; the people wear civilized clothing, work at fishing, in the sawmill, or in the cannery for six days in the week, and rest on the seventh, attending church service in the edifice which they erected with their own

*hands, and which is a piece of architecture which would be called
beautiful in any land. Except for their color, and for the peculiar
gait, which seems common to all these fishing Indians, these people
and their wives and children could hardly be told from any civilized
community of a thousand souls anywhere in the country. It took
many years for Mr. Duncan to change these Indians from the wild
men that they were when he first met them, to the respectable and
civilized people that they now are.*

William Duncan graciously invited the expedition members
into his home and then took them on a tour of the public buildings, entertained them with stories about the Tsimpsian, and later
preached a sermon in the church to a large congregation of the
tribe. Grinnell recalled that "some of the dwellings are two stories
and a half in height, comfortable in appearance, and neatly kept,"
and as he strolled through the village it "was like an old-fashioned
New England hamlet in its peaceful quiet." And with respect to the
sermon: "It would be hard to imagine a more decorous and atten-
tive audience; obviously their thoughts were fixed on the discourse
to which they were listening, and neither man, woman, nor child
turned eyes toward the company of strange white people which
crowded in the church behind them."

While studying the congregation, Charles Keeler, an author,
ornithologist, and adventurer who had sailed around Cape Horn
and explored the South Seas, was struck with the realization that in
a matter of only thirty years they had gone from "wild cannibals" to
"ladies and Gentlemen." John Burroughs believed that these people
"took more kindly to our ways and customs and to our various man-
ual industries" than those Indians he had observed in the States and
Territories. Harriman was duly impressed with these people, and,
always the capitalist, mentioned that if they could speak English
"they could be largely used in the development of the territory."

The expedition departed New Metlakatla and moved on to Sitka,
the capital of Alaska, where they were received by Governor John
Green Brady. No doubt Brady related to George Grinnell the story
of his youth, when he had run away from home to save himself
from an abusive, drunken father. He had been found there on the

streets of New York City by Theodore Roosevelt, Sr., the father of the future twenty-sixth president and Grinnell's friend. The elder Roosevelt had arranged for the "orphaned" Brady to be sent to a western family by paying for his transportation and other necessary expenses. He lived in Indiana with a judge's family, and eventually attended Yale University. Governor John Brady had become a lawyer, minister, and co-founded a college for Alaska Natives—all because of the kindness of one wealthy man.

George Grinnell and his peers were introduced to Tlingit leaders, as well as Americans who could be useful in directing them to subjects for study. Grinnell made the acquaintance of Navy Lieutenant George Thornton Emmons, who was an expert in Tlingit culture. Emmons was part of the unit that was responsible for the stability of the region and over the years had become fascinated with the local Natives. He had studied them for nearly twenty years, and understood their traditions, such as weaving, their hunting techniques, their feasts and feuds, and had even mastered their language. Emmons treated those scientists who were interested to a tour of ceremonial artworks that were not generally displayed to outsiders.

Grinnell wrote: "Here we had an opportunity not only to see something of the Indians and of how they lived in their old-time way, but also to examine the Sheldon Jackson Museum, and in some of the stores, a great deal of material in the way of primitive implements which are now practically discarded." Those items included elaborate dancing masks, shaman's hats, and Chilkat blankets. Edward Harriman had brought a graphophonic recording machine and was able to record a song sung by native Tlingits.

Grinnell was not able in his time with Emmons to gather an intimate profile of these Natives—their economic and political issues or how they were now educated. He recorded nothing more than second-hand accounts related by Emmons, which severely limited his ability to utilize his talents at ethnography, those customs that set Native people apart from others.

Grinnell desired to witness Natives in the field. He wanted to write about what he personally observed rather than another person's perspective. With that in mind, he traveled to Yakutat Bay where three camps of Natives living in temporary canvas tents or bark-covered shelters were engaged in hair seal fishing. An estimated three to four hundred people were there looking for seals.

Grinnell observed:

The seals are hunted in small canoes, usually occupied by two persons. The two seal hunters in the canoe may be two men, or a man and his wife, or a man and boy. The hunter sits in the bow and his companion in the stern. To the right of the bowman, and so of course immediately under his hand, are his arms, usually a Winchester rifle, or double-barrel shotgun, and a seal spear ten or twelve feet in length. When the seal is about due at the surface the paddlers stop and look for him, the hunter holding his gun in readiness to shoot. If the seal appears in range a shot is fired, and if the animal is wounded both men paddle to him as fast as possible, and the hunter tries to spear him, either by throwing or thrusting the spear.

Grinnell estimated that this hunt had produced perhaps as many as a thousand seals combined from the three camps.

Inside the shelters, Grinnell noted poles from which had been hung delicacies of various sorts from the hair seal. "There are flippers, sides of ribs, strips of blubber and braided seal intestines. All these things are eaten; and, in fact, during this fishing the Indians must subsist chiefly on the flesh of the seal. The flippers appear to be regarded as especially choice. We saw many women roasting them over the fire." Grinnell also offered detailed instructions about the process of butchering the seal, which was a task handled by the women of the tribe.

"The Indians," he noted, "kill the seals not for the flesh, although this is eaten, nor for the hides, though these are used, but for the oil, which is a necessity to them. They drink it; preserve berries in it; and use it for cooking, so that it really forms a considerable and important part of their food."

Grinnell admitted that the Tlingit, "are now greatly changed from what they were when the Russians first came to Alaska," and that "until the white man came and changed all their life, they lived well." Still, he wrote down everything he could learn about the tribe. At Cape Fox village, which was deserted by the people at the time, he described their totem poles, architecture, burial grounds, and artwork and crafts that he found in the houses before the *Elder* sailed away from that fascinating place.

It should be added that, although Grinnell failed to mention it, the village at Cape Fox was not left undisturbed. Edward Harriman ordered his crewmen to remove several totem poles and grave monuments, which were later donated to various scientific institutions in the United States, including the Peabody Museum. Pieces of artwork were also taken from homes; Harriman justifying his actions in the name of science. It should be noted that the villagers had moved away when the plundering took place, but the artifacts that remained behind had been left there to honor ancestors.

Not everyone aboard the ship was pleased with the display of seal hunting and did not approach it as a topic for study as did Grinnell, rather as a reason for revulsion. Ornithologist Charles Keeler called this hunt "one of the filthiest, bloodiest places" he had ever witnessed and quickly walked away. John Muir refused to go near the site of the killing but was nonetheless haunted by the hunted seals that were "barking or half-howling in a strange, earnest voice." He interpreted the sounds as the seals mourning their dead. Edward Curtis, although sickened by the odor of rotting seals, approached the women who were cutting up the animals and snapped some photographs. These Natives were reluctant to pose, but he was able to cajole them into allowing him to take their photos, a talent that would serve him well in his future visits to Indian villages.

At the same time, Edward Harriman was negotiating for a souvenir pelt from the nearly extinct sea otter. He bought the thickest pelt displayed, rumored to have cost five hundred dollars. Grinnell noted that the Natives at Juneau were already taking advantage of the tourist trade when he observed Tlingit women "sitting on the wharves offering their baskets and other simple articles made for trade."

During the course of their studies, these scientific explorers were able to catalog the plentiful animals, plants, and marine life, and mapped out geological and glacial formations. In addition, they also viewed the results of the Klondike Gold Rush, finding both positive and negative aspects. This was one instance when Grinnell recorded his own opinions rather than his usual factual observations. He described the relationship between the gold miners heading for Nome and the Eskimos at Port Clarence:

White men, uncontrolled and uncontrollable, already swarm over the Alaska coast, and are overwhelming the Eskimo. They have taken away their women, and debauched their men with liquor; they have brought them strange new diseases that they never knew before, and in a very short time they will ruin and disperse the wholesome, hearty, merry people whom we saw at Port Clarence and Plover Bay. Perhaps for a while a few may save themselves by retreating to the Arctic to escape the contaminating touch of the civilized, and thus the extinction of the Alaska Eskimo may be postponed. But there is an inevitable conflict between civilization and savagery, and wherever the two touch each other, the weaker people must be destroyed.

Grinnell could have just as well have been writing about the Plains tribes that he had visited across the West.

There were, as might be expected, monotonous days with only the sea for sightseeing. The scientists made the best of these days by working on their various research projects. There was scenery lining the shores along the way, of course, such as spectacular glaciers, many of which were explored by the scientists and there were also those isolated out-of-the-way Indian villages. Edward Harriman wanted to experience everything he could and would upon occasion row ashore with members of his family or a group of scientists. On some days Harriman relaxed and spent time enjoying his children by playing games with them on board. In the evenings, guests would assemble in the auditorium and listen to fascinating lectures of thrilling discoveries that was almost a daily occurrence. The scientists relished the opportunity to reveal their findings and gauge the response of the audience to prepare themselves for their trip-ending essays or for further lectures after the expedition. Many of them would return to their classroom to influence the way future generations would view this frozen land.

During this voyage, George Grinnell and John Muir could be found together quite often, each one said to have had an appreciation for the other's company. Although they were friends, it is anyone's guess how the spirited conversations between these two men had remained entirely civil. Muir was an advocate, a zealot, for leaving wilderness areas pristine and not permitting use of any kind in them—much like Edward Abbey after him. Grinnell, on the other hand, firmly believed that laws and regulations should be placed to protect and preserve these wild lands, but that they should be used for purposes beneficial to the greater public. Neither man would be able to convince the other that his opinion was the right one, but they debated this subject, each one learning from the other and in the end respecting the other man's position.

No doubt other scientists debated their positions with their scholarly peers in an informal atmosphere, but there were no reported rivalries that would warrant anyone being confined to the brig. Perhaps a lesson can be learned from these scholarly men with opposing opinions working to find middle ground without hurling expletives and threats and insults at each other.

Another example of the civility displayed between men with contrary beliefs can be found in a most unexpected relationship that occurred on board. John Muir had decided to go on this expedition although he had a prior personal distaste for Edward Harriman, particularly because he believed that hunting was a barbaric practice. As time went on, however, Muir had a change of heart and came to like and respect Harriman. In fact, Harriman and Muir became life-long friends on the voyage, and the wealthy man was instrumental in helping Muir win protection for the Yosemite Valley in 1905. Muir would give the eulogy four years after that at Harriman's funeral.

Harriman's ability to charm a man with Muir's unshakable contradictory values and principals speaks volumes for the reason he had been successful in business despite his lack of formal education. He had an innate intelligence, a street smarts, likely blessed with a primitive glibness that could charm the scales off a lizard's back if it was to his advantage. That is not to imply that Harriman was disingenuous, only that he was adept at every aspect of personal relationships. And, as the expedition itself shows, he did have a passion for scholarship, and likely could hold his own with any of his invitees.

Harriman's conversations with John Muir had not lessened his zeal to go bear hunting and kill a trophy for his wall that he could admire for years to come. He directed that the *Elder* head toward Kodiak Island, where the population of bears was said to be plentiful. It was there on Kodiak Island that Edward Harriman bagged his bear, a mother and cub. He had now obtained the trophy that gave him bragging rights in social circles when he returned to New York.

John Muir caustically wrote that Harriman had killed a "mother and child." Muir was no stranger to bears, having had one interesting encounter with a bear in the Sierras some years earlier. Muir and the bear had come upon each other unexpectedly, and rather than either of them running away they had engaged in a staring contest. The naturalist hoped that his "human stare would finally overcome the beastly one." Fortunately, on that day Muir prevailed. The bear sauntered away. Muir was pleased and professed that the inhabitants of the world are as one.

It was beyond Annette Island where the expedition encountered salmon fishing and the canneries. George Grinnell was dismayed at how the industry was mere exploitation of wildlife and humans alike. In his essay, he summarized the existence of the salmon as it went through its life cycle. Then, he explained the process used to capture and can the fish. "When the fish have at last congregated at the mouths of the rivers, the work of the canners begins. When the salmon are visible the seine, from three to five hundred fathoms long, is swept through the water, and the captured fish are loaded on to the steam tug, which then takes them to the cannery. The fishermen who manage the small boats and sweep the nets are either Indians or Aleuts. The crews of the tugs are usually white men, while the workmen on the wharf and in the cannery proper are all Chinamen, except for an occasional foreman or skilled mechanic."

Thusly, Grinnell described the fishing and cannery operations in detail, as he had observed it. Just as he had with the exploited Natives, he could not hold back his opinions of this industry and its effects on the people. He noted that:

Not only are salmon taken by the steamer load, but in addition millions of other good fish are captured, killed, and thrown away. At times also, it happens that far greater numbers of salmon are caught than can be used before they spoil. Competition is so very sharp between the great canning companies, as well as between the smaller individual concerns which run the canneries, that each manager is eagerly desirous to put up more fish than his neighbor. All these people recognize very well that they are destroying the fishing; and that before very long a time must come when there will be no more salmon to be canned at a profit.

The canners work in a most wasteful and thoughtlessly selfish way, grasping for everything that is within their reach and thinking nothing of the future. Their motto seems to be, "If I do not take all I can get somebody else will get something." The canners reply, "Yes, we know you are quite right; it is wrong. We do not wish to do what we are doing, but so long as others act in this way we must continue to do so for our own protection. Speak to our rivals about this. We will stop if they will.

Congress had already passed laws meant to protect Alaska's salmon industry, but they were almost impossible to enforce in remote Alaska. These laws provided for the Natives to take as many fish as they wanted and were not subject to the same laws as the canneries. Grinnell also pointed out that the industry was exploiting Natives because the salmon streams were owned by local families who caught the fish for their own daily subsistence, but these people would also sell all the fish they could catch to the canneries.

Grinnell made the case for the development of this natural resource at a slower pace than the hurried harvesting of the greedy companies. The debate has continued to this day and has been the source of conflict with the rich resources that Alaska has available for the taking.

John Muir was dismayed when he observed the men brought up there from San Francisco and were working for poor wages. "Men in this business are themselves canned," he wrote.

They passed a cannery at Orca, where they had dumped rotting fish into the water, causing the surface to shine with an oily sheen for miles along the coast. Two members of the expedition refused to participate in anything related to this industry. Artist and explorer Frederick Dellenbaugh turned his back on the disgusting canneries and sketched the mountains instead. Edward Curtis regarded the view from high up on the mountain preferable to the carnage below.

It is interesting to note that the diverse group aboard the *Elder* arrived at different conclusions about the salmon industry. There were those, like George Grinnell, who believed that the practices of the canneries that thrived on Native labor were akin to slavery, while others viewed these operations as smooth-running, admirable businesses doing the best they could to maximize profitability. This view of quick profit as opposed to sensible preservation has often demonstrated the shortsightedness of business in not planning for the future. In the mind-set of industry, when a resource panned out, they simply moved on to another one rather than take steps along the way to preserve their bread and butter for decades to come.

The ship had visited Prince William Sound, and named a fjord in the northwest corner of that body of water "Harriman Fjord." They sailed to Popof Island and the Shumagin Islands, where several scientists set up a camp to study the region while the ship went on to Siberia. Harriman's wife wanted to say she had stepped foot in Siberia, so a small party landed at Plover Bay to fulfill her wish.

The expedition set up camp at Disenchantment Bay in late July. The offshore islands a half mile away posed a fascination for John Muir, who professed that he could smell the fragrance of the wildflowers from over there. John Burroughs disagreed and called the area "weird" due to all the birds and wildflowers found there along with the "savage" ice.

The nearby glaciers, however, quickly captured the attention of the scientists—and the wonderment of members of the passenger list. In a show of the congenial companionship between scientists and "civilians," while mapping the ice fields there, Henry Gannett and William Healey Dall offered a lesson in "Glacier 101" to sixteen-year-old Cornelia Harriman and her cousin Elizabeth Averill. The young girls, dressed in formal ankle-length Victorian dresses and fashionable shoes, happily danced on the slick surface while class was in session.

By this time, Harriman had fulfilled his primary objective by killing the two bears and was now anxious to return home and go back to work. He directed the ship to Popof Island where they picked up those scientists camped there and steamed for home. The *George W. Elder* docked in Seattle on July 30 after two months at sea.

By the end of the voyage, this groundbreaking expedition had yielded around six hundred as yet undiscovered species, including thirty eight new fossils. There were 344 insects out of over eight thousand found that had been previously unknown to scientists, thousands of shellfish, birds and small mammals, and a few large mammal specimens. The bounty of specimens was packed in over one hundred trunks and included more than five thousand photographs. Grove Karl Gilbert wrote a study of glaciers that broke new ground for future scientists. This natural history treasure trove, now at the Smithsonian Institution, retains great research value even today about Alaska's ecosystems of a century ago.

Edward Harriman and his wife financed the publication of the expedition's discoveries, first in a two-volume collector's set, and then thirteen volumes, which took over fifty specialists interpreting the work twelve years to complete beginning in 1901. John Burroughs was named the official scribe and wrote most of the first of the volumes; the rest, edited by C. Hart Merriam, highlighted the findings of all the scientists on board.

This series, which can be downloaded for free from the Smithsonian, is not casual reading, rather much of the text was written for other scientists and includes technical aspects and terminology. In addition, the custom back then was to write long-winded descriptions of the flora and fauna that would quickly glass over the eyes of today's reader. The essays do serve as a perfect example of how scientists thought and processed their findings at that time in history, however. These men worked as a team and shared information with each other to better solve scientific mysteries. All of the writers, however, wrote in one voice when raving about the breathtaking beauty and grandeur of the coastline along which they had sailed.

Entomologist Trevor Kincaid later wrote in his memoirs: "The expedition was a thoroughly deluxe affair without any regard to expense. The party included a number of interesting personalities.

Harriman himself, of course, was the center and dynamo of the expedition. He was reputed to be worth sixty million dollars, and was of the type that issues orders and expects them to be obeyed."

George Bird Grinnell had met Native people from the Aleut, Southern Eskimo, and Coastal Indian groups, but was disappointed that the encounters were "hasty and superficial," given that the *Elder* rarely spent more than a day in any port. Nevertheless, Grinnell employed the talent and technique honed from thirty years among the Plains tribes and created a valuable overview of Alaska Native life at the turn of the century.

His essay titled "The Natives of the Alaska Coast Region" appeared in the first of the thirteen volumes that cataloged the expedition's discoveries. After describing the people, villages, and customs, Grinnell concluded that the outlook and the future of the Alaskan Native population, unless protected from interference, would suffer a fate similar to that of the vanquished Plains tribes. He added another essay detailing Alaska's salmon industry from the point of view of a naturalist rather than that of a profiteer. His condemnation of this wasteful business that exploited both fish and people had a profound effect on the public, but changes in that far-away land were slow to come.

Upon his return from the expedition, Grinnell resumed his work at *Forest and Stream*, as well as going off on his annual summer excursions to hunt and study Native Americans in the West.

In the spring of 1902, he planned a visit to the Southern Cheyenne Reservation in Oklahoma to inspect grazing leases at Dakota Territory's Standing Rock Sioux Reservation at President Roosevelt's request. George extended an invitation to a young Boston widow by the name of Elizabeth Williams to accompany him and take photographs for his planned book about ordinary Cheyenne life. Elizabeth had been "attracted" to Grinnell since September 1892—at age fourteen—when she had read an article that he had written for *Scribner's Magazine* titled "The Last of the Buffalo," and she accepted his invitation.

Evidently the attraction was mutual and blossomed into love— on August 21, 1902, fifty-three-year-old George Bird Grinnell married twenty-four-year-old Elizabeth Curtis Williams in New York

City. Elizabeth would be his constant companion for the remainder of his life and would accompany him on his visits to the West and would supply photographs for his books. The couple would not have any children.

Now happily married, there was one issue that had nagged Grinnell for years and he could not get it out of his mind. In northwestern Montana, there was a breathtaking, pristine wilderness that was being threatened by commercialization, and he believed that it should be preserved for the enjoyment of public. With the odds stacked heavily against him, Grinnell set out on another mission, this time to establish a new national park.

CHAPTER ELEVEN:
GRINNELL'S GLACIER

After you have exhausted what there is in business, politics, conviviality, and so on—have found that none of these satisfy, or permanently wear— what remains? Nature remains.
—WALT WHITMAN

IN *1885* GEORGE GRINNELL HAD RECEIVED AN ARTICLE AT *Forest and Stream* that greatly intrigued him and fueled his imagination. "To the Chief Mountain," had been submitted by James Willard Schultz, a white man who lived with the Blackfeet or Piegan tribe—and had even joined them for raids on enemy tribes—in a wild, little-known region of northwestern Montana.

"To the Chief Mountain" was about hunting mountain goats and bighorn sheep and catching twelve-pound trout in sparkling blue lakes "walled-in by stupendous mountains, peak after peak of jagged mountains, some of them with shear cliffs thousands of feet high. Beyond the head of the lake is a long, wide, densely timbered valley, and on the upper left-hand side of this valley is a mountain, the top of which is a true glacier at least 300 feet thick."

The article fueled Grinnell's adventurous spirit, and he was anxious to see these fantastic sights for himself to ascertain if the author's description was factual or not. This was exactly the type of exploring that suited Grinnell best—new and wild country, different and intriguing wild animals, and a welcome escape from editing duties at the magazine.

In August, Grinnell boarded a Northern Pacific train destined for Helena, Montana, stopped for a week's stay at Yellowstone Park, and was a passenger on a mail wagon over one hundred miles of bumpy road the rest of the way to Fort Benton. He stepped from the stage carrying his bedroll and personal gear, a Sharps .45-caliber rifle, and his custom-made bamboo fly rod. He was met there by the article's writer, James Schultz, who would serve as guide to escort him to this remote walled-in lake country.

Schultz had been born into a wealthy family at Booneville, New York, in 1859, and learned how to find his way around the woods from the earliest age by accompanying hunters and explorers into the Adirondack Mountains. At eighteen, he had left home and eventually settled at Fort Conard, Montana, where he would eventually establish a trading post. In 1879, he had married into the nearby Piegan Blackfeet tribe, choosing a fifteen-year-old maiden named Natahki, or, Fine Shield Woman, and receiving the Piegan name Apikuni, translated meaning, "White Buffalo Robe." The couple had one son, Hart Merriam Schultz, or Lone Wolf, named after Schultz's boyhood friend, Clinton Hart Merriam, who had accompanied George Bird Grinnell on the Harriman Expedition when he was Chief of the Bureau of Biological Survey.

Grinnell had published several articles written by Schultz over the previous years, the first in 1880 titled "Hunting in Montana," but the one that had intrigued him most was this new one, "To the Chief Mountain." And now he had a chance to see for himself the area named Saint Mary Lakes that had been romanticized about by James Schultz in that article. Grinnell and Schultz would be joined on the trip to these lakes walled in by mountains by a half-white half-Blackfeet man named Charles Rose, who was an employee of the elite American Fur Company that had been founded by John Jacob Astor in 1808.

On September 1, the three men made their way into the mountains with a wagon laden with provisions, a ten-foot wall tent, an iron cook stove, and a fourteen-foot skiff. That first night out, Grinnell unpacked his fly rod and caught a dozen trout.

In the following days, the men hunted sheep above the tree line on a mountain where a "keen wind and drenching fog penetrated to one's very marrow." Grinnell would explain in *Forest and Stream*:

"The life of a sheep hunter is not one of luxurious ease. He must breast the steepest ascents, and must seek his game over ridges, along precipices and up peaks, and follow it to its home among the clouds…The man who kills a sheep usually earns it several times over before he gets the meat to camp."

Although the weather was cold and drizzly, this spectacular territory was everything that Grinnell had anticipated. The breathtaking beauty of the land, with its high mountains, active glaciers, rushing mountain streams, waterfalls, and abundant wildlife, was difficult for even a writer with the talent of Grinnell to adequately describe. He endured blinding snowstorms to explore and hunt, and even attempted to climb a huge glacier. Grinnell did manage to bring down a trophy bighorn ram with one shot, and James Schultz graciously named the mountain where it happened "Singleshot Mountain" in honor of Grinnell's success.

On their way back to the fort, Grinnell's party happened upon a group of about twenty-five Blackfeet warriors. These men were on the trail of 150–200 of their horses that had been stolen during the night by Crow raiders. Although the thieves had a twelve-hour head start, the Blackfeet trackers managed to catch up to them and regain their stolen horses, arriving in camp safely with the animals the following morning.

Grinnell was overwhelmed by the grandeur of the Saint Mary region, and wrote:

> An artist's palette, splashed with all the hues of his color box, would not have shown more varied contrasts. The rocks were of all shades, from pale gray, through green and pink, to dark red, purple and black, and against them stood out the pale foliage of the willows, the bright gold of the aspens and cottonwoods, the vivid red of the mountain maples and ash, and the black of the pines. In the valley were the greens of the deciduous shrubs, great patches of the deep maroon of the changing lobelia, lakes turbid or darkly blue, somber evergreens; on the mountainside foaming cascades, with their white whirling mist wreathes, gray blue ice masses, and fields of gleaming snow. Over all arched a leaden sky, whose shadows might dull, but could never efface, the bewildering beauty of this mass of color.

Perhaps the highlight of the trip for Grinnell was when his guide introduced him to the Piegan, or Blackfeet tribe, which inhabited the region. To his delight, he was welcomed into their camp with open arms. Tribal leaders, including Red Eagle who was Schultz's wife's elderly uncle, embraced this congenial man who wanted to know every detail of their history, traditions, and daily life. During this first visit, the Blackfeet made him an honorary member of the tribe, bestowing upon him the name Pinut-u-ye-is-tsim-o-k, or "Fisher Cap."

At Red Eagle's camp, Grinnell brought gifts of tea and tobacco, and was the honored guest at a Bear Pipe Dance, a ceremony meant to bring health and long life to those assembled there. After singing several songs and chanting, Red Eagle unveiled the sacred pipe by peeling away a dozen silk handkerchiefs of various brilliant colors. The old Blackfeet man smoked, and then handed the pipe to Schultz to smoke, and he in turn handed the pipe to Grinnell who smoked, and on around the circle, all the while there the sounds of men praying as they carried out this sacred ceremony.

Over the next several days, Grinnell soaked up as much of the Piegan-Blackfeet customs and culture as he could. He watched them work harvesting grain, and visited the graves of their beloved old ones, and learned about their daily life and the struggles of the preceding years. He loved to hear about the roots of the tribe, and when and where they had taken up residence over the years.

Researchers have found evidence of human presence in north-central Montana said to date as far back as five thousand years, and buffalo jumps—the high rock formations used to kill buffalo in large quantities by stampeding them over the edge—were there as early as AD 300. More recently, DNA of an infant's remains that was said to be over twelve thousand years old has been traced to existing Native American people. Those ancient Indians were likely the forerunners of this Blackfeet tribe whose recorded history can only be traced back to 1730, although contact with the white man was likely not to have occurred until late in that century when a trapper from the Hudson Bay Company happened upon an encampment in the province of Alberta, Canada.

In those early days, the Blackfeet, not to be confused with the

Blackfeet band of the Lakota Sioux, occupied a stretch of land from the Saskatchewan River in Canada to the Missouri River in Montana. They had originated in the Great Lakes region and moved westward when the more powerful Cree tribe pushed them out of the area. They were not a typical nomadic Plains tribe of hunter-gatherers who lived in teepees and hunted buffalo for their main subsistence. They did hunt buffalo, but they also grew some crops and camped in the same place for extended periods of time. They were a spiritual people, believing that a sacred force permeates all things and was represented symbolically by the sun whose light sustains all things. To the Blackfeet, the mountains of that area around them were regarded as the "Backbone of the World," Chief Mountain and Two Medicine in particular.

They had boasted an estimated population of up to twenty thousand in the early 1800s, but diseases brought west by white people—smallpox and measles in particular—would decimate their numbers until by the late 1800 they were down to about 5,000 people.

In January 1870 the Blackfeet had been victims of the Marias Massacre, one of the worst slaughters of Indians in our nation's history but also one of the least known. The US Army on patrol mistook a friendly group of Blackfeet led by Chief Heavy Runner for a hostile band under Mountain Chief. Most of the men had gone out hunting, and this peaceful village on the Marias River was unprotected as the cavalrymen surrounded it. An army scout named Joe Kipp then realized that this was the wrong camp. He protested to the officer in charge, Major Eugene Baker, but was silenced. Baker, whom Kipp claimed was drunk, placed the scout under arrest to stop him from warning the camp as the army prepared to attack.

When the first shot was fired, Chief Heavy Runner came forward waving a safe conduct paper. In that initial volley from the cavalrymen, the Chief was shot and killed, and by the time the command to cease fire was given, 173 lay dead—mostly women, children, and the elderly. Every dead Blackfeet man was thrown into the fire and burned. Another 140 members of the tribe were briefly captured but turned loose to face the brutal winter without horses, food, or proper clothing. These refuges made their way to Fort Benton, ninety miles away, but by then many of them had frozen to death or were quite ill. Meanwhile, Mountain Chief and his renegade band escaped into Canada.

General Philip Sheridan managed to prevent any official investigation into the massacre, although a few voices called for a thorough examination. Sheridan even went as far as to vouch for Major Baker's competence and sobriety, thereby avoiding an ugly political scandal for the US Army.

By the time of Grinnell's visit, the Blackfeet were trying to recover from years of hardship. War and meager food supplies had plagued them, and then in 1882, which became known as the year of starvation, their annual buffalo hunt failed to provide enough to feed them. Grinnell had noted earlier that wild game in the vicinity of the camps had been hunted out. This story of hardship was typical of the tribes Grinnell visited, owing to turmoil caused by neighboring enemy tribes and advances of what the white man called progress.

George Grinnell returned to New York and chronicled his adventure in Montana on the pages of *Forest and Stream* in a series of fifteen weekly articles. In his heart he knew that this trip would be the first of many. His summers from now on when possible would include visits to Blackfeet country to learn everything he could about them, as well as the captivating Saint Mary Lake region. He would not neglect trips to the camps of other tribes, especially the Cheyenne, but the Piegan, partially due to their proximity to the spectacular glaciers, would always be high on his list.

He also understood that publicity from his articles in the magazine about the glacier and its surroundings could invite commercialization. With that in mind, he persuaded the Forestry Commission to include this Montana region in a new forest reserve in order to curtail attempts at logging and other commercial intrusions.

Grinnell did not return to Montana in 1886, but instead traveled to Yellowstone, and then spent time at his Shirley Basin ranch. He had as guests at the ranch his friends Lute North and George Gould, a banker from California whose brother had been a classmate of Grinnell's at Yale. The men lounged around the ranch, and went hunting, having limited success—"an elk or two, a few deer, and a few antelope all that I killed," Grinnell noted.

The next year, with George Gould accompanying him, Grinnell once again traveled to this mysterious Saint Mary glacier region of Montana. With James Schultz, Apikuni, serving as his guide, the three men set off on October 1 on a week-long journey to lower Saint Mary Lake. Grinnell decided another man was needed for hunting and visited a whiskey trader's camp at Pike Lake to hire a man named J. B. "Jack" Monroe. The hunt was successful right from the start when Grinnell managed to shoot a mountain goat that had stood still for too long on a narrow shelf.

The hunting trip was halted for three days when a blizzard roared in and it was not only cold but visibility was poor. Gould decided to leave for home, and Monroe accompanied him out. Grinnell and Schultz resumed hunting but did more sightseeing than shooting. They came upon an army detachment led by Lieutenant John H. Beacom. The lieutenant put in for a furlough and returned to their camp after being invited to join the hunt. Grinnell had been taking photographs of a huge glacier from afar but wanted to study it.

The next day, Jack Monroe returned, and the four men traveled along a stream above a lake that had been named by Schultz after George Grinnell, now Lake Josephine, and arrived on the shoreline of a glacial lake just below the majestic glacier that Grinnell had seen from a distance. After an arduous climb, they arrived at the edge of the glacier, which lay in a basin two miles wide and three miles long.

The men decided to climb this icy monster that occupied three thousand feet of that mountainside. After about three hours of strenuous hiking, moving past "a seemingly bottomless abyss, where the ice had melted next to rock," they reached fresh, soft snow that helped with their footing. They had stopped to eat a lunch of bread and cheese when Schultz spotted a bighorn sheep about two hundred yards away. Grinnell readied his rifle and fired, and the ram dropped dead.

The weather turned overcast and threatening, so they made their way back down the mountainside, carrying the fresh meat. When finally they reached their camp at Lower Saint Mary Lake—after passing what was now called Grinnell Mountain—Lieutenant Beacom bid them farewell.

Before he departed, however, Grinnell handed the army officer a rough but detailed map of the area. Grinnell had undertaken the task of mapping the places they had visited, naming peaks and landmarks for his friends and business associates. This map was later borrowed by the US Geological Survey, which retained most of those original names. The huge glacier that stands as the centerpiece of the region was named by Beacom "Grinnell's Glacier" in Grinnell's honor and remains so to this day.

The men had spent ten days braving the stormy weather, falling snow, and treacherous terrain. Grinnell decided that he would like to visit Victoria, British Columbia, while he was in the vicinity. Once there, he was surprised to learn that he was being given credit for discovering the first glacier in the United States. Beacom had evidently trumpeted the news of their climb up the glacier, and no one had heard of such a feat, although it was said that geologist and mountaineer Clarence King had been to that glacier a decade earlier.

Grinnell wrote to George Gould about this pioneering effort of mapping the area: "Gould's Mountain and Grinnell's Basin will probably appear on maps of the St. Mary's region, which is to be made by a young army officer who was with us for a day or two about the Lakes. He went up Swift Current with us and from afar saw the glories of my glacier, and after my return I saw him again and made a diagram of the country. The reason I possess a basin and a glacier is because this young man insisted in naming both after me."

Grinnell returned to "his" glacier the next year, 1888, in the company of James Schultz, Jack Monroe, and his friend from the Plains, army scout Lute North. Grinnell had his rifle, but also carried scientific tools that would measure altitudes and bearings on mountaintops in an effort to improve on the crude map that he had given to Lieutenant Beacom. Gould and North both killed a mountain goat, but Grinnell was more interested in studying the glacier. He was dismayed to discover that "his" glacier was melting and decreasing in size.

The party moved on to Saint Mary Lake where Grinnell and North both shot a sheep on "Singleshot Mountain." While traversing the mountainside, Grinnell slipped and wrenched his back, an injury that would plague him from then on. Regardless, he climbed a mountain that he measured at 3,800 feet above the lake.

Before returning home, George Grinnell paid a visit to his friends at the Blackfeet reservation. He found that all was not well. Several tribal leaders, including Little Dog and Little Plume, informed him that the local Indian agent, M. D. Baldwin, was dishonest and had been allowing white cattlemen to graze their stock on Indian land, had sold goods from the agency to non-Indians, and was personally making money off starving the tribe to death. All these transgressions were against the rules and regulations for the conduct of an Indian agency.

Grinnell was shocked to hear of such blatant corruption. He promised them: "I come from the east a private man. My business is to write. Many thousands hear my words, more people perhaps than live in all of Montana."

Grinnell went right to work and wrote to the Commissioner of Indian Affairs T. J. Morgan to complain that the agent was "wholly unfit for his position." He went on to state that: "I sympathise [sic] deeply with these Indians. I have known the tribe for some years…they ought to be helped instead of hindered…I am no eastern sentimentalist on this question, for I have been familiar with Indians in their homes in the west for nearly 20 years, have lived with them on terms of intimacy and have met them in war, but I believe that the government might to, at least partly, to fulfill its treaty obligations, and give these people a chance to survive." He later added: "Although far away, they are human beings whose sufferings are as real as ours are to us." He requested that the corrupt Indian Agent be replaced.

Grinnell followed up this protest with fiery essays throughout mainstream media, including his own *Forest and Stream* and the *New York Times*. Once again, Grinnell rallied the public to come to his aid for a worthy cause.

Consequently, the Blackfeet received a new agent, and they showered Grinnell with praise for making it happen. Tribal Chief Whitecalf said: "Don't quit helping us. I guess the Great Father still listens to you for he knows you. He knows you have a good heart." The New York *Evening Post* would publish the letters from the Blackfeet to Grinnell thanking him for his efforts.

In 1890, Grinnell and Gould, with Jack Monroe as their guide, braved inclement weather—barbed-wire wind and deep snow—to further explore and map the Montana glaciers. Grinnell wrote: "Glaciers were on every Mt. almost. A number on the Mts. about head of St. Mary's were very large. One especially on S. Fork of St. Mary's covers the whole Mt., a very large one, from summit as far down as we could see it without a break. We call it the Blackfeet glacier and the Mt. the Blackfeet Mt." Grinnell decided then and there that he would return the following year and explore every foot of that monstrous glacier.

The trip to Montana was brief because Grinnell was anxious to visit the camps of the Pawnee, the Cheyenne, and the Arikaras before heading back east. His efforts to fill his notebooks with more historic campfire information, however, was thwarted by an unexpected event—the religious fervor surrounding the Ghost Dance that had affected every reservation and would lead to a terrible tragedy.

In 1889 a Paiute Indian named Jack Wilson, who called himself *Wovoka*, allegedly had a spiritual experience that prompted him to create the messianic Ghost Dance, a religion based on the premise that the white man would disappear, and the buffalo would return to western lands. The religion was quickly embraced across Indian Country. Most tribes accepted the Ghost Dance as a peaceful doctrine; not so the Lakota Sioux, who converted the ceremony to conform to their hostility toward the white man.

Indians at the Pine Ridge and Rosebud reservations began to defy their agents to the extent that the outbreak of war was feared by the army. The government responded by sending additional troops of soldiers to the two reservations. General Nelson Miles ordered the arrest of medicine man Sitting Bull, who had embraced the turmoil caused by the Ghost Dance. Sitting Bull resisted and was killed by his own people acting as policemen. Miles also surprisingly ordered the arrest of Chief Big Foot, who was known as a peacemaker. Big Foot feared for his life. He and 350 of his people slipped away from the Rosebud reservation with intentions of visiting Pine Ridge. General Miles dispatched troops from the Seventh Cavalry to prevent Big Foot from reaching his destination.

Twenty miles from Pine Ridge, in the valley of Wounded Knee Creek, five hundred soldiers and four cannons surrounded the Indian caravan. When the Sioux were ordered to give up their firearms, a struggle ensued, a shot was fired, and within seconds a barrage of rifle and cannon fire ensued. When the firing stopped, eighty-four Lakota Sioux men and boys, forty-four women, and eighteen children, including Chief Big Foot, lay dead on the frozen ground. Seven more who had been wounded would later die. The soldiers suffered nineteen killed and thirty-three wounded.

No doubt George Grinnell was heartsick that such an excessive use of force was employed by the army against these people. He could only wonder when and if this war against the Plains tribes would ever end.

Grinnell returned to northwest Montana in 1891, this time again with James Schultz as guide but not Jack Monroe. Monroe had been caught selling whiskey to the Blackfeet and was expelled from the reservation. Grinnell hired a new guide to replace him, an old acquaintance from Custer's Black Hills Expedition of 1874, William "Billy" Jackson.

Jackson, was the son of a white tailor and a Blackfeet woman, likely born near Fort Benton. He was about eighteen years old when he started scouting for the Seventh Cavalry in 1873 and rode with Custer on the Yellowstone Expedition. He went into the Black Hills the following year and had been part of Major Marcus Reno's battalion at the Little Bighorn Battle, where he barely survived.

During Reno's cowardly every-man-for-himself retreat to the hilltop, Jackson had become trapped in a harrowing situation when he was left behind in the timber with several others while the rest of the command scrambled for the bluffs across the river. After dark, with Sioux warriors virtually everywhere in the vicinity, the four men managed to catch two horses and were riding upstream when they were challenged by an enemy. Jackson galloped away and subsequently hid in some willows until the following evening when he made his way safely to Reno's perimeter on the hilltop.

Two other men accompanied Grinnell on this trip to Saint Mary country—an attorney named William H. Seward Jr., who was the grandson of President Lincoln's secretary of state; and Henry L. Stimson, a Yale graduate who in later years would become secretary of state under President Hoover and secretary of war under both Franklin Roosevelt and Harry Truman.

Grinnell had brought his rifle, but was more concerned with his other gear, a compass and a plane table—a device used to make field drawings, charts, and maps. The land through which they passed was described by Grinnell as "absolutely virgin ground...no sign of previous passage by human beings; no choppings; no fires; no sign of horses." He would attempt to survey the territory as best as he could.

Grinnell had visions for the future of this vast territory. On September 17, 1891, he wrote:

> *How would it do to start a movement to buy the St. Mary's Country, say 30 x 30 miles from the Piegan Indians at a fair valuation and turn it into a National reservation or park...This is worth thinking of and writing about.*

George Grinnell visited the Blackfeet and "his" glacier often during the ensuing years and was pleased to see that the new agent was taking good care of the tribe. Captain Lorenzo Cooke had kept whites out of the area, stopped traders from cheating the people, and had limited whiskey sales. Grinnell believed that the tribe needed increased annuities and wrote to Secretary of the Interior Hoke Smith to recommend that they be given twenty-five percent more cattle—three thousand cows and calves—and three additional threshing machines for spring planting. The secretary agreed.

Grinnell was troubled, however, by the influx of prospectors that had been trespassing in Blackfeet country. The years 1893 and 1894 saw more and more miners invade the territory in and around the two Blackfeet reservations when gold was located on the southern slopes of the Little Rocky Mountains. Settlements sprang up overnight, bringing all the vices of civilization, and the government was compelled to save what they could from destructive commercialization.

In March 1895, the interior secretary appointed a commission under the Indian Appropriations Act that would negotiate with the Blackfeet to sell a portion of their reservations. Grinnell was asked to be a member, and, although reluctant, he finally agreed. He envisioned the land that would be purchased by the government as a future national park and believed that the Blackfeet would approve of this usage.

The Blackfeet viewed the sale as inevitable and wanted three million dollars for the land. Grinnell assured them that the government would never pay that much, and the deal was presented for one and a half million. The money would allow the tribe to buy essential livestock and implements necessary for acculturation. With Grinnell's encouragement, the deal was signed on September 25. Grinnell wrote: "In the afternoon it was accepted and tonight everybody is glad. Many Indians made good speeches thanking me."

Grinnell returned to New York and noted: "It grieved me to think of that beautiful country being defaced by civilization and improvements so called, but there seemed no way to avoid facing conditions that existed."

It was in the summer of 1900 when George Grinnell was visiting the Blackfeet tribe that he became aware of indications that the presence of whites had taken a toll on his beloved Saint Mary country. Miners and temporary developments had damaged timber and waterways, and wreaked havoc on the landscape. He wrote a letter to chief forester Clifford Pinchot complaining of this serious threat. He had watched this happen all across the West, but now it was personal—this was where his mountain and his glacier were located.

He returned home to learn that an article titled "The Crown of the Continent," that he had written years earlier had been published in the September issue of *Century* magazine. In the article Grinnell argued that the spectacular Saint Mary Lake region of Montana should be set aside as a national park, and all commercialization should be banned. The timing was perfect. Grinnell launched his own campaign in *Forest and Stream* to encourage Congress to create a national park before it was too late.

Elizabeth Grinnell made her first visit to her husband's beloved Saint Mary Lake country in the summer of 1903. They had married the previous summer, after she had accompanied him to Indian Country in Oklahoma. On this trip, she was introduced to the

Blackfeet tribe on the fourth of July, and soon after they headed out into the wilderness with now redeemed Jack Monroe as guide and another couple, the Whites, accompanying them. Their first order of business was to climb Chief Mountain, where Grinnell wrote that "the women climbed with extraordinary pluck and facility. At the very first they had a little difficulty, but in a very few minutes Elizabeth came to understand how to walk and balance."

Unknown to Grinnell, his wife had a nightmarish fear of heights. At home, she dreaded those part of their trips that would take her up the high peaks, and for that reason she occasionally remained in camp, begging off due to illness. It would be some time before she summoned the nerve to confess her fears to her husband. She did, however, appreciate the beauty of the region, and would never consider staying in New York while George went exploring out West.

Grinnell and Theodore Roosevelt had a serious disagreement in 1903 that threatened their close relationship. *Forest and Stream* had published an article from a man identified only as "hermit" from New Hampshire that was highly critical of John Burroughs, calling him a "bad naturalist."

Roosevelt had recently enjoyed a delightful time with Burroughs at the dedication of Yellowstone National Park, and together they had visited the wonders of that park. Grinnell had published Roosevelt's speech to the 3,five-hundred people gathered there in its entirety in his magazine. But Roosevelt, always loyal to friends, thought the article about Burroughs was a cheap shot and responded angrily to this personal attack.

"I have just seen the long letter by 'Hermit,' to *Forest and Stream* attacking John Burroughs," Roosevelt wrote to Grinnell, "and incidentally furnishing the most ample reason for distrust of Hermit's truthfulness in narrating or else his power of accurate observation. I will say frankly that I am surprised that a paper of the standing of *Forest and Stream* should publish such an article, especially unsigned. It is thoroughly discredible of Hermit not to have attached his real name, and when *Forest and Stream* permits an article to be published without the name it, of course, in the eyes of the public, itself becomes responsible for the attack on Mr. Burroughs."

Roosevelt was accusing Grinnell of being personally responsible for this devastating article about Burroughs. It is not known what response Grinnell might have shot back at Roosevelt, or if he ever did respond, but he never did leak this letter to the press. Perhaps he was not pleased with the article, either, but believed for some reason that he had an obligation to publish it. His reasons will never be known. Grinnell had maintained a cordial relationship with Burroughs through the years, including the trip to Alaska with the Harriman Expedition four years earlier.

"Hermit," by the way, was a recluse from Bond's Hill, Massachusetts, by the name of Mason A. Walton. He had written the book *The Hermit's Wild Friends; or, Eighteen years in the Woods* that same year. It would be possible that Mason had a problem with Burroughs's work and felt compelled to write about it. George Grinnell and Theodore Roosevelt were both critical of those they called "nature fakers," and Roosevelt's letter was possibly based on his friendship and not his intimate knowledge of Burroughs's ideas, some of which went beyond mere naturalism and into the realm of spiritualism and religion.

Roosevelt and Grinnell remained for the most part estranged after this rift, and the following year Grinnell went ahead and edited alone—for the first time without Roosevelt—the Boone and Crockett Club's fourth book, *American Big Game in Its Haunts*. Grinnell, however, apparently made an attempt to patch up relations with Roosevelt by using "Wilderness Reserves" by Roosevelt as the lead article and also publishing it in *Forest and Stream*.

Grinnell wrote that "Mr. Roosevelt's account of what may be seen [in Yellowstone] is so convincing that all who read it and appreciate the importance of preserving our large mammals, must become advocates of the forest reserve game refuge system." Grinnell went on to praise the president for his work on behalf of nature and the common man.

During the summer of 1904 Grinnell was chained to his editing desk at *Forest and Stream* when others in the office were either ill or away.

He wrote:

Sometimes I feel as if I should like to drop work for two or three months and simply go off to the Rockies and loaf and camp until I was tired of it.

His daydreaming also included that ambition to see a national park established in the Saint Mary country. "I should be very glad to do anything that I could to help forward a project to make a national park of any part of the region," he wrote to Francois Matthes, who had written an article in *Appalachia*, the journal of the Appalachian Mountain Club titled "The Alps of Montana."

The following year, Grinnell launched an aggressive campaign to push a bill through Congress that would establish that national park. Unfortunately, his contacts at the capitol were less than enthused. Grinnell then changed his strategy and began to promote the idea in *Forest and Stream*. "It is a region of marvelous lakes, towering peaks, vast glaciers and deep, narrow fiords," he wrote. "Few people know these wonderful mountains, yet no one who goes there but comes away filled with enthusiasm for their wild and singular beauty."

It was not until December 1907 that Montana senator Thomas Carter introduced a bill to create Glacier National Park. Grinnell tried to drum up support for the bill, but the proposal failed. A second bill in February 1908 was passed by the Senate, but changes made by the House could not be reconciled and that bill died.

A third bill, introduced by Senator Carter in June 1909, was supported by influential Montana representative Charles Pray. George Grinnell asked the readers of *Forest and Stream* to petition Congress for a quick vote before enthusiasm waned. "Let everyone now put his shoulder to the wheel and push," he wrote. The bill became stalled and was on life support. Grinnell rallied all the assistance he could from influential allies, such as members of the Boone and Crockett Club, and friends, and sympathetic congressmen—and his faithful readers.

Finally, on April 13, 1910, the bill passed, and was signed into law by President Taft on May 10, 1910. Glacier National Park, which covered three million acres of mountainous country, had been established mainly through the efforts and vision of one man— George Bird Grinnell.

When congratulated by friends after the president had signed the bill, Grinnell, who was always humble, said: "To receive credit for good work well done is pleasant but a reward far higher comes from the consciousness of having served the public well."

The establishment of Glacier National Park was Grinnell's final crusade as editor and owner of *Forest and Stream*. In 1911, one year after the park bill had been signed by the president, Grinnell believed it was time to leave, and sold the magazine that he had been part of for more than thirty years.

Grinnell had been the driving force behind this magazine that had come to be known as the "voice of the sportsman." In that capacity, he had inspired and enhanced the careers of a legion of outdoor writers, photographers, artists, and others associated with conservation. Even more so, Grinnell became the chief catalyst, conscience, and overall pulse of the nation's fledgling conservation movement. The magazine later was incorporated with another publication to form *Field and Stream*, a monthly that exists to this day in a different format and with less advocacy.

Grinnell's conservation work, however, did not end with the sale of the magazine. He spent considerable time helping people who desired to draw on his vast well of knowledge. "With the passage of years," he observed, "the West has ceased to be wild and lost much of its attraction to me…Most of the old Indians have passed on and the young fellows that have grown up do not know as much about Indian matters as I know, myself. In fact, they often come to see me for information…my life seems to be devoted chiefly to keeping up a large correspondence."

Grinnell remained active in natural history affairs by dedicating his later years to public service. He had played a significant role in most of the environmental campaigns of his day, and his opinion was sought out by those who now carried the torch of conservation.

In addition to offering advice, he helped guide various organizations that had missions promoting conservation and natural resources. He was a fellow of the American Ornithologists' Union, which was formed in 1883 with the mission of advancing the scientific knowledge and the conservation of birds. He was instrumental in the founding and served as director of the American Game and Propagation Association, the forerunner of today's Wildlife Management Institute, which played a leading role in establishing pioneering wildlife laws.

One of Grinnell's successes was the Migratory Bird Treaty Act, which was signed by President Taft on March 13, 1913, only the second federal law after the Lacey Act to protect the environment. Passage of this law put a stop to spring duck shooting while stimulating sportsmen to initiate enactment of new laws in their respective states, soon limiting and finally halting the rampant slaughter and commercial sale of wildlife in the absence of federal and state laws. Grinnell would serve on the first advisory board for that Federal Migratory Bird Law.

He chaired the Council on National Parks, Forests, and Wildlife; succeeded Herbert Hoover as president of the National Parks Association; was a trustee of the American Museum of Natural History in New York City; was a member of the Washington, DC, Biologists Field Club; as well as a member of the New York Academy of Sciences and Archaeological Institute of America; and a member of the *Century*, Cosmos, Rockaway, Mayflower Descendants, Authors, Explorers, Narrow Island Clubs, and the Society of Mammalogists.

In 1921, Yale conferred on George Grinnell an honorary Litt.D degree, Doctor of Letters, awarded in recognition of achievement in the humanities. He had toiled long and hard for the Peabody Museum in his younger days, and had become an excellent alumni role model for Yale, so it was only fitting that the institution would recognize him.

He busied himself writing books and essays, and in the spring and summer of 1924, George and Elizabeth toured Europe. Just as with the trip with his parents after his junior year in college, Grinnell had little to say about his experiences overseas.

In 1925, commemorating his extraordinary contributions to conservation, Grinnell stood in the East Room of the White House and was presented the Theodore Roosevelt Gold Medal by President Calvin Coolidge, who remarked: "Few have done as much as you, none has done more to preserve vast areas of picturesque wilderness for the eyes of posterity in the simple majesty in which you and your fellow pioneers first beheld them."

Grinnell's humble character—and perhaps his droll sense of humor—was displayed when he wrote to Lute North: "I went to Washington and with two other people [Gifford Pinchot and teacher Martha Berry] stood up, listened to a speech by the President, and received the medal. It is big enough to knock a man down with, and, I suppose, is actually something to be gratified about."

That same year, he visited Glacier National Park on his way home from a trip to the West Coast. He spent time with James Schultz, Jack Monroe, his Blackfeet friends, and had the privilege of meeting another notable Montanan—artist Charley Russell. He noted several paintings in the studio that Russell had been working on—a prospector discovering gold, Father DeSmet speaking to a tribal camp, and a Native American approaching a wounded buffalo. Russell would pass away later that year.

George, with Elizabeth at his side, made his final visit to Glacier National Park in July 1926. They were not recognized when they checked into a room at the Many Glacier Hotel. Grinnell was seventy six years old, and worried that he might not be able to climb his namesake mountain or glacier but was determined to give it a try—just one last climb. As he gazed at the icy monster, however, he did fret over the condition of the glacier, which was melting. He prophetically wrote: "All these glaciers are receding rapidly and after a time will disappear."

George would not be climbing the glacier alone. He was eventually recognized in the lobby by Morton J. Elrod, a professor of biology at the University of Montana, who was spending the summer as a naturalist at the Park. Elrod gathered together a group of people, and the following day at 11 a.m. the party of twenty started off on horseback, headed toward Lake Josephine. Elizabeth had suffered her usual "mountain sickness," and choose to remain at the hotel.

After lunch, early in the afternoon, roped together for safety, they commenced climbing over the glacier's lateral moraine and onto the icy surface. It had been thirty-nine years since Grinnell first visited this spectacular place, and he was troubled to see how it had changed. The ice had fallen some one hundred feet, and even the ice caves that he had Elizabeth had viewed three years earlier were gone. The going was difficult, but he would not quit this climb for anything.

Late in the afternoon, Grinnell had worn himself out, and he fell twice on the descent. "Leg weary," he wrote, "Everyone was sympathetic about my progress." He briefly rested, and then continued on down to where they had tethered the horses. The trip ended at the hotel at about 9 p.m. That was the last time George Bird Grinnell would see his beloved glacier.

In July 1929, Grinnell was struck down by the first of a series of incapacitating heart attacks. He remained in grave condition for over a month but managed to recover enough to walk a few steps and then would spend most of his time seated in a chair. In those days when he was bedridden, Grinnell would ask his secretary to read to him at his bedside—and not from just any book. He wanted to hear the stories in the "Jack" series that he had written for boys.

He became confined to a wheelchair and, although his mind was sharp, he was a prisoner to nostalgia as he thought about all those friends who had already left him—Theodore Roosevelt, Charley Reynolds, even Lute North was now gone. No doubt he dreamed of one more shot at an elk, one more Cheyenne campfire to warm himself, one more mountain to climb, one more bone-hunting adventure exploring the wilderness, and one more conservation issue in which his pen and his ideas could make a difference. But it was not to be.

George Bird Grinnell died in New York on April 11, 1938, in his eighty-ninth year.

The obituary in the New York Herald Tribune wrote that his passing "cuts a strong strand in the remnants of the thinning cable that still links America with the age of the frontier. Aside from Grinnell's prophetic vision, his forthrightness, his scholarship in the field of zoology and Indian ethnography, and the drive that empowered him to carry so many causes to successful conclusion, his outstanding personal characteristic was that of never-failing dignity, which was doubtless parcel of all the rest. To meet his eye, feel his iron handclasp, or hear his calm and thrifty words—even when he was a man in his ninth decade —was to conclude that here was the noblest Roman of them all."

The obituary in the *New York Times* summed it up best when it bestowed upon George Bird Grinnell the title of "the father of American conservation."

CHAPTER TWELVE:
PRESERVING THE LEGACY

*What a noble gift to man are the forests! How pleasantly the shadows of
the wood fall upon our heads when we turn from the glitter and
turmoil of the world of man!*
—SUSAN FENIMORE COOPER

GEORGE BIRD GRINNELL JOURNEYED TO THE WEST WHEN
huge bison herds and Native cultures remained intact on the Plains.
He not only experienced the wilderness but became part of it by
getting as close to nature on his visits as possible. His writings as
a naturalist and ethnographer are important legacies, for much of
what he saw and heard soon vanished forever. His curiosity about
nature and Native Americans led him on adventures that most people could only dream about, and he told the public about his experiences on the pages of *Forest and Stream* magazine.

Grinnell helped awaken the nation to the beauty and importance
of our natural resources, and he lived long enough to see many of
his preservation efforts fulfilled. His influence in various fields—
paleontology, natural history, ethnology, conservation, wildlife
preservation, Native American rights—was very great at a crucial
time and proved of lasting benefit to the nation.

Grinnell understood that saving the wildlife meant protecting
the habitat. Those natural places where birds and animals make
their homes were just as important to him when pushing for sensible hunting and fishing laws, which was why he and Theodore

Roosevelt worked to set aside forest preserves, national forests, and wetlands—and the animals that lived there.

It would be reasonable to state, however, that Grinnell would be dismayed to learn that many of the causes for which he so bravely fought and sacrificed to bring about are being abused or neglected or amended to suit commercial interests.

While it cannot be said that without George Bird Grinnell, we would not have national parks or protected wilderness areas, unquestionably it is him that we owe the largest debt of gratitude for their establishment and protection from commercialization. And it would be safe to assume that Grinnell would be proud that our national park system has endured and flourished, but he would be disappointed by its current state.

Admittedly, national parks and recreation areas remain a huge success and something about which Americans can be justly proud. The beauty alone defies description, with each park boasting a uniqueness and allure. In recent years, however, these public lands have been subjected to increasing stress. Much of that stress is the result of issues that Grinnell fought against, namely the increasing pressure by private interests to engage in commercial endeavors— logging, mining, and oil and gas drilling, to name a few. In fact, the Department of the Interior has been reviewing standards that have protected the parks from the impact of oil and gas drilling within their boundaries, which could have a devastating effect if regulations are weakened.

The most stress, however, can be attributed to the success of these parks in attracting people. Annually, more than 300 million people visit national parks, and with them comes traffic, noise, garbage, crime, stress on wildlife, and pollution. The number of park rangers has remained relatively constant for years, but the budgets in terms of inflation have actually decreased.

In Grinnell's day, the national parks were expected to generate the revenues they needed to cover operating expenses, which worked quite well. This practice has been changed to tax funding, which has promoted overuse, poor management, and politicization of decisions. Perhaps worst of all, Park Rangers, who should be free to manage the resources and educate the visitors with interpretive programs, have been turned into policemen who spend much of their time dealing with crime, such as drugs, drunkenness, disturbances, assaults, and fugitives who hide out in campgrounds.

It was at Yellowstone National Park, our first national park, where George Grinnell made the first survey of wildlife and natural resources and submitted a protest about their abuses, and later saved the last wild buffalo herd in the country from slaughter by poachers. This park entertains more than four million visitors a year who enjoy the stunning scenery, incredible geysers, and abundant wildlife.

The bison herd has thrived in Yellowstone over the years and has reached a population of about five thousand animals. However, more and more encounters of buffalo and visitors have been reported recently, with people being gored, trampled, and interfering with young animals. The Park Service runs a program that reduces buffalo numbers each year through slaughter or hunting. They believe that the ideal number of animals for the entire park would be about three thousand. Activists are pushing for the buffalo to be added to the Endangered Species Act to keep the herd intact and stop the culling process, but the government has been fighting against it.

Grizzly bears are another success story at the park. In 1970 there were about one hundred bears, now this number has risen to seven hundred. The bears have experienced a lack of food at times with the decline in the cutthroat trout population and the dying off from disease of whitebark pine, the seeds of which the bears eat. The incidence of a grizzly attack is rare, but in this time when selfies are all the rage, people have been pressing their luck by getting too close to these dangerous animals.

The grizzlies are also threatened by the Fish and Wildlife Service, which, for purely political reasons, wants to delist the bears as an endangered species. Many people, and Native Americans in particular, are opposed to this move and are fighting to preserve these animals from a political death.

Another threat to wildlife at the park is that certain species have migration corridors that take them outside of the boundaries into unprotected areas. Grizzly bears and wolves in particular are not aware of boundary lines, and there is a frequent conflict between people and wildlife, which can upset the natural balance. The wandering ways of wolves, which can travel as far as thirty miles in a day and may journey five hundred miles from their home range, are especially troubling. The confines of Yellowstone cannot contain them, and their presence outside the park is not welcome.

Wolves became a targeted animal when the Wyoming legislature, the home state of Yellowstone, decided to permit their killing outside of the park by any means, with no limit, day or night, after the animal was removed from federal protection in 2017. Wolves can be poisoned, snared, incinerated, run over by a truck, an ATV, or a snowmobile, and, of course, shot on sight. Millions of dollars have been spent to bring the wolf back from the brink of extinction, but Wyoming has adopted a nineteenth century mentality and believes that wolves are enough of a threat to livestock and people that they must be totally eliminated.

This attitude and policy in Wyoming directly contradict the efforts of George Grinnell and his fellow members of the Boone and Crockett Club. He was alarmed by the fact that in his day people could kill any animal, at any time, in any amount, without any law to stop them. The result of this lack of rules and regulations that pertain to the wolf in Wyoming nearly caused the extinction of the buffalo. Those who say "Good riddance" to the wolf have never heard that mournful howl on a moon-lit night that epitomizes the romance of the western wilderness. The wolf belongs to that land just as much as the buffalo, or the elk, or the grizzly. Hopefully, a resolution can be found that will protect wolves from extinction.

Research indicates that recent changes in the climate have had a negative impact on not just Yellowstone but all the national parks. There are worries about growing seasons, and snow run offs, the possibility of increased fire frequency, plant growth rates, pollen production, soil conditions, and water levels.

George Grinnell did not have to face the climate change debate, also known as global warming, which is perhaps the most mischaracterized and politicized issue of our time. This change to the climate and the natural systems that support us threatens our health, our fragile environment, and our future prosperity. It would be fair to speculate, however, that Grinnell would not have fallen prey to hysterical claims and skewered data, rather he would have become the voice of reason. He had heard the shouts of wild-eyed doom-sayers' countless times telling him that the world was going to end soon. He did not live to see the world end—and it is unlikely that we will, either.

If Grinnell were alive today, he would wonder why irresponsible, self-serving American politicians believe that to fix this problem our country must revert to the Stone Age when we are not the primary culprit. He would face the facts that certain foreign countries, such as China and India, are the indiscriminate polluters on this planet. To reverse the course of man-made climate change, those countries must be dealt with, not so much the American people who have made great strides in cleaning up the air and water and are now watching the ozone layer begin to heal. We must be vigilante, how-ever, to ensure there is no relapse, and we must continue to move forward with programs to improve our earth's health.

George Grinnell would have trusted the wonders of science to develop a solution to climate change. He was a great believer in the capabilities of the scientific community, of which he was a member. Historically, we have always adapted to any threat. But until climate change is not being kicked around in the political arena, and data in reports is not altered or amended to suit an agenda, the voice of the scientist, and reason, will be drowned out by nearsighted, uninformed pseudo-experts, and we will be left to the hands of fate.

Sadly, even at Grinnell's "Crown of the Continent," Montana's Glacier National Park, the wildlife and land face a variety of threats—from commercial and residential development, hard-rock and coal mining, and extraction of oil and gas on bordering land. Worse yet, however, is the status of the glaciers themselves. In 1911, when the park was established, there were one hundred fifty glaciers of twenty-five acres or larger—but, as witnessed back then by Grinnell, they were gradually melting away. By 2018, there were only twenty-six active moving masses of ice remaining. Grinnell's prophetic prediction about the glaciers eventually disappearing was apparently coming true.

But there is hope for Glacier National Park. In Spring 2019, the park service quietly removed signs posted that warned tourists that all the glaciers would be gone, melted away, by the year 2020. The US Geological Survey computer models were modified to show that due to colder weather and heavy snowfall, the glaciers were actually increasing in size rather than decreasing. George Bird Grinnell would be pleased.

While writing about national parks, we would be remiss if we did not salute those Americans who work in conservation jobs across the country. They are often underpaid, live and work in substandard facilities and challenging conditions, and sacrifice much in the way of a comfortable lifestyle to preserve and nurture our wildlife and natural resources and to enforce the laws. These individuals deserve our respect, our admiration, and our complete cooperation. Check with local offices of the Forest Service and other agencies if you wish to volunteer your time to a good cause. They are truly carrying on the legacy of George Bird Grinnell.

Grinnell's first love was birds, fostered by his close relationship to the Audubon family as a child, and he would be proud to know that the Audubon Society has thrived after all these years. He had served as a director of the National Association of Audubon Societies for twenty-six years. Birds, however, remain under myriad threats.

Wild birds serve as our best connection to the natural world. We love birds—we feed them, watch them, and even keep them in cages for our amusement. Birds are enduring; they have an ability to master their environment, which has allowed them to thrive for millions of years longer than humans have been on the planet. However, humans are constantly changing the planet, and birds are presently having a difficult time adapting.

Women no longer decorate their hats with dead birds, but our feathered friends are nonetheless threatened by other insidious means. In the United States, feral and house cats maliciously rip to shreds at least one billion birds and over six billion small animals every year—an astounding number. In recent years, domestic cats have been directly responsible for the death of around two-and-a-half billion birds and the extinction of at least thirty-three bird species worldwide. Yet, laws restricting a cat's freedom to slaughter these birds are basically nonexistent, especially in comparison to the restrictions placed on domestic dogs. The only solution appears to be with the owner, who must keep these cats inside or be complicit in this carnage.

It has been reported that forty percent of the ten thousand or so bird species are in decline. The Audubon Club has predicted that half of all North American bird species face extinction from climate change, although detractors claim the club has used flawed data in order to solicit donations. Whatever the number, there can be no doubt that many species are on life support.

The primary threats to birds are oil drilling and mining operations, as well as development that eliminates habitat and oil pits that birds mistake for water. Recent data indicates that power lines account for an estimated 25 million deaths per year, collisions with vehicles cause over two-hundred million deaths, glass windows kill six-hundred million, and 72 million die from poisoning.

Another effective, new, and fast-growing bird killer are wind turbines, which account for at least 230,000 dead birds every year, and that number is on the rise. The bases of these machines are usually littered with the remains of its victims. The turbines are especially deadly to raptors—hawks, eagles, and kestrels. Perhaps as bad or worse than just killing the birds, these wind factories also result in the loss of bird habitat to development. Proponents claim that wind farms are clean, green energy, but there are reports of damage to farm animals, and humans' health as well. More research is needed before these killing machines can be acceptable—although politicians favor the impact turbines have on local, county, and state coffers.

The Migratory Bird Act that George Grinnell fought so hard to implement is in danger of being amended in favor of business interests for the first time in more than one hundred years. This law has protected over one thousand migrating species, with ten percent of them federally listed as threatened. Now, the government wants to put these birds in the line of fire. The federal government will permit the "incidental" killing of birds by energy production, buildings, and other industry death traps without repercussions.

Other relaxed rules detrimental to our feathered friends include a repeal of the ban on lead ammunition, which poisons countless eagles, among other birds, each year. Eagles were successfully brought back from near extinction due to the pesticide DDT in the 1960s. Now they are threatened again by a problem that had already been solved. The US Geological Survey estimates that about twenty-five percent of all bald and golden eagles have some form of lead exposure. This condition makes it difficult for them to breathe, they suffer from convulsions, and eventually they cannot digest their food and die. These deaths are unconscionable, unnecessary, and preventable.

Birds, which are said to the descendants of dinosaurs, have survived all this time against natural odds but may have met their match by the selfish acts of mankind. It could be speculated that George Grinnell would be trumpeting his call to save the birds today just as he did when they were threatened by the millinery business.

Grinnell served as active president of the Boone and Crockett Club (1918–27) and was made honorary president for life in 1927. The club's mission and purpose remain basically the same now as it did in his day—preserving and protecting game animals and habitats for future hunters. It also maintains a system for scoring trophy animals and recognizes hunters who achieve excellence with medals or certificates which are awarded at an annual banquet.

Grinnell was the perfect example of a true sportsman, a hunter-naturalist, a man who respected the wild game he hunted and had the foresight to work to preserve every species he could as well as its habitat. In *Forest and Stream*, he constantly called attention to any threat that could destroy our precious animals, birds, and fish. In his lifetime, he worked to save the lives of not only an untold number of birds and bird species and game animals but lobbied for sensible hunting laws to preserve them for the future. Perhaps more importantly, he made the public aware of conservation issues at a time in history when few laws and little enforcement protected our wildlife, and hunting was not regulated. People could kill animals at will, which often upset a natural balance in a region and threatened the extinction of various species.

Hunting is frowned upon by many environmentalists who believe, like John Muir, that it is a barbaric practice. But if we banned all hunting, the negatives of that rash act would far outweigh the positives. Our cities would be overrun with unwanted wildlife—deer would devastate gardens, bears would raid trash cans, coyotes and foxes would feast on family pets, and with them comes disease and danger to human lives. Many animals would cruelly starve to death due to overpopulation and the competition for food.

In addition, hunting and fishing license fees support conservation programs, and that amount of money can make a difference in maintaining viable habitat and healthy wildlife. Hunting is a pure form of environmental responsibility, and we have dedicated game wardens across the country who make certain that people abide by the laws. Hopefully, we have hunter-naturalists who follow those laws and respect their prey as much as those protecting them. A day in the field shooting can be a safe and enjoyable outing for families to share.

There are some Americans, mainly those who live in rural and remote places, who supplement their annual food budget by hunting animals in season. Studies show that eating wild game provides essential fats, which are components of a healthy diet, and help reduce cholesterol, and other disease risks, and is a good source of protein and minerals. The wild meat contains no hormones or antibiotics and is said to be more flavorful than meat from farm-raised animals. Hunters who do not eat the game they kill often donate the meat to food pantries. For non-hunters and hunters alike, certain restaurants specialize in wild boar, venison, quail, buffalo, elk, and other exotic game on their menus, and the prices are sky high.

Sport fishing, one of Grinnell's favorite hobbies, has also made a positive impact on our waterways and the scaly creatures that swim within them. Over the years, states have cleaned up streams, rivers, and lakes, when necessary, and stocked them with native fish from fisheries. Consequently, people who fish and organizations that support fishing have been responsible stewards of the water and have added considerably to the economy and the well-being of the earth. Practices such as catch-and-release have ensured the quality of fishing by maintaining a balance in high-pressure areas and is one example of protecting the environment. Fishing has proved to be a stress-reducing, family-oriented activity that is enjoyed by millions of Americans.

The Endangered Species Act did not exist in George Grinnell's day, but he would have given it his wholeheartedly support. Although he was a paleontologist hunting the remains of extinct animals, he had dedicated his life to making sure that existing species did not go extinct. He would have fought the real threat, Congress, which does the bidding of business and makes stealth attempts, provisions hidden in obscure bills, to try and pass legislation favorable to economic interests and detrimental to imperiled species. Wildlife organizations watch for these stealth bills and inform their members, but the public at large needs to become more aware of this threat to wildlife.

The World Wildlife Fund released a report stating that humans are directly responsible for killing off sixty percent of the world's mammals, fish, birds, and reptiles since 1970—all due to our insatiable appetite and over-exploitation of earth's natural resources. Our need for energy, water, and land use for commercial activities, not to mention food production, must be controlled for people and nature to live in harmony. George Grinnell believed that civilization, commercialization, and conservation could flourish together, but we must make the right choices and take into consideration the needs of our wild things.

While on the subject of healing our globe, unfortunately, recent political changes in this country are making that challenge all the more difficult. Portions of the Clean Water Rule are being repealed, which threatens the health of our waterways. The Department of the Interior is planning to grant developers access to areas previously closed to offshore gas and oil drilling. The Clean Power Plan has been repealed, which had reduced emissions from energy development.

These few examples of recent modifications favor business and ignore the environmental impact. Our earth is being battered, and beaten, and abused like never before. Regulations that have been in place for over a century are being tossed aside. If we do not find the means to stop this rampant destruction, there is no telling how much damage will be done. The earth is resilient, but it can only regain its proper form if we step in and guide it with values prescribed years ago by Grinnell and his contemporary conservationists.

Another issue that was dear to the heart of Grinnell was the plight of Native Americans. He enjoyed many a day living with one tribe or another on the Plains, sharing their campfires—and their lives. They had a mutual friendship and respect. Sadly, Grinnell would be appalled by what he would see today on a visit to most of Indian Country.

Native Americans have been treated with shameful disregard. This attitude is reflected by statistics that indicate that the Native American lags far behind the average in life expectancy, years of schooling, and employment—in fact, unemployment rates on many reservations, most of which are isolated ghettos, run as high as eighty percent. Infant mortality among Native Americans is three times the national average. Alcoholism and drug addiction affect a staggering number of Native Americans, and the likelihood of them committing suicide is far higher than the national average.

A controversial issue that did not exist in Grinnell's day but is very much a puzzle today is the mysterious disappearance of thousands of Native American girls and women across the western United States each year. The National Crime Information Center received over 5,700 reports of killed or missing Native American girls and women in 2016. On some reservations, women are killed at a rate ten times the national average. The Justice Department claims to have taken steps to address this issue, but concerned Native Americans believe that there would be more urgency if the victims were non-Native.

Overall, Native American tribes have been devastated by poverty, prejudice, and hopelessness by a society that misunderstands or ignores their culture and proud heritage. At the same time, society carries a guilt complex that fosters a pseudo-concern by vocally defending these people without doing anything to benefit them. Native people are without question this nation's forgotten citizens, its most abused minority—in part the result of a failure to acknowledge historical blunders that may prove embarrassing.

Thanks to the research and writing of George Bird Grinnell, however, we do possess a recorded history of tribal affairs that predates the takeover by the government and the confinement of these Indigenous Peoples to reservations. We can, if we care to seek it, have a better understanding of the roots and culture of these people, and perhaps find a clue to their needs within Grinnell's narratives.

The Black Hills, where Grinnell accompanied Custer's Seventh

Cavalry on an 1874 expedition in search of gold, is now a tourist-friendly destination and home of Mount Rushmore, the Crazy Horse Memorial, and the historic gambling town of Deadwood. The Lakota Sioux, however, are still at war with the United States over this mountainous region that was given to them by the Fort Laramie Treaty of 1868.

In 1889, the government forcibly removed the Lakota Sioux from the Great Sioux Reservation and placed them on five smaller reservations west of the Missouri River. That same year, North and South Dakota gained statehood, and the government sold nine million acres of Black Hills region land to ranchers and farmers, who struggled to grow crops. The poor farming techniques in the Dakotas, such as plowing up grass that supported the earth, was said to have led to the Dust Bowl crisis of the 1930s.

In 1980, the Lakota Sioux tribe sued the United States government, claiming that the Black Hills had been taken from them illegally. The Supreme Court ruled in favor of the Native Americans and awarded them 120 million dollars as compensation. The Lakota refused to accept this money—they wanted the return of the Black Hills instead. It was the belief of the tribe that if they took the money it would be admitting that the United States owned the Black Hills. The awarded money has remained in an interest-bearing account all these years and now amounts to over one billion dollars.

On that July afternoon in 1874 when George Grinnell and Lute North were camped near French Creek in the Black Hills and speculated about how now that gold had been found that the Sioux would declare war, they could not have imagined that the war would continue being fought to this day.

Grinnell dedicated much of his young adult life to the Peabody Museum at Yale University. He loved cataloging, and analyzing, and discussing theories about the specimens that Professor O. C. Marsh would receive from all over the country. The mission of the Peabody remains the same today as it did in Grinnell's day—"advancing our understanding of earth's history through geological, biological, and anthropological research." The Peabody contains several of the world's most important collections, including one of vertebrate paleontology partially collected during Grinnell's employment. Perhaps the most well-known feature of the museum is the mounted skeleton of a juvenile *Brontosaurus* in the Great Hall of Dinosaurs. George Grinnell said that he would have been quite content to have spent his entire life working at the Peabody, but he had a higher calling and rightfully departed New Haven to accept the responsibility as editor of *Forest and Stream* magazine.

Whether you believe that humans are subconsciously drawn to the grasslands and streams of their African origin, or if you believe the biblical story of creation that finds mankind in the Garden of Eden, or even if you have never thought about it, there can be no denying that humans have an inherent spiritual connection to nature. We may nurture house plants in a high-rise apartment; feed backyard songbirds; vacation in a national park or at an ocean shore; cast a line for panfish; hunt for wild game; plant a flower or vegetable garden; backpack into the wilderness; or just take a casual stroll with the dog at a local park—all of which proves that we have an unexplainable need to get outside and commune with nature. We are an inseparable part of the natural world. Therefore, it would stand to reason that it is naturally within us to protect and preserve the habitat and creatures that give us so much comfort.

What can be done to preserve nature for future generations? What can I do? What can we do? What can anyone do? There are no simple answers. We may think that we are prisoners of our circumstance, setting priorities of work, family, entertainment, recreation, and have little power to influence any environmental issue. However, George Bird Grinnell proved that common people banding together have more influence than we may think, but it must be used wisely and properly.

It would be taking the easy way out by stating that Edward Abbey got it right in his novel *The Monkey Wrench Gang*. All we need to do is send out gangs of thugs to damage and destroy construction equipment, blow up dams, spike trees, burn billboards, and terrorize corporate executives until they holler "uncle," and they will leave nature alone. Bad idea. Extremists often go too far with their activism, and cause harm to innocent people or animals and sabotage their issue with their criminal activities. Violence and terrorism are never the answer and are counterproductive in winning the hearts and minds of the general public. Being reasonable rather than radical could have been George Grinnell's motto—and it worked. Abbey wrote a fun book, however, if you read it with tongue planted firmly in cheek.

The urgent needs of nature in this critical time in history should outweigh any commercial project that threatens our natural resources. And when it does not, the people must mobilize against it. Anyone can become an activist, because every community is presently or will eventually be the target of nature destroyers—illegal wildlife trade and poaching; deforestation; invasive oil and gas drilling; habitat loss due to development; wind farms; industrial and agricultural pollution; mining; quarries, just to name a few. Wildlife can coexist with potentially dangerous elements if a fair and equitable balance is reached, but too often the commercial interests overrule conservation interests without anyone watching out for those abuses in the fine print.

Not all corporations are enemies of the environment, however, and only those whose profits are dependent upon tampering in some way with our natural resources are even suspect. George Grinnell walked away from Wall Street, but he did not abandon the capitalistic principles that make this country great. He was a savvy investor, which was how he and his father gained controlling interest in *Forest and Stream* magazine, and he believed that businesses and the earth could coexist. Our economy and lifestyle require a certain amount of fossil fuel to thrive, and we need timber professionals to manage forests to prevent devastating forest fires, and we must extract resources from the ground, and so on and so forth.

Grinnell was a champion of the environment—no one did more to protect and preserve it—but he was a practical man. He vehemently opposed those businesses that harmed our wildlife and natural resources. But Grinnell understood that nature is ready and willing to share its rich bounty with us. He did not intend for every acre of our country to be a preserve rather than used in a responsible manner for our benefit. We are not betraying the environment by removing those resources for our own use that provide a comfortable lifestyle—as long as we restore them and do not deplete them. Grinnell believed that civilization, commercialization, and conservation could live together happily ever after, without us having to sacrifice our lifestyle of abundance.

And, yes, it is all so dizzying to try and figure out the next step that a violator of nature might take until it is too late. Involvement and knowledge are the answer. Just one person raising his or her voice can rally the multitudes into action. There exists a silent majority of closet nature lovers in this country—tending to their house plants or feeding backyard birds—that need to be told that it is all right for them to protest abuses.

By all means, seek out a conservation organization or two or more to join that fits your particular interests, and support them. There are countless worthy clubs, many with local chapters, that will keep you informed about issues and put you in touch with other like-minded people. You may even wish to volunteer your time and talents to help—and there are never enough volunteers. Your presence would always be welcome at local city or county meetings where environmental issues are being discussed. You do not have to be an expert and speak your piece; you can simply listen and learn, if that is more comfortable for you.

Do not forget that children are the future. Little kids love to get muddy, sandy, wet, draw in the dirt with sticks, and throw rocks at things. They are curious about spiders, and grasshoppers, and butterflies, and frogs, and how seeds grow into plants and flowers. Encourage them. They are instinctively drawn to the natural world, and it is up to us to nurture that interest. As they grow older, they may drift away from the outdoors in favor of video games and phones and hanging out. But if we start early, taking them to a nature center, a zoo, an animal park, go birdwatching, take a hike, go camping, plant a garden, let them take care of a pet, or other healthy outdoor activities, they just may fall in love with nature for life. And along the way, if you explain to them their duty toward nature, how we must take care of the earth, they just may grow up to be a responsible environmentalist.

George Grinnell used *Forest and Stream* as a platform from which to inform and inflame the public, and other magazines and newspapers picked up his stories. The population of the country has exploded since his days when national conservation organizations protesting abuses were a new concept and virtually nonexistent.

Consequently, today there is not one voice as powerful as *Forest and Stream*, and the various nature and sportsman's organizations often have agendas that clash, which prevents them from working together. We are so diverse in this country that every club or organization is demonized by some sector of society or by each other. For this reason, conservation organizations should make an effort to hold their noses and set aside differences and band together as much as possible. Combined voices are louder and more credible than just one lone voice crying from the wilderness—after all, it is all for the good of nature.

Rules and laws will never be strict enough to protect our air, water, wildlife, and natural resources to satisfy everyone. Concerned citizens should never become complacent—the fight must never end. Persistence was the watchword for George Bird Grinnell. It may have taken him years to push important legislation through Congress, but he did not just give up and move on to the next shiny object. He came back time and time again until the job was finished.

Thankfully, apart from all the social and political turmoil, there is nature. There comes a time when the sights, and smells, and clamor of the city renders us dazed and confused. Our tasks at work become mundane, our colleagues bore us, our almond milk Frappuccino tastes sour, and even our phones fail to provide entertainment.

Our lives in the city are a radical change from our ancestors' over the past thousands of years. Our forebearers were mainly farmers, hunters, and fishermen, tended to livestock, and lived an outdoor fresh-air life, not a mere existence within a cramped cubical. We have the blood of our ancestors flowing through our veins reminding us that now and then we require a refuge from the concerns of our working day. It is then that we know that it is time to commune with nature.

The pleasure of experiencing nature does not need to be a visit to a national park or a wilderness area. It can be as close as your own backyard. It is a place where you can be alone with the wind, or a walk in the rain with the joy you had as a child, or jump into that inviting snowdrift, or just relax and inhale the sweet scents of the season. Nature is a source of inspiration that offers freedom from everyday irritations. Resolve to celebrate the beauty of nature more and the ills of the human condition less.

Out where wildflowers bloom and songbirds serenade awaits a

whole new magnificent and mystifying world to explore each time you enter it—a place where every leaf is a map, every shadow conceals a secret, every raindrop has an answer, and every stream is rippling with songs and stories. If you listen closely, you can sense the rhythm of the earth and awaken to the realization that you, too, belong in nature's master plan.

And when the wind and sun are just right, and the clouds open up to offer a glimpse, perhaps up there on a distant ridge through the trees just below the rocky crevasses we can recognize the silhouette of a person carrying a walking stick, or a camera, or a rifle, or a fly rod, or a geological hammer, or an open notebook, and we know that all is right with the world—the legacy of George Bird Grinnell is being preserved.

BIBLIOGRAPHY

NEWSPAPERS

Bismarck Tribune
Chicago Inter-Ocean High Country New
New York Evening Post
New York Herald Tribune
New York Times
New York *Weekly Herald*
Rocky Mountain News
Sioux City Journal
St. Paul Daily Pioneer

COLLECTIONS/MANUSCRIPTS

Birdsall, Amelia. "A Woman's Nature: Attitudes and Identities of the Bird Hat Debate at the Turn of the 20th Century," Senior Thesis, Haverford College, 2002.

Burroughs, John. "Journal of the Expedition." The Huntington Library, San Marino, CA.

Cart, Theodore Whaley. "The Struggle for Wildlife Preservation in the United States, 1870-1900: Attitudes and Events Leading to the Lacey Act," PhD. Diss., University of North Carolina, 1971.

Charles Keeler Family Papers, Bancroft Library, Berkley, CA.

Custer, George Armstrong. "Pages from the Black Hills Expedition Order and Dispatch Book," July 1 to August 25, 1874. Yale University Beinecke Rare Book and Manuscript Library.

Grinnell, George Bird. "Collection of Journals, Field Notes and other Materials on the Plains Indians, 1870–1930." Southwest Museum Library, Los Angeles, CA.

Grinnell, George Bird. Collection. Yale University, New Haven, CT, and on microfilm at Mansfield Library, University of Montana, Missoula.

Grinnell, George Bird. "Memoirs." MSS 204, Box 4, Folder 20, K. Ross Toole Archives, Mansfield Library, The University of Montana, Missoula.

Grinnell, George Bird. "Dairy of an Expedition." Southwest Museum.

Hough, Emerson. Papers at the Universities of Wyoming and Iowa.

Letter Book, The. Unpublished Grinnell correspondence. K. Ross Toole Archives, Mansfield Library, University of Montana Missoula.

Morton J. Elrod Papers, K. Ross Toole Archives, Mansfield Library, University of Montana, Missoula.

Newton Horace Winchell Manuscripts, Minnesota Historical Society.

Ninth Annual Report of the Sheffield Scientific School of Yale College. New Haven: Sheffield Scientific School, 1874.

Roosevelt, Theodore. *Papers.* Washington, DC, Library of Congress, Manuscript Division.

South Dakota Department of History, Collections VII.

Wilson, James. "Journal of a Trip to the Yellowstone Park, July, August, and September 1875." Yale University Beinecke Rare Book and Manuscript Library.

GOVERNMENT DOCUMENTS

Annual Report to the Commissioner of Indian Affairs, 1875.

Custer, George Armstrong. *Report of the Expedition to the Black Hills under Command of Brevet Major General G. A. Custer*, 43 Cong., 2 sess., Sen. Exec. Doc.32.

Grant, Madison. "Early History of Glacier National Park Montana." Washington, DC: Government Printing Office, 1919.

Indian Appropriations Act of March 2. Statutes at Large. Vol. 28. 1895.

Jenny, Walter P. *Report on the Mineral Wealth, Climate and Rainfall and Natural Resources of the Black Hills of South Dakota*, 44 Cong., 1 sess., Exec. Doc. 51

Kappler, Charles J. *Indian Affairs: Laws and Treaties*, vol. 2, Washington, DC: Government Printing Office, 1904-41.

Lacy Act of 1894, The. "An Act to protect the birds and animals in Yellowstone National Park, and to punish crimes in said park." U.S. Statutes at Large Vol 28 May 1894.

Ludlow, William. "Report of a Reconnaissance from Carroll, Montana Territory, on the Upper Missouri, to the Yellowstone National Park, and Return, Made in the Summer of 1875." Washington, DC: Government Printing Office, 1875.

Ludlow, William. "Report of a Reconnaissance of the Black Hills of Dakota, Made in the Summer of 1874." Washington, DC: Government Printing Office, 1875.

Report of the Superintendent of the Yellowstone National Park for the Years 1872, 1877, 1878, 1880, 1883, 1886, 1887, 1889, 1891, 1902. Yellowstone National Park Archives, Gardiner, MT.

U. S. Congress. House. *Protection of Game in Yellowstone National Park*. 53d Cong. 2d Sess. April 4, 1894.

U. S. Congress. Senate. *An Agreement Made and Concluded September 26, 1895, with the Indians of the Blackfeet Reservation, Montana*. 54th Cong. 1st Sess., 1896 S. Doc. 118, 8. Serial 3350.

U. S. Congress. Senate. *The Glacier National Park*. 61st Cong, 2d Sess. S. 2777, Congressional Record, Vol. 45, no. 5 (April 14, 1910).

U. S. Congress. House. *Glacier National Park*. 61 Cong, 2d Sess. H. R. 2777, Congressional Record, Vol. 45, no 5 (April 26, 1910).

U. S. Congress. House. *Glacier National Park*. 61 Cong. 2d Sess. H. R. 1142, House Reports, Vol. 3, Serial 5593.

PERIODICALS

Allen, J. A. "An Ornithologist's Plea," *New York Times*, November 25, 1897.

Anderson, Harry H. "The Benteen Base Ball Club: Sports Enthusiasts of the Seventh Cavalry," *Montana, the Magazine of Western History* 20, no. 3, summer 1970.

Barnette, LeRoy. "Ghastly Harvest: Montana's Trade on Buffalo Bones." *Montana*, summer 1975.

Betts, Charles Wyllys. "The Yale College Expedition of 1870," *Harper's New Monthly Magazine* 43, no. 257, October 1871.

Blackwell, Alice Stone. "Ballots and Millinery," *New York Times*, May 3, 1910.

Calloway, Colin G. "The Inter-Tribal Balance of Power on the Great Plains, 1760–1850," *Journal of American Studies* 16, 1982.

Danker, Donald E. "The Journal of an Indian Fighter," *Nebraska History* 39, no. 2, June 1958.

Davis, Theodore R. "The Buffalo Range," *Harper's New Monthly Magazine*, January 1869.

Fisher, Albert K. "In Memoriam: George Bird Grinnell." *The Auk*, 56, no. 1, January 1939.

Forest and Stream magazine. 77 volumes. August 14, 1873 to December 30, 1911.

Grant, Madison. "George Bird Grinnell." *The American Review of Reviews* 71, January-June 1925.

Gray, John. "The Last Rights of Lonesome Charley Reynolds." *Montana*, Summer 1963.

Grinnell, George Bird, ed. "A Chapter of History and Natural History in Old New York." *Natural History* 20, 1920.

Grinnell, George Bird. "Mountain Sheep." *Journal of Mammalogy* 9, February 1928.

———. "An Old-Time Bone Hunt," *Natural History* 23, July-August 1923.

———. "Audubon Park: A Brief History to 1886." *The Auk*, 1920.

———. "Old-Time Range of Virginia Deer, Moose and Elk." *Natural History* 25, 1935.

———. "On a New Crinoid from the Cretaceous Formation of the West." *American Journal of Science and Arts*, 12, July 1876.

———. "Pronghorn Antelope." *Journal of Mammalogy* 10, May 1929.

———. "Recollections of Audubon Park." *Auk* 37, July 1920.

———. "Review of Professor Marsh's Monograph on the Odontornithes, or Toothed Birds of North America." *American Journal of Science* 21, April 1881.

_____. "Sketch of Professor O. C. Marsh." *The Popular Science Monthly*, September 1878.

_____. "The Character of John James Audubon," *Audubon Magazine*, October 1887.

_____. (Writing as "Ornis") "The Green River Country," *Forest and Stream*, November 13, 1873.

_____. (Writing as "Ornis") "A Day with the Sage Grouse," *Forest and Stream*, November 6, 1873.

_____. (Writing as "Ornis") "Buffalo Hunt with the Pawnees," *Forest and Stream*, December 25, 1873.

_____. "Destruction of the Buffalo." *Forest and Stream*, October 16, 1873.

_____. "A Trip to North Park." *Forest and Stream*, September 25, 1879.

_____. "The Audubon Society," *Forest and Stream*, February 1886.

_____. "The Return of the War Party: Reminiscences of Charley Reynolds," *Forest and Stream*, December 26, 1896 and January 30, 1897.

_____. "The People's Park." *Forest and Stream*, January 18, 1883.

_____. "Save the Park Buffalo," *Forest and Stream*, April 14, 1894.

_____. "Park Poachers and Their Ways," *Forest and Stream*, May 26, 1894.

_____. "A Premium on Crime." *Forest and Stream*, March 24, 1894.

_____. "Protection for the Park." *Forest and Stream*, May 12, 1894.

_____. "A Step Forward." *Forest and Stream*, April 21, 1894.

_____. "Game Protection Fund." *Forest and Stream*, May 5, 1884.

_____. "New Publications: *Hunting Trips of a Ranchman*." *Forest and Stream*, July 2, 1885.

_____. "Famine Winter." *Forest and Stream*, October 16, 1885.

_____. "To the Walled-In Lakes." *Forest and Stream*, December 10, 1885 to March 18, 1886.

_____. "Bird Destruction." *Forest and Stream*, January 14, 1886.

_____. "Songs or Feathers." *Forest and Stream*, March 11, 1886.

_____. "An Audubon Magazine." *Forest and Stream*, February 11, 1886.

_____. "A Review." *The Audubon Magazine* 1 No. 1, February 1887.

_____. "Membership in the Audubon Society." *The Audubon Magazine* 1 No. 1, February 1887.

_____. "The Rock Climbers." *Forest and Stream*, December 1887 to January 19, 1888 and January 26 to May 3, 1888.

_____. "The Last of the Buffalo." *Scribner's Magazine* 12 No. 3, September 1892.

_____. "Charley Reynolds." *Forest and Stream*, December 26, 1896.

_____. "Climbing Blackfeet." Forest and Stream, October 8, 1880.

_____. "The Mutual Interests of Farmers and Sportsmen." *Forest and Stream*, March 11, 1880.

_____. "Make Forest Preserves Game Preserves." *Forest and Stream*, February 16, 1901.

_____. "The Crown of the Continent." *The Century Illustrated Monthly Magazine* 62, September 1901.

_____. "The Appalachian National Park." *Forest and Stream*, October 12, 1901.

_____. "The Forest Preserves and Game Preserves." *Forest and Stream*, December 7, 1901.

_____. "Our Forest Reserves." *Forest and Stream*, March 8, 1902.

_____. "More National Parks." *Forest and Stream*, September 9, 1905.

_____. "More National Parks." *Forest and Stream*, October 14, 1905.

_____. "Proposed Glacier National Park—I." *Forest and Stream*, December 12, 1908.

_____. The Glacier National Park—II." *Forest and Stream*, December 26, 1908.

_____. The Glacier National Park—III." *Forest and Stream*, January 9, 1909.

_____. The Glacier National Park—IV." *Forest and Stream*, January 25, 1909.

_____. "Glacier National Park." *Forest and Stream*. February 20, 1909.

_____. "Glacier National Park." *Forest and Stream*, August 10,

1909.

_____. "The Glacier National Park." *Forest and Stream*." March 5, 1910.

_____. "Speak for the Glacier National Park." *Forest and Stream*, March 19, 1910.

_____. "Glacier Park Bill Passes House." *Forest and Stream*, April 23, 1910.

_____. "The Glacier National Park." *Forest and Stream*, May 21, 1910.

_____. "A Chapter of History and Natural History in Old New York." *Natural History*, vol. XX, 1920.

_____. "The King of the Mountain." *American Forests and Forest Life* 35, August 1929.

Grinnell, George Bird, and Dana, Edward S. "On A New Territory Lake Basin." *American Journal of Science and Arts* 11, February 1876.

Jacobs, John Cloud. "The Last of the Buffalo," *The World's Week*, January 1909.

Johnson, Carole M. "Emerson Hough's American West," *Books at Iowa* 21, November 1974.

Merchant, Carolyn. "Spare the Birds: George Bird Grinnell and the First Audubon Society," *University Press Scholarship Online*: January 2017.

Mitchell, John G. "A Man Called Bird." *Audubon* 89, no. 2, March 1987.

Reiger, John F. "A Dedication to the Memory of George Bird Grinnell," *Arizona and the West* 21, no. 1, Spring 1979.

Riley, Paul D. "The Battle of Massacre Canyon." *Nebraska History*, vol. 54, no. 2, 1973.

Roosevelt, Theodore. "The Boone and Crockett Club." *Harper's Weekly*, March 10, 1893.

Shellenberger, A. C. "The Last Pawnee-Sioux Indian Battle and Buffalo Hunt." *Nebraska History Magazine*, vol. 16, no. 3, 1935.

Schultz, James Willard. "To Chief Mountain." *Forest and Stream*, December 3, 1885.

Thatcher, Mary. "The Slaughter of the Innocents," *Harper's Bazar*, May 22, 1875.

Utley, Robert M. "The Celebrated Peace Policy of General Grant," *North Dakota History* 20, July 1953.

Wall, Henry. "Restless, Troubled Opportunist: Portrait of a Pioneer Photographer," *Ramsey County History* 4, no. 1, January 1968.

BOOKS

Abbey, Edward. *The Monkey Wrench Gang.* New York: Lippincott, Williams & Wilkins, 1975.

Ames, Charles Edgar. *Pioneering the Union Pacific: A Reappraisal of the Builders of the Railroad.* New York: Appleton-Century-Crofts, 1969.

Anglin, Ronald M. and Larry E. Morris. *The Mystery of John Colter: The Man Who Discovered Yellowstone.* Lanham, MD: Roman and Littlefield, 2016.

Audubon, John James. *The Birds of America.* New York: Macmillan Publishing Company, 1937.

Audubon, Maria R. ed., *Audubon and His Journals.* New York: Charles Scribner's Sons, 1897.

Austin, Jane G. B*etty Alden: The First-Born Daughter of the Pilgrims.* Boston, New York: Houghton, Mifflin and Company, 1896.

Barber, Lynn. *The Heyday of Natural History, 1820-1870.* Garden City, New York: Doubleday, 1980.

Barrus, Clara. *The Life and Letters of John Burroughs.* 2 vols. Boston: Houghton Mifflin, 1925.

Barsness, Larry. *Hides, Heads, and Horns: The Compleat Buffalo Book.* Fort Worth: Texas Christian University Press, 1982.

Bishop, Joseph Bucklin. *Theodore Roosevelt and His Time: Shown in His Own Letters.* 2 vols. New York: Charles Scribner's Sons, 1920.

Blum, Stella. *Victorian Fashions and Costumes from* Harper's Bazar, 1867-1898, New York: Dover Publications, Inc., 1974

Boughter, Judith A. *The Pawnee Nation: An Annotated Research Bibliography.* Lanham, MD: Scarecrow Press, 2004.

Brinkley, Douglas. *The Wilderness Warrior: Theodore Roosevelt and the Crusade for America.* New York: HarperCollins Publishers, 2009.

Brown, Dee, ed. *Pawnee, Blackfeet and Cheyenne: History and Folklore of the Plains from the Writings of George Bird Grinnell.* New York: Charles Scribner's Sons, 1991.

Bruce, Robert. *The Fighting Norths and Pawnee Scouts.* New York: Brooklyn Eagle Press, 1932.

Burroughs, John. *Camping and Tramping With Roosevelt.* Boston: Houghton Mifflin, 1907.

Carroll, John M. and Lawrence A. Frost. *Private Theodore Ewert's Diary of the Black Hills Expedition of 1874.* Piscataway, NJ: CRI Books, 1976.

Cody, William F. *The Life of Hon. William F. Cody, Known as Buffalo Bill, The Famous Hunter, Scout, and Guide: An Autobiography.* Lincoln: University of Nebraska Press, 1978.

Colbert, Edwin H. *The Great Dinosaur Hunters and Their Discoveries.* Reprint. New York: Dover Publications, 1968.

Conniff, Richard. *House of Lost Worlds: Dinosaurs, Dynasties, & the Story of Life on Earth.* New Haven, CT: Yale University Press, 2016.

Cornett, James W. *The Roadrunner.* Palm Springs, California: Nature Trails Press, 2001.

Crittenden, Hiram Martin. *The Yellowstone National Park*, Cincinnati: Robert Clark, 1905.

Custer, Elizabeth Bacon. *Boots and Saddles: or, Life in Dakota with General Custer.* New York: Harper & Brothers, 1885.

Cutright, Paul Russell. *Theodore Roosevelt: The Making of a Conservationist.* Urbana: University of Illinois Press, 1985.

Danker, Donald E., ed. *Man of the Plains: Recollections of Luther North, 1856-1882.* Lincoln: University of Nebraska Press, 1961.

Dary, David A. *The Buffalo Book: The Full Saga of the American Animal.* Athens, OH: Swallow Press, 1989.

DeLatte, Carolyn E. *Lucy Audubon: A Biography.* Baton Rouge: LSU Press, 1982.

Ellsworth, Lincoln. *The Last Wild Buffalo Hunt.* New York: Privately printed, 1916.

Farr, William F. *The Reservation Blackfeet, 1882-1945: A Photographic History of Cultural Survival.* Seattle: University of Washington Press, 1986.

Frost, Lawrence A. ed., *With Custer in '74: James Calhoun's Diary of the Black Hills Expedition*. Provo, UT: Brigham Young University, 1979.

Goetzmann, William H. *Exploration and Empire: The Explorer and the Scientist in the Winning of the West*. New York: Alfred A. Knopf, 1966.

Goetzmann, William, and Kay Sloan. *Looking Far North: The Harriman Expedition in Alaska 1899*. Princeton University Press, 1982.

Grinnell, George Bird, ed. *American Big Game in Its Haunts*. New York: *Forest and Stream* Publishing Company, 1904.

_____. *The Harriman Alaska Expedition*, 1899. Privately printed.

_____. *American Duck Shooting*. New York: *Forest and Stream* Publishing Company, 1901.

_____. *American Game-Bird Shooting*. New York: *Forest and Stream* Publishing Company, 1910.

_____. *Two Great Scouts and Their Pawnee Battalion*. Lincoln: University of Nebraska Press, 1973.

_____, *Pawnee Hero Stories and Folk-Tales; With Notes on the Origins, Customs and Character of the Pawnee People*. Lincoln: University of Nebraska Press, 1961. (New York: *Forest and Stream* Publishing Company, 1889).

Grinnell, George Bird, and Charles Sheldon, eds. *Hunting and Conservation*. New Haven: Yale University Press, 1925.

Gunnison, J.W. *A History of the Mormons*. Philadelphia: Lippincott, Grambo & Co., 1852.

Hagedorn, Hermann. *The Boys' Life of Theodore Roosevelt*. New York: Harper & Brothers, 1918.

Haines, Aubrey L. *The Yellowstone Story: A History of Our First National Park*. Yellowstone National Park: Yellowstone Library and Museum Association, 1977.

Hampton, H. Duane. *How the U. S. Cavalry Saved Our National Parks*. Bloomington: Indiana University Press, 1971.

Hanna, Warren I. *Stars Over Montana: Men Who Made Glacier National Park History*. West Glacier, MT: Glacier National History Association, 1988.

Hatch, Thom. *The Custer Companion*. Mechanicsburg, PA: Stackpole Books, 2002.

_____. Black *Kettle: the Cheyenne Chief Who Sought Peace But Found War*. New York: John Wiley & Sons, 2004.

_____. *Glorious War: the Civil War Adventures of George Armstrong Custer*. New York: St. Martin's Press, 2014.

_____. *The Last Days of George Armstrong Custer: the True Story of the Battle of the Little Bighorn*. New York: St. Martin's Press, 2015.

Herrick, Francis Hobart. *Audubon the Naturalist: A History of His Life and Time*. 2 vols. New York: Appleton, 1917.

Hyde, George E. *Red Cloud's Folk: A History of the Oglala Sioux Indians*. Norman: University of Oklahoma Press, 1937.

Ise, John. *Our National Park Policy: A Current History*. Baltimore: Johns Hopkins University Press, 1961.

Jackson, Donald. *Custer's Gold: The United States Cavalry Expedition of 1874*. New Haven, CT: Yale University Press, 1966.

Johnson, Willis Fletcher, ed. *Addresses and Papers of Theodore Roosevelt*. New York: Unit Book Publishing Company, 1900.

Klein, Maury. *The Life & Legend of E. H. Harriman*. University of North Carolina Press, 2000.

Krause, Herbert and Gary D. Olson. *Prelude to Glory: A Newspaper Accounting of Custer's 1874 Expedition to the Black Hills*. Sioux Falls: Brevet Press, 1974.

Laut, Agnes C. *John Colter-Free Trapper: The Fur Trade in America*. New York: Macmillan Company, 1921.

Lazarus, Edward. *Black Hills/White Justice: The Sioux Nation versus the United States, 1775 to the Present*. New York: Harper Collins, 1991.

Luberkin, John L. *Jay Cooke's Gamble: The Northern Pacific Railroad, The Sioux, and the Panic of 1873*. University of Oklahoma Press, 2014.

Lunde, Darrin. *The Naturalist: Theodore Roosevelt, a Lifetime of Exploration, and the Triumph of American Natural History*. New York: Crown Publishers, 2016.

Mead, Margaret, and Ruth L. Bunzel. *The Golden Age of American Anthropology*. New York: George Braziller, 1960.

Merington, Marguerite. *The Custer Story: The Life and Intimate Letters of General George A. Custer and His Wife Elizabeth*. New York: Devin-Adair, 1950.

Merriam, C. Hart. *A Review of the Birds of Connecticut*. New Haven: Tuttle, Morehouse and Taylor, 1877.

———, ed. *Harriman Alaska Expedition*. 13 vols. New York: Doubleday Page and Company, and Washington, DC: Smithsonian Institution, 1901-1914.

Morison, Elting E., and John M. Blum, eds. *The Letters of Theodore Roosevelt*. 8 vols. Cambridge: Harvard University Press, 1951-54.

Moulton, Gary E., ed. *The Journals of the Lewis and Clark Expedition*. 13 vols. Lincoln: University of Nebraska Press, 2002.

Muir, John. *Our National Parks*. Boston and New York: Houghton Mifflin and Company, 1901.

Murray, William H. H. *Adventures in the Wilderness; Or, Camp-life in the Adirondacks*. Boston: Fields, Osgood & Company, 1869.

Nash, Roderick. *Wilderness and the American Mind*. New Haven: Yale University Press, 2001.

Parker, Watson. *Gold in the Black Hills*. Lincoln: University of Nebraska Press, 1982.

Punke, Michael. *Last Stand: George Bird Grinnell, the Battle to Save the Buffalo, and the Birth of the New West*. Washington, DC: Smithsonian Books, 2007.

Reiger, John F., ed. *The Passing of the Great West: Selected Papers of George Bird Grinnell*. New York: Winchester Press, 1972.

Reiger, John F. *American Sportsmen and the Origins of Conservation*. Norman: University of Oklahoma Press, 1986.

Remsburg, John E. and George J. *Charley Reynolds, Soldier, Hunter, Scout and Guide*. Kansas City, MO: H. M. Sender Co, 1931.

Rhodes, Richard, ed. *The Audubon Reader*. New York: Everyman's Library, Alfred A. Knopf, 2006.

Robinson, Donald H. *Through the Years in Glacier National Park*, West Glacier, MT: Glacier National History Association, 1960.

Roosevelt, Theodore. *Hunting Trips of a Ranchman; Sketches of Sport on the Northern Cattle Plains*. New York and London: G. P. Putnam's Sons, 1885.

_____. *Works*. National Edition. 24 vols. New York: Charles Scribner's Sons, 1926.

Roosevelt, Theodore, and George Bird Grinnell, eds. *American Big-Game Hunting*. New York: *Forest and Stream* Publishing Company, 1893.

_____. *Hunting in Many Lands*. New York: *Forest and Stream* Publishing Company, 1895.

_____. *Trail and Camp-Fire*. New York: *Forest and Stream* Publishing Company, 1897.

Russell, Don. *The Lives and Legends of Buffalo Bill*. Norman: University of Oklahoma Press, 1960

Sage, Rufus B. *Scenes in the Rocky Mountains*. Philadelphia: Carey and Hart, 1846.

Sandoz, Mari. *The Buffalo Hunters: The Story of the Hide Men*. New York: Hastings House, 1954.

Schneider, Paul. *The Adirondacks: A History of America's First Wilderness*. New York: Owl Books, Henry Holt, 1998.

Schuchert, Charles and Clare Mae Le Vene. *O.C. Marsh, Pioneer in Paleontology*. New Haven: Yale University Press, 1940.

Schultz, James Willard. *Blackfeet and Buffalo: Memories of Life Among the Indians*. Norman: University of Oklahoma Press, 1962.

Schullery, Paul and Lee H. Whittlesey. *Myth and History in the Creation of Yellowstone National Park*. Lincoln: University of Nebraska Press, 2003.

Smith, Sherry Lynn. *Reimagining Indians: Native Americans Through Anglo Eyes, 1880-1940*. Cary, NC: Oxford University Press, 2000.

Steele, Joan. Captain Mayne Reid. Woodbridge, CT. Twayne Publishers, Inc., c/o Macmillan Reference USA, 1978.

Trefethen, James B. *Crusade for Wildlife: Highlights in Conservation Progress*. Harrisburg, PA: Stackpole Books, 1961.

Vinton, Stallo. *John Colter: Discoverer of Yellowstone Park*. New York: Edward Eberstadt, 1926.

Welker, Robert Henry. *Birds and Men: American Birds in Science, Art, Literature and Conservation, 1800-1900*, New York: Atheneum, 1966.

Whitney, Casper, George Bird Grinnell, and Owen Wister, eds. *Musk-Ox, Bison, Sheep and Goat.* New York: Macmillan, 1904.

Williamson, J. W. *The Battle of Massacre Canyon: The Unfortunate Ending of the Last Buffalo Hunt of the Pawnees.* Whitefish, MT: Literary Licensing, LLC, 2011.

Wilson, Edward O. *The Social Conquest of Earth.* New York: Liveright, 2012.

Wilson, R. L. *Theodore Roosevelt: Hunter-Conservationist.* Missoula, MT: Boone & Crockett Club, 2009.

Wolfe, Linnie Marsh, ed. *John of the Mountains: Unpublished Journals of John Muir.* Boston: Houghton Mifflin Company, 1938.

Wooster, Robert. *The Military and United States Indian Policy, 1865-1903.* New Haven, CT: Yale University Press, 1988.

Wylder, Delbert, *Emerson Hough.* New York: Macmillan, 1981.

INDEX